MW00780161

BEFORE THE COLORS FADE

GENERAL GEORGE S. PATTON, JR.
Photograph by Peer P. Johnson, M.D.

BEFORE
THE COLORS FADE

PORTRAIT OF A SOLDIER

George S. Patton, Jr.

BY FRED AYER, JR.

With a Foreword by General of the Army
OMAR N. BRADLEY

illustrated with photographs

★ ★ ★ ★

Cherokee Publishing Company
Atlanta, Georgia

Ayer, Frederick.
  Before the colors fade; portrait of a soldier: George S.
Patton, Jr., by Fred Ayer, Jr. With a foreword by Omar
N. Bradley. Boston, Houghton Mifflin, 1964.
    xvii, 266 p. ports. (part col.) 22 cm.

1. Patton, George Smith, 1885–1945.   ɪ. Title.

E745.P3A9   923.573   64–18329

Library of Congress   ₅₎

This book is printed on acid-free paper which conforms to the American
National Standard Z39.48-1984 *Permanence of Paper for Printed Library
Materials.* Paper that conforms to this standard's requirements for pH, alka-
line reserve and freedom from groundwood is anticipated to last several
hundred years without significant deterioration under normal library use
and storage conditions.

Manufactured in the United States of America

ISBN: 978-0-87797-368-3 Hardcover

ISBN: 978-0-87797-369-0 Paper

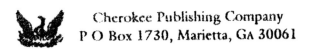
Cherokee Publishing Company
P O Box 1730, Marietta, GA 30061

DEDICATION

TO MY FATHER, FREDERICK AYER,
THE MOST COMPLETELY HONEST MAN
I HAVE KNOWN AND ONE OF A HANDFUL
OF THE TRULY COURAGEOUS

FOREWORD

by

General of the Army Omar N. Bradley

A LEADER — military or civilian — must be judged by results. Patton was certainly a successful battle leader. He had a battle sense — a sixth sense if I may call it that — which enabled him to foresee situations that were developing and make dispositions to meet them. Some officers commented about this even in maneuvers held just prior to World War II. I remember one outstanding wartime example. After crossing the Moselle River near Coblenz with about three divisions and moving rapidly south, he suddenly stopped his advance and collected his forces. Some members of my 12th Army Group staff expressed surprise and wondered why he did not keep going as the advance was going so well. Knowing Patton's feel for the battle, I suggested there must be a reason which George felt but which was not apparent from the information we had. True, the next day he was hit by a strong counterattack which he was able to repel because he had stopped and regrouped. He then continued his advance.

I think that one of the greatest examples of his being a real soldier was that although he was my senior by six years' service and I had served in his command as a subordinate in

Africa and Sicily, he never questioned the decision that placed him in my command in Europe as my subordinate, commanding the Third Army of my 12th Army Group. He was a loyal and a sincere friend to the end.

George Patton was a man with a many-sided character. In the first place, he was an actor — almost everything he did was designed to create a dramatic effect. I understand that this trait was in evidence even while he was a cadet at West Point. Even his language was designed to attract attention. He was profane, but he was also reverent. He strutted imperiously as a commander, but he knelt humbly before his God. For example, the evening before the attack on Gafsa in March 1943, he told his II Corps staff and unit commanders, "Gentlemen, tomorrow we attack. If we are not victorious, let no one come back alive." With that, George excused himself and retired to his room to pray.

Patton was rough on offenders for relatively minor infractions of discipline, for he thought that profanity was the most convincing medium of communication with his troops. But while some chuckled delightedly over the famed expletives he employed with startling originality, many were often shocked and offended. I felt that he failed to recognize the difference in education and standards between the prewar soldier and the wartime soldier.

Yes, when you add up all the pluses and minuses — all of his good points and his faults — and consider his accomplishments, we must conclude that General Patton was a great leader in battle.

AUTHOR'S PREFACE

THIS is not a biography of my late uncle, George S. Patton, Jr.; it is not a history of his campaigns, nor an attempt at military analysis. The references to military matters in these texts are mostly personal in nature — an aid, I hope, in throwing brighter sidelights onto the widely accepted Patton portrait. Or else they deal with certain events of a controversial nature which occurred when the author himself was in the area; events such as the German escape through the Avranches corridor, the Nijmegen–Arnhem disaster, the Battle of the Bulge, the Battle for Trier, and the Hammelburg rescue mission involving Patton's son-in-law. I have also dealt with the famous slapping incident and the reasons for which Patton was relieved of his Third Army command.

In essence: this is written to be a portrait of the man I knew for more than twenty years, from the time when as a small boy I sat at his fireside through to his last year of the war in Europe and the end of his life.

In these pages, I have tried to show more than the façade George Patton presented to the press and to the public, and to look for the influences, the basic traits of character which made him inevitably what he became. In doing so, I have told of many incidents which I believe serve to illustrate or reflect these influences and characteristics; incidents which are intimate or public, trivial as well as crucial, the somewhat ridiculous and those no less than splendid.

In sum, I have tried to show more than just George S. Patton, Jr., leader of men in training and in battle or as the subject of military legends. It is my earnest hope that the reader can see him here through the eyes and ears of some of us who knew him, as well as in the light of his own words, both those written and those spoken aloud; see him as a member of his family; a friend among his friends and a challenge to his enemies; as a thinker as well as a prankster; as a scholar as much as an athlete; and as a leader who in the end had still to obey; that is to say, as a man, even if one who lived on a scale just a little larger than life.

To assure chronological and geographical accuracy, and even to be certain of correct names I have consulted: *War As I Knew It,* by Patton himself (Boston: Houghton Mifflin); *A Soldier's Story,* by General Omar N. Bradley (London: Eyre and Spottiswoode, Ltd.); *Portrait of Patton,* by General Harry Semmes (New York: Appleton, Century, Crofts); *Patton and His Pistols,* by Perry-Parke (Harrisburg, Pa.: Stackpole Company); *Duel for France,* by Martin Blumenson (Boston: Houghton Mifflin), and *Lucky Forward,* by Robert S. Allen (New York: Vanguard Press). I have also had access to the written reminiscences of Don Benito Wilson; George Patton's memoirs of his early life with his own father; and that George S. Patton, Jr.'s, recollections in turn of his father, the George Patton who was killed in the Civil War. I have likewise studied the journal kept by Van S. Merle-Smith, Jr., who was Patton's aide-de-camp during the last four months of his life. All material quoted from the late General Patton's writings are from papers which are in the possession of his family and by them made available to me. The same is true of the photographs which I have used.

I have had also the benefit of numerous personal interviews. Among those who have thus helped me are: General Omar N. Bradley, who has graciously consented to write the foreword to this book; Ruth Ellen Patton Totten; Frederick and Hilda Ayer, my parents; George C. Murnane of Long Island; General (ret'd) Jess Larson of Washington, D.C.; Carl A. Russell of Beverly, Massachusetts; Mr. and Mrs. George Kreissmiller of San Marino, California; Mr. and Mrs. Gordon C. Prince of Hamilton, Massachusetts; Edward P. Creed of Beverly, Massachusetts; Raymond P. Daniell of the *New York Times* and Ottawa, Canada; the Hon. Carl McArdle of Washington, D.C.; Colonel (ret'd) J. Hunter Drum of Washington, D.C.; James S. Nolan of Washington, James B. Hallett of Greenwich, Connecticut, John H. Perry of Cincinnati, General Harold E. Watson, U.S.A.F., Mme. Jacqueline Rethoré of St. Cloud, France, Henri Tardieu of Bayeux, France, Joseph Ekeland of Stockholm, Sweden; Lieutenant Colonel George S. Patton IV, and Anne Moody Ayer, my so patient wife.

To all of these persons I am grateful. Their assistance has helped me in trying to accomplish my aim, to paint a living portrait for those who can still remember that this man was on earth during their lifetime — as well as for those who cannot. Obviously, this portrait is not complete, and only a part of the whole story has here been told. I felt most strongly compelled, however, to do at least this much before half a million printed words, names of people and places no longer remembered and a few faded photographs come to be all that is left of George S. Patton, Jr., U.S.A., 1885-1945.

FREDERICK AYER, JR.

Washington, D.C.
October, 1963

CONTENTS

★ ★ ★ ★

ILLUSTRATIONS

★ ★ ★ ★

Frontispiece

General George S. Patton, Jr.

following page 44

Grandfather Patton, circa 1860.

Susan Glassell Patton, circa 1860.

Grandfather Don Benito Wilson, circa 1850.

Grandmother Margaret Hereford Wilson and Hereford child, circa 1860.

Father, George S. Patton, Jr., at Virginia Military Academy in 1873, and circa 1885.

Mother, Mrs. George S. Patton, Jr., circa 1888.

G. S. Patton, Jr., 1891.

The second G. S. Patton, Jr., and father, California, 1901.

G. S. Patton, Jr., Santa Catalina, California, 1905.

West Point, 1909.

Beatrice Ayer Patton, 1909.

George S. Patton, Jr., and Beatrice Ayer Patton, 1910.

The groom's father and Beatrice Ayer Patton.

Uncle George, Bea Jr., Aunt Bea, Ruth Ellen, 1914.

following page 108

Pershing's aide — Mexico, 1915.

"There's life in the old man yet." Riding off
Walter Dillingham, Hawaii, 1927.

Fort Meyer, Virginia, 1920.

"My war face," 1927.

With son George S. Patton IV, Hamilton, Massachusetts, 1929.

National Capitol Horse Show, same year.

Honolulu, 1939, just prior to departure for California:
G. S. Patton, Jr., Francis Graves, Beatrice Ayer
Patton, Joe Ekeland, G. S. Patton IV, and Suzuki.

G. S. Patton, Jr., with Beatrice Ayer Patton, Jr.,
Hamilton, Massachusetts.

G. S. Patton, Jr., James W. Totten, Ruth Ellen
Patton Totten.

At daughter Ruth Ellen's "Gone With the Wind" birthday
party, 1940.

"Green Hornet."

Night before leaving for North Africa.

following page 236

General Noguès and G. S. Patton, Jr., at Residency
just after French surrender.

An autograph, somewhere in Tunisia.

Landing in Sicily.

Across France to . . .

Belgium and Prince Baudouin.

Luxembourg, March 1945.

"And that was for the Rhine," March 23, 1945.

Bedford Airport, June 1945.

G. S. Patton, Jr., Frederick Ayer, Beatrice Ayer Patton.

June 1945 — Boston, Massachusetts.

G. S. Patton, Jr., and Beatrice Ayer Patton, July 1945.

June 1945, back home at "Lake Vineyard" in California.

Beatrice Ayer Patton, Tufts College, Medford, Massachusetts. Universal Military Training Speech, 1952.

Hamm, Luxembourg. "Not by the last bullet."

BEFORE THE COLORS FADE

CHAPTER I

"This is my war face"

★ ★ ★ ★

"THE only way for a soldier to die is by the last bullet in the last battle of his final war." That is what the man had just said, a tall, fair-haired man standing in dramatic pose before the open fire. His young listener heard him say it and, even not quite understanding, believed the words. Truthfully, however, he was more interested, even still a bit bemused, by the wonderful gift the man had just given him.

The helmet was created from an old-style hard derby hat. Its rim had been cut away, ear and nosepieces added in heavy cardboard. Then the whole had been carefully gilded. The flaring crest was made of the business end of a russet-colored hearthbrush. Breastplate and greaves and shield were cut from cardboard also, then finished in bronze and gold paints. The throwing spear and the Grecian hoplite's short, heavy cutting sword were carved of soft white pine; yet they were that day more real than real to me — the little boy who had received them.

That boy had sat throughout the afternoon before a bright wood fire in the living room of an old dark house perched on a rocky bluff above the cold Atlantic. Even indoors he had been able clearly to hear the crunching of the seas against the rocks below and had felt the power of their pounding. He had also listened to the metered words of the *Iliad* read aloud: and they were just as real to him then as was his brand-new sword. They belonged to today as well as to the ages. He had heard of the Greek ships and the angry jealousy of Agamemnon, and of the "Broad oars which in order smote upon the wine-dark sea," and of Ajax the Mighty who struck his foes to the ground "and loud their armor rang," and of Patroclus, beloved friend of Achilles who at the end "crashed upon the earth and darkness filled his eyes."

The little boy sitting there in open-mouthed attention knew that the lines rang true. He was even, for the moment, standing by himself somewhere within the shadows of the beached Greek ships, resting for a little while before returning to glorious battle. The man who read them knew also that the lines rang true because he believed with all his self that he had once fought upon the plains of Troy, and in another age with Caesar's terrible Tenth Legion, and still again with the Highlanders for the rights and hopes of the House of Stuart, and very lately against the brutal Hun in France. The man *knew* also that he would fight for his country at least once more in this present life, and most certainly again in some later incarnation. To the boy he said then and many times later, "The greatest privilege of citizenship is to be able freely to bear arms under one's country's flag."

On that day, before the fire-bright hearth, the man also gave to the little boy another gift; the beautifully bound volumes of Lord Derby's translation of the *Iliad*. "The greatest story told by man, and you must read it all." Although only eight at the time, the boy that very night began to do as he was told.

The books stand today in a shelf to the left of my own fireplace. So far as I know the suit of cardboard armor rests somewhere in a carton far back in the attic of my mother's house. And over my desk hangs a photograph, now nearly forty years old, of the man who made these gifts: a brash young major of cavalry named George Smith Patton, Jr.

He was my uncle, but he became also my godfather. He was the latter by my choice, since someone had forgotten until quite unusually late to observe the formalities of christening my brothers, my sister and me. A lineal male ancestor of mine had been hanged as a sorcerer in the Salem of 1692; and this event had precipitated a certain long-lasting coolness between our family and the Church. But in 1927 christened we finally were, not in church, of course, but in the living room of Avalon, the house of my uncle, Keith Merrill, in Pride's Crossing, Massachusetts.

At that time George Patton was stationed at Schofield Barracks on the Island of Oahu, Hawaii, and thus could not be present in person even for so important an event. He did, however, do his best. He sent the photograph I have referred to, and with it an explanatory note. "This is my war face which I have been practicing before a mirror all my life. I'm going to use it again to scare hell out of the Germans." This was a strange thing to say a scant nine years after the end of World War I. Uncle George felt strongly, however, that we had left things unbalanced by Versailles, that disarmament was dangerous and that certainly there would be another major war. Sometimes he said it would be against the Japanese, sometimes against the Russians; but he was always sure that it would come. It is possible, also, that he was repeating his father's expressed convictions. The senior George Patton had studied C. A. L. Totten's books about predicting the future on the basis of measurements of the Great Pyramid of Cheops; and himself believed in the power of prophecy.

I also received a letter of godfatherly advice, some of which is fit to print. It made various recommendations; for instance, "Any idiot can spell a word the same way time after time. But it calls for imagination and is much more distinguished to be able to spell it several different ways as I do." Also, "Never be obscene or use profanity in conversations unless the obscenity is so splendid or the profanity so outstanding that people will be so interested they will forget to be shocked."

The letter concluded with what could only in charity be called a poem "which is among the most profane in the English language. I should know because I wrote it myself. You should memorize it and recite it to some of your more pious uncles and aunts. It will do them a lot of good." I have since forgotten the poem except for its concluding stanza:

> The sun came out so bright and clear
> That it dried up all the rain
> So the god-damned spider son-of-a-bitch
> climbed up the spout again.

I was then barely past eleven years old and not at all a sophisticated child in the worldly sense of today. I accordingly did as I was told. I do not recall in whose house it happened, but I do know that parents and relatives were present. Someone had mentioned the name of Uncle George and something he had done. Then came a pause for chewing during which the chubby and somewhat buck-toothed child that I was piped up, "Guess what, Uncle George sent me a letter when we were christened. It had a poem in it and it goes like this —"

There was a moment of rather stunned horror. Then came quick action by the end of only two lines. But there was no punishment since, after all, I had merely followed the orders of the man responsible for my religious instruction. And anyway, I now know that the poem was far from the most profane, and even further removed from the most obscene in the language. Still, it sufficed for the occasion.

My godfather brought up his own children much as he had been brought up himself. He was sometimes too stern toward them and was jealously protective of his daughters. He believed in punishment as well as reward, and he hammered home the words of the scriptures, the great stories of history, and what he felt was the best poetry. Highest on his list ranked the *Iliad* and the verse of Rudyard Kipling.

Uncle George learned from everything he read, and remembered nearly all of it. I recall very well his long quotings from the *Barrack-Room Ballads;* including long ones such as "Danny Deever." I have sat in rapt attention as he recited verse upon verse of the Bible, Shakespeare, and Lord Macaulay.

More impressive, however, were to be his performances in 1944 and 1945 at his headquarters in France and Luxembourg when he proved superior in historical accuracy to a visiting Harvard professor, and in the contents of the Bible to a ranking Prince of the Church. His aide, the late Colonel Charles Codman, told me about the occasion. The men were Bruce Hopper and Cardinal Spellman, and Codman was researcher as well as referee.

In addition to reading or reciting the beloved poetry to

his family, Uncle George starred as a teller of tales of all his favorite ancient heroes. Quite often he added a deft mastery of the inventive. His imagination in this field was almost unlimited. One of his finest recitals ran in serial form for his children and sometimes for me, and its hero was one of the men he claimed long ago to have been. The man bore the magnificent name of Reginald Sharkfoot the Black, which memory vaguely tells me was because Reginald's mother was a mermaid. I am certain, however, about one of his more splendid abilities, that of burglar supreme. Wearing a complete suit of head-to-foot armor he would back up to dining table or sideboard, lower the drop seat of his cast-iron pants and stuff in the jewelry or silverware of his choice. He would then make his swift and silent escape by flushing himself down the nearest toilet.

In the summer of 1935 when I was nineteen, and about to become a Junior at Harvard, I discovered that Uncle George's encyclopedic knowledge was no accident. Together with my younger sister, I paid a month's visit to the Pattons at their quarters at Fort Shafter on Oahu. Like too many army posts of those days, officers' quarters were homely square structures of ocher-painted clapboards arranged in an arc and occupied in descending size according to descending rank. Uncle George's was number three. Numbers one and two contained a general and a full colonel, respectively, and each contained a teen-age daughter. Neither to me seemed even remotely attractive. No matter; as a young visiting male it was my duty under Army protocol to call on them and invite them out. Only after this had been done, to the mutual distaste of all parties concerned, was I permitted to look to greener pastures.

The Patton house had very little extra space. Accordingly, the quarters assigned to me consisted of the curtained-off end of a rectangular screened porch. This area contained also a considerable portion of Uncle George's library. In looking back it seems to me there must have been nearly five hundred volumes on the shelves. All but a few of these, detailing the care and management of the horse, dealt with history, biography, and political or military memoirs.

At first I thought, "Of course he hasn't read them! Where could he find the time between doing whatever a Lieutenant Colonel did, and shooting, sailing, fencing and playing polo? Obviously the books had been inherited or were the gifts one would customarily present to a professional soldier to be exhibited only for show." Late one night, however, I began idly to leaf through some of the volumes and saw how wrong I had been. Every one I examined had in many places been carefully underlined, and others bore marginal notes, just like my more challenging college textbooks. Many of the notes referred to the works of other authorities; to corroborate or to contradict. I no longer can remember particular titles or the precise notations although quite a few were very personal. I can, however, still see one. "Man's a damned liar. I know because I was there."

It is more than probable that Patton had, in fact, been there. He had attended Virginia Military Institute, West Point, and in 1912 and 1913, the Military School at Saumur in France. There he had studied advanced fencing under Adjutant Cléry, a world-famous teacher of the sport. As a result Patton was named the United States Army's Master of the Sword. At Saumur also he came for the first time under the influence of Lieutenant Jean Houdemon, then cavalry instructor and later to become in two World Wars one of the great heroes of France. The two men studied, argued, fenced, shot and rode horseback, but mostly they pored together over accounts of wars and battles. General Houdemon's daughter, Mme. Jean Rethoré, recently told me, "They were great friends. Every evening Uncle Georgie, for he was this to me even when I was three years old, used to study with my father, especially about the campaigns of Napoleon. More than thirty years later, my father, who was a great connoisseur of history, told me that the great strikes of the 3rd Army reminded him of Bonaparte's Italian campaign, from overall strategy right to the psychological approach of the commander himself."

General Houdemon himself wrote in September 1947, "Yes, I first knew him at Saumur in the French Cavalry School, and I still see his proud and elegant figure, accompanied by Mrs. Patton, brightening the threshold of my house — a tall, thin cavalry man with a keen eye and a firm hand either to wield a sword or guide a horse (my horse) riding over the racetrack obstacles at Saumur."

Early in 1913 both officers became convinced that war with Germany would come, and quickly. So, it was then that Houdemon promised his American friend that if the United States stayed out of the coming conflict he would see to it that he received a commission in his own regiment of cavalry. Although this never happened, George Patton did do things more or less spectacular in places scattered far apart. I shall write of them later but feel they should at least be listed here. He represented his country in five events during the 1912 Military Olympics in Stockholm, paying his own way since our government provided no

other funds. He was later Black Jack Pershing's very com-
bative aide in the punitive expedition against Pancho Villa
in Mexico. During World War I he was the first United
States Commander of Armor, suffered a serious wound and
received the Distinguished Service Cross for action in the Argonne Battle.

He had otherwise traveled widely, been variously stationed
about the United States and was once offered the post of
Military Attaché to the Court of St. James's. He served as
Master of Foxhounds in Virginia and captained the polo
teams of several Army commands. He twice sailed for assignment to the Hawaiian Command, the second time as both
G-2 and G-3 (Intelligence and Plans and Operations, respectively). On this second trip, furthermore, he arrived on a
45-foot schooner, by self-taught navigation, with an amateur
crew and in near record time.

These things have been recorded; other events have not,
although Uncle George was certain that they had happened
because he so strongly believed them. As I have mentioned,
he *knew* he had been to France before as a Roman legion-
naire, but he *knew* also that he had been there later encased
in knighthood's armor on his way to the Crusades. He
experienced *déjà vu* and sometimes claimed the power of
prophecy.

On other levels, he was also remarkable. Witness an incident in 1910 at "Avalon," the house of his fiancée Beatrice
Ayer in Pride's Crossing, Massachusetts, on the very staid
North Shore. Obviously I was not there, but members of the
family have told me about it many times. There is a wide
terrace running the length of the same huge living room in
which my brothers, sisters and I were later christened. It

overlooks a fine slanting lawn and a steep drop to the Atlantic. The lawn and terrace are connected by a flight of some twenty cut-stone steps. This day on the terrace were assembled a family group. My grandfather, magnificent in his broad white beard; the younger men in the narrow trousers, blazers and high hard collars of the day; the ladies in broad hats and voluminous summery organdy dresses. Then Lieutenant George S. Patton, Jr., came to call: twenty-four years old, slender, erect, with wavy hair and on a horse. There was nothing unusual about this in 1910. It was, however, somewhat of a surprise when the young officer clattered his horse up all the steps, rode across the terrace and dismounted to bow at his fiancée's feet.

The same man would, because ever since childhood he had believed he would, lead one of the two largest armies ever to march under the flag of the United States. His sister, Anita Patton, told me that even as a little boy in Los Angeles County he used to stride martially about carrying a wooden sword into which he had burned "Lt. Gen. G. S. Patton, Jr." I do not know how old he was then, but believe that he was not more than ten. And he was to lead his army well, lead it the blazing miles from Rabat and Casablanca to the tip of Sicily, from the beaches of Normandy westward to Brest and east to the gates of Prague. He was to occupy thousands of square miles of enemy territory, seize and inflict on the Germans on the continent of Europe alone just short of a million and a half casualties, seize great quantities of enemy material, and do this all with an extraordinary low casualty rate among his own troops.

He would also, because he was a profound student of the past, be able accurately to foretell much of the future. He would, because this is in the nature of things, be ridiculed and bitterly criticized for having always kept in the forefront of his mind, and so spoken clearly and loud of, that which he believed best for his country. He would, since this was his basic make-up, shock, anger, but also charm many people; and he would hurt himself badly in the eyes of others. He would not, however, die by the last bullet of his final war. He would instead be mortally injured in a tragically needless auto accident, live nine days longer than allotted him by two of the best neurosurgeons of the world. He would say toward the last, "This is a hell of a way for a soldier to die."

CHAPTER II

From history comes prophecy

CHRONOLOGICAL recitation of each fact of a man's life from hour and date of birth onward may be necessary to the usual biography. To a written portrait of a man I think that it is not. There are, however, certain matters of ancestry, schooling, family relationships and household atmosphere without knowledge of which any real accuracy of understanding remains most difficult.

George S. Patton, Jr.'s, maternal grandfather was Don Benito Wilson, who began his career in the late 1820's as an Indian trader in Tennessee and ended it as one of the largest landholders in Southern California. His intervening adventures were by any standards extraordinary. In California, leading a group of Spaniards in what was then Mexican territory, he killed Joaquín, the notorious half-breed murderer and bandit. In a simultaneous exchange, Wilson was left with a poisoned arrowhead embedded in his shoulder. He survived the resulting long illness to lead a troop of Mexicans and Americans against the tyrant General Micheltorena in 1845, and to go on a punitive expedition against some Indians who had wiped out a white settlement near Bear Lake.

He returned from the latter foray with several wicker baskets containing the gory heads of those responsible for the massacre, to prove conclusively to the provincial governor that he had fulfilled his mission. He also fought and killed a large grizzly bear with only a knife as a weapon. His first wife was Ramona Yorba, daughter of the deputy to Pio Pico, governor of the province, and he was called Don Benito because the Mexicans considered him one of their own. Nevertheless, at the end of the U.S.-Mexican War in 1848, Commodore Stockton offered him, and he accepted, a captaincy in our own Army because he was so much trusted by Mexicans and Americans alike that he could keep the peace in his district.

After Ramona's death he married Margaret S. Hereford, a handsome widow who had been born in Virginia and raised in Richmond society. To them were born three daughters of whom Ruth and Annie survived. Ruth married George S. Patton, Jr., the father of my Uncle George.

Don Benito was a tough and imperious man. In later life he never, as he wrote and told his children, carried a gun. He was afraid of his lightning temper. Once, however, he broke his rule. He had loaned one of the early members of the Spreckels family $5000 and had come to collect. Spreckels demanded a note of hand as receipt but Don Benito stated firmly that in his circle a handshake was enough. Spreckels did not agree. Don Benito went home for his pistol and returned to ask the Spreckels clerk, "Young man, have you ever watched death? No? Well just wait about one minute!" There was no death that day, but the debt was quickly repaid, and in cash.

Don Benito's photographs show strong almost fiercely chiseled features and a look of domineering arrogance. Those of his daughters reflect much of their father's looks, softened it is true by feminine lines, but holding a stubborn strength. Thus, there ran a commingling of very rugged blood in the veins of George Patton's mother.

Uncle George's grandfather on his father's side was a third-generation Virginian, and one of eight brothers. Their ancestry ran back through the Patton family of Bermuda to Scotland from which they had fled as Jacobite refugees. Ten of the eighteen barons who signed the Magna Charta are represented on the Patton genealogical chart, as are also a Plantagenet king and an aunt of George Washington.

The Virginian George Patton served with the Kanawah Rifles when they went to fight John Brown at Harper's Ferry; and when Virginia seceded there was no question in his mind as to where his loyalties lay; nor was there in the minds of his brothers. Robert William, John M., Isaac W., Waller Taswell and James French all became officers in the Confederate Army. Hugh Mercer and William Mercer Patton did not, only because they had not yet reached their teens. Waller Taswell was killed at Gettysburg. George as Colonel of the 22nd Virginians fought valiantly in many engagements and was three times wounded, the third time by a rifle bullet in the abdomen. He told his commander General Henry Heth, "I am hit in the belly. It is all over." General Heth probed the wound with an unwashed finger, "I think not George," and extracted a twenty-dollar gold piece which had halted the lead. This dented coin rests today in the family safe deposit box in Los Angeles.

The fourth bullet, however, proved fatal and this George S. Patton, Jr., died from wounds received at the Battle of Winchester. His Negro body servant, Peter, hiding by day and

moving furtively by night, at last managed to bring his saddle and saber home to Patton's beautiful widow Susan Glassell Patton and her sons. One of them, George, Jr., has written of this event in his memoirs; and the saber is kept shined
to this day.

At the age of twelve this boy, the second George S. Patton, Jr., went in 1866 to California with his mother and three
brothers with money furnished by her Uncle Glassell. After
reaching the age of sixteen he returned to Virginia Military
Institute where he studied law and later taught.

While still at the Institute he at last managed to receive ap-
proval from the federal government for his family's request
that Uncle Taswell Patton be disinterred from alien Yankee
soil and reburied where he belonged in Winchester, Virginia.
This permission was granted only on the condition that the
reburial be conducted secretly and at night. After all, this
was only 1873 and violence could still flare dangerously in
the bitter South. Accordingly, young Patton and three companions loaded the coffin onto a train, took it at nightfall to
Winchester, and from that station on a horse-drawn wagon
down the dark dirt road to the cemetery.

As he drove through the night Patton became conscious
first of dim figures slipping from behind hedges and between
trees to follow along behind the wagon, then of a strange soft
cadenced thumping. Arriving at the cemetery he saw a company of men slowly form ranks on either side of a new-dug
grave immediately next the headstone of George S. Patton, Jr., of the 22nd Virginia. All were in Confederate uniform and had marched there with muffled drums, risking
long imprisonment, to honor their dead friend and former
comrade in battle.

As Taswell's coffin was being lowered, it bumped the older one holding brother George's body, knocking off the boarding of one side. Young Patton later told that his uncle looked to him exactly as he had in life, although the light of the torch he held was flickering and dim.

I hope that enough of the same blood still runs in the living Patton children. If it does they might carry out their mother's wishes despite our government's official refusal. They would then move her ashes from Massachusetts and place them with those that are marked by a plain white cross at Hamm in Luxembourg, a cross which bears the name "General George S. Patton, Jr."

Returned to California, Patton conducted a successful law practice and became in fact District Attorney for Los Angeles. Although recurrently ill from tuberculosis, incurred no doubt during the times of hardship and deprivation of the war years, he won, on behalf of the state of California, a major lawsuit against Mr. Huntington and his Southern Pacific Railroad. People in those days in California just did not oppose the Huntingtons; nevertheless, afterwards the two men became great friends.

Later in his life Patton ran for the United States Senate, at the same time campaigning for Woodrow Wilson. He lost the Senate race and never quite forgave the new President for not offering him the one job in the world he wanted, that of Secretary of War.

It was in the first years after the Civil War that the widow Patton became friendly with Mrs. Don Benito Wilson, another lady from Virginia, and their children became friends. In the course of time Ruth Wilson, whose diaries and letters show she had loved him since the age of nine, married the handsome young lawyer.

The portraits of the George Patton killed at Winchester, save for the presence of a militant mustache, show features, the mouth in particular, far more gentle than those of Don Benito. His face seems to me, to reflect the truth that pure strength is inborn, and therefore of no particular credit to the owner; but courtesy and gallantry are characteristics which can only be acquired. Patton's father had a face which was very similar, with wavy hair, high forehead, and the same gentle mouth under a fine mustache. By any standards he was a very good-looking man, who dressed perfectly and with meticulous attention to detail. All those who remember him well tell me that his features clearly told the truth; he was quietly generous, courteous, but he had what could be called a certain flair for living. Although he lived in California, he remained in character a landowner of Virginia.

Certainly the characteristics of both Don Benito Wilson and George Patton of the Kanawah Rifles and the 22nd Virginia reappeared in the features of their grandson. In his character, they did not so much merge as conflict. It seems to me that the Wilson looks and the Patton personality were dominant but that Uncle George wished at times that they were not; that he tried sometimes subconsciously, but more often deliberately, to suppress them. Perhaps he succeeded too well in hiding his ingrained gentleness beneath a surface toughness. Certainly there constantly recurred strong contradictions in his behavior which may become more easily explicable if we know a little about the boyhood of the third George S. Patton.

The family of George and Ruth Patton lived for a time reasonably well. Then the trusted manager of the Wilson estate absconded with much of the family funds. Addition-

ally, owing to George Patton's various sicknesses, he was for
quite a while unable actively to continue his law practice
and was forced bit by bit to sell off at a pauper's price much
of the large family holdings of land. Even so the family appeared outwardly to live richly, still holding considerable
acreage, employing many servants, and with access to ample
farm and livestock produce. All that they lacked was money.
At one point, according to my uncle, his father had to borrow
from a bank the cash needed to buy him an ordinary shotgun for his twelfth birthday. It was to be a long time before
financial conditions gradually improved.

It must have been a strange household, a stranger early upbringing for a young boy. Ruth's sister Annie Wilson lived
with the couple and their children, Anita and small George.
Annie Wilson doted on the weak and often sickly little boy
and would not let his mother punish him. She was by far the
dominant one of the two sisters and often enforced her will
by taking to bed and screaming for the doctor when she felt
that her wishes were being unreasonably thwarted. What is
more, abetted by his indulgent father, she was able by such
tactics to prevent Uncle George from being sent to school until he was eleven. As a result he did not learn either to read or
write until after that age.

Young George Patton adored his father; no wonder. The
man read to him by the hour from the great works, especially
the *Iliad*, taught him to swim, shoot, hunt and fish, even
coached him in sailing and carpentry. Inevitably, he took
the boy to visit the Civil War battlefields and impressed on
him the heroism of his ancestors. And, of course, he told him
of being taken himself as a little boy by his father to view the
body of J. E. B. Stuart, "the greatest cavalryman who ever

lived"; and of his own reburial of Uncle Taswell at Winchester. Throughout Uncle George's written remembrances of his father there appears the great sympathy and love which existed between them. There is, however, not the slightest doubt that the young man was very spoiled, not only by his Aunt Annie but also by his father, who taught him everything that even borrowed money could buy: guns, expensive fishing gear and horses.

No doubt the most spectacular entertainment provided for the young man was that which marked his sixteenth birthday. The entrepreneur was Mr. Hancock Banning, who was some sort of second cousin to the Pattons and the uncle of Ellen Banning Ayer who would become George Patton's mother-in-law. Mr. Banning was a rich, impressive and delightful man who owned Santa Catalina Island and most of Pasadena. He believed in doing things properly and acted according to his beliefs. On this occasion he acquired an old inter-island steamer, and loaded it entirely full of every conceivable form of fireworks. He then had the ship towed out into the channel, set afire, and cast adrift. Those of the family who were present say it was a sight not easy to forget.

It was also on this birthday that George Patton's doting Aunt Annie gave him a ring. It was of gold in the form of a scaly snake wrapped around itself, and in the head were set ruby chip eyes and a glittering sapphire topknot. This ring he was to wear on the third finger of his left hand throughout every day of his life. As of this writing it has just been given to his grandson Michael Totten upon the occasion of his college graduation.

After his marriage Uncle George wore four rings. Next to the snakes on his left hand was a gold-set diamond given him by his wife, on his right he carried his 1909 West Point class ring and a Camora marriage band of two hands clasping a golden heart; on his powerfully long, well-tended hands so many rings did not look out of place.

As mentioned, Uncle George never once doubted that he would be a famous soldier, never since the days of his wooden sword; and his father encouraged him. The senior Patton, sick as he sometimes was himself, applied for a commission in our Army for the Spanish-American War of 1898, asserting that it was his clear duty even as a man in his forties to fight. About the same time, he gave his son a cavalry saber with which to practice fencing cuts. When young George was about to leave in his turn for the life of a cadet at Virginia Military Institute, he writes that when he told his Uncle Glassell Patton that he was afraid he might be a coward, and he was answered: " 'No Patton could be a coward,' I told this to Papa and he said that while ages of gentility might make a man of my breeding reluctant to engage in a fist fight, the same breeding made him willing to face death from weapons with a smile. I think that this is true."

George's father was on the Board of Visitors at West Point and was, of course, present at his son's graduation. After that, except at Uncle George's wedding, the two saw very little of each other for three years. His father did, however, write him several times with the advice to moderate his language and expressions of opinion in public. He also accompanied him to the 1912 Olympics in Stockholm and to New York when he sailed for France with the A.E.F.

During the next to last year of his life, in 1926, his father told Uncle George "that the very fortunate career I had had in the army was fate and that I was being especially prepared for some special work. He felt that the end of our civilization was at hand and that war was sure. When I used to bemoan the fact that wars were getting scarce and that all the time I had spent getting ready would be wasted for lack of opportunity he used to assure me with the greatest confidence that I would yet be in the biggest war in history . . . I have always felt the same thing concerning myself."

Uncle George's father died after an operation for tuberculosis of the kidneys on June 10, 1927, while his son was on duty in Hawaii. Uncle George came home at once, and here is the conclusion of his own account of his father's life written only four weeks later.

The morning I arrived I wore my uniform and went alone to his grave. The whole lot was covered with flowers all of which were wilted save the sheath of red roses over the spot where he lay. These to me seemed fresh, vivified by the great soul of him who lay beneath them.

For an hour I stood there, and the knowledge came to me that the grave no more held Papa than does one of his discarded suits hanging in a closet. Suddenly I seemed to see him in the road wearing his checked overcoat and with his stick which he waved at me as he had been used to do when he was impatient and wanted to go somewhere.

I knelt and kissed the ground and saluted, not Papa, but the last resting place of that beautiful body I had loved. His soul was with me and, except for the density of my fleshly eyes, I could have seen and talked with him.

As I write this in his office where we smoked and talked so often, he is here. I like to remember not the symbol of his gallant spirit which I saluted in the churchyard, but rather Papa, the last time I saw him alive wheeled out (in the hospital) to die perhaps, and to think of his words so true of our present temporary separation when he smiled at me and said, "Au revoir, son."

Oh, darling Papa. I never called you that in life as both of us were too self-contained but you were and are my darling. I have often thought that life for me was too easy, but the loss of you has gone far to even my count with those whom before I have pitied.

God grant that you see and appreciate my piteous attempt to show here your lovely life. I never did much for you and you did all for me. Accept this as a slight offering of what I would have done.

Your devoted son,
G. S. PATTON, JR.
July 9, 1927

Remember that this was not written by a boy. It was set down by a man just short of forty-two who had fought one war and was preparing for and waiting for the next. It was written by one who to some seemed a hard, callous man. His natural gentleness was sometimes hard to see since, spoiled as a child, he still saw himself as he had during that boyhood: as a descendant of warriors, still a Virginian, and above all the most important person he himself knew, and so clearly destined for greatness.

I believe I can now know how he must have been when young, because in basic things he never changed. To him things tinged with the mystical, things glowing in a romantic light were almost always the very real.

To him an army without cavalry was not really an army at all; and an officer without a horse was just barely an officer and certainly not quite a gentleman. He saw a horse as the winged Pegasus, as the Bucephalus of Alexander the Great, as the steeds of Napoleon's Imperial Guard "which now dies but will never surrender." He saw it also as the iron-gray "Traveller" under saddle to the great Robert E. Lee, and as one of the ghostlike horses of J. E. B. Stuart's midnight raiders, or as the mist-shrouded sentry horse in the famous sketch by "Snaffles" who nods "Pass, friend" to the nighttime fox. But he saw also in the horse a creature which he must dominate, by brute strength if need be.

When the brasses sound and the drums roll and the flag comes by, one man feels an urge to shoulder arms and march, another will choke up. Clearly George Patton was both men. Some, when they hear the notes of taps think of Memorial Day, the off-key high school band and a speech by some long-winded town selectman. Patton could think only of the white horses and flag-draped caisson before the gates of Arlington Cemetery, as one more fellow soldier he had loved who went to his rest too early and with too little recompense.

Even when his professional star was high Uncle George could still too vividly remember the days when many restaurants and bars displayed placards which read "Dogs and Soldiers Not Allowed Inside." These were the early thirties, the same gloomy times when Patton was told, "You won't get any appropriations recommended by the Military Affairs Committee, Georgie, even if you can drive those tanks up to Capitol Hill loaded with votes."

To George Patton "The Long Gray Line" was not just the Corps of Cadets marching on a fall Saturday into a concrete stadium. He deeply felt the full meaning of the words as first they were written. Behind each man at the Academy paced another who had stood his post, and now was gone; and behind that gray shadow a dimmer ghost, and back of that man another, and behind that one last man more. To him, in a more than half-understood way, the line stretched somehow back through history even to the gallant Spartan three hundred who had barred the pass of Thermopylae against the hordes of Persia, and died in their places, the three hundred whose common grave was marked even by their bitter rivals the Athenians, "Stranger, go tell to the Spartans that we lie here according to their law." He likened this law to the admonition of the West Point motto "Duty, Honor, Country," and it ruled his life.

There was something in Patton which reacted with equal intensity to a raging victory or a gallant defeat. He could, and did, talk of "ripping the guts out of the filthy bastards," or using their bowels to grease the tractor treads of his tanks. Yet he could also talk with tears in his eyes of the rusted bayonets which still projected above ground in the "Trench of Bayonets" at Verdun, or of the sentry who, as the lava cast of his body still shows, stood unflinching beside his spear under the deadly flow from Mount Vesuvius, "faithful unto death."

He was most gallant to women, but not always. Certainly he did not look at every attractive one with the eye of a brother. As a matter of fact this knight once at gunpoint rescued a beautiful girl from forcible abduction by automobile at the hands of two swarthy men. It developed, however, that the girl did not in the least wish to be rescued. Uncle George was philosophic about it all. He had for the ladies a wonderful way with words in this as in many other respects, not profane or obscene words such as he sometimes used, but courtly and flowing words. A good example is his "Toast to the Ladies" at a West Point dinner in Kansas City, April 5, 1924:

Good water is the greatest gift to set before a King,
But who am I, that I should have the best of everything?
Let monarchs gather round the pump and pass the dipper
    free.
Gin, whiskey, wine and even beer are good enough for me.

In quoting the above I refer simply to the feeling of unworthiness expressed and not in the horrid idea of excessive potations, for in toasting The Ladies, similar feelings of unworthiness oppress me.

Had I been called upon to toast Horseflesh, or Profanity, or some other subject on which I may possess erudition, I would have been less abashed. As it is, the timorous modesty of my nature and my well-known celibate instincts are compounded. I am at a loss.

I might raise my glass to those generous-spirited ladies of the Paris boulevards; but abstain out of regard for the feelings of some, and from the knowledge that there are others here better qualified to sing their praises than I.

And so, in a lighter vein, I might review women (ladies, if you will), brown, mauve or painted; dressed or "au nature"; but should I do so it were a sacrilege to later offer you the toast I shall propose.

In the chapel at Leavenworth, on the monument at Riley, on the walls of Cullum Hall, are names: names of officers dead on the field of honor; bits of marble, slate or bronze commemorating the fact that Lieutenant Willie

Jones made the choice and without ostentation or hope
of reward, did his duty even unto death. The little
plaques tell the story and fame, such as it is, and high
honor from us who know, are accorded Willie. But
where is Mrs. Willie's tablet?

Such were the women who year on harrowing year
made homes for officers in these bleak western posts;
such the women who today uncomplainingly share the
luxury of cantonment quarters.

Think of the horror of the slow torture of suspense between the night of Wounded Knee or Château Thierry,
and the morning at the cemetery. Think of it and thank
God for the quick mercy of the bullet.

Gentlemen, I reverently pledge you: The Ladies who
have shared our lives from the Equator to the Arctic; the
Ladies who have condoned our reverses, and inspired,
but to applaud, our successes.

May we live to make them happy, or, and the Great
Day come, so die as to make them proud. The Army
women God bless them.

This man felt that good bourbon was made to be drunk,
not sipped. He was vain and confident in his own prowess in
anything to which he chose to put his hand. His drive and
determination, however, were such that he became very
nearly as good as he thought he should be in a variety of pursuits. He felt certain of his destiny to greatness; of success in
all things. Yet, he raged and ranted at people, objects, or
events which he felt had been placed unfairly in his path.
He demanded attention, feeling it was only his just dessert.
In sum, he was too highly emotional, but he was extremely
brave.

If I were to pick out just one touchstone of his character it would be this. Some men can look at an ancestral portrait and smile at the waxed mustache, the somewhat foolish high collars, or the emblem-bearing thick gold chain across the vest. I do not believe that George Patton could have looked at such a portrait and felt anything other than this: "I know his eyes are still on me, that he is watching and judging me. I wonder am I man enough always squarely to look back."

CHAPTER III

Enfant terrible

IN UNCLE GEORGE then there was more than a little of the enfant terrible. His humor was not always kindly, nor necessarily in the best of taste. He could appreciate Marlowe's protagonist in *Dr. Faustus* who, under a cloak of invisibility, caused panic to a consistory of cardinals by tossing lighted squibs and petards into their kneeling midst. But Patton would have acted in one way quite differently. He would never have been invisible. He would not have wanted to be even if he could.

My very first picture of him, admittedly, is a little cloudy, composed of what I have been told since childhood and what I can, with total clarity, recall. The mis-en-scène, however, comes clear. It is the front hall of my family's house; a house built by a misanthrope named Sias, who was mortally afraid of robbers or assassins in the night. It was built of heavy stone, and boasted sliding metal grilles to bar the windows after dark. It was very gloomy with black and heavy furniture; and there are those who called it Middle Pullman architecture. The whole ground floor of the house was surrounded by glassed-in and covered porches keeping out all but a dim funereal light. It was, in short, a very homely house which Father bought for Mother when she was bedridden with pneumonia and a double mastoid infection. She wept when she saw it and threatened never to live in it — not ever. Her three youngest children were born there and there she and Father still live. But the front hall is still homely and much too dark. And that is where I was sitting, probably in the chair with the carved griffon claws gripping walnut spheres.

I think the year was 1919. Without knocking, there crashed spectacularly into the gloom Colonel George Patton, tall, piercing of voice and gorgeously arrayed. I can remember that voice, then brick red riding breeches and slender highly polished boots. He had come precipitate from somewhere, possibly the hospital where he had been treated for wounds, to call on Mother, and was annoyed to find her not yet home. When she finally arrived it was to discover her baby son seated on the military knees and receiving precise instructions, "And now, again, repeat after me, Goddammit to hell, Mother, why are you so goddam late?"

Mother still grins when she relates this incident. She was very fond of Uncle George but did not hesitate to fight him tooth and nail when he was too outrageously wrong or behaved, in her opinion, too badly. I am sure these times could not well be counted on the fingers of two hands. The early instruction of her eldest son in strong language she did however not number among them. In dealing with recalcitrant horses, yapping dogs, and hooligan children she used some of that language herself.

I remember in its full glory another Patton arrival at our house. He had again found no one at home; that is, no one was readily available on the ground floor. Accordingly, with what could have been interpreted as a Rebel yell, he grabbed with each hand a three-foot carved balustrade from the stair railing, ripped them loose and charged roaring into my room, waving the broken balustrades. "Goddammit, when I come to this house I expect people to be downstairs to meet me. Next time I'm going to rip things up even worse."

You may well wonder how Mother put up with this sort of invasion and vandalism. She did, however, for several reasons. The first was relatively simple: "This is a horrible house, a homely house and I've always hated the sight of that stair railing." The railing is incidentally still there, homely as ever, although repaired. Secondly, Mother was often amused by Uncle George's outrages because she really understood his motivations better than he did himself; thirdly she has a splendid sense of humor. Mother has always been blessed with beauty and the capacity for great patrician dignity. She can terrify or totally freeze the rude or presumptuous if she wants to and can, with or without strong language, make a balky horse take a fence merely by yelling at it. I have, despite this, all my life tried out on her all the questionable stories I thought had merit. If she looked me straight in the eye and said, "That is not one bit funny," and then seconds later laughed, I knew my judgment had been correct. She also asserted quite regularly, "Anything that any of you can say, I can think of — but need not say — something much worse; and 'any of you' includes your Uncle George." Uncle George himself was well aware of this.

The next time he came to the house he did not rip things up. Instead he brought me a splendid gift, my very first dog. He answered to the name of Bowser, was a powerful, pure-white British pit bull, had pink eyes and bit horses. He was a firm confidant and friend who listened patiently to my recitals of what a dreadful unreasonable bitch was my French governess. Bowser bit horses because he considered that in so doing he was protecting me. I am sure of this, since he bit only horses on which I was mounted. For this Bowser was all too soon banished to another home, an action I felt to be grossly unfair.

Uncle George over the years owned several of these pit bulls. Some members of the family claimed he kept one around so that he could practice imitating its prognathous jaw and belligerent aspect. One which he owned for many years was named Tank and was a prodigious lover and fighter. His last was named Willy and was certainly the homeliest dog I have ever met socially. He accompanied his master across Europe, was an honored guest in the General's mess, and survived him by quite a number of years.

As a thing bright and wonderful to us children in those younger years there was Uncle George on the Fourth of July, or to put things in more proper order, there was the Fourth of July and sometimes with it, Uncle George. This number one holiday was, now nearly twoscore years ago, observed in the manner intended by those who originated it. "That now and henceforth let this day be marked by bells, bonfires, music and cannon across the land," wrote John Adams. Every child I then knew saved his allowance to comply, begged more, and ran additional errands in order to lay in a respectable supply of fireworks. These we hoarded, counted and gloated over against the coming dawn of the glorious day. From then until the last trailing rocket spark had winked into darkness close on midnight, the air was hideous, or magnificent, with sound. It stank, or according to us, was incense-laden, with the fumes of spent powder. Some of our cannon crackers were of such power that they could blast metal ash barrels twenty to thirty feet into the air.

In those days also there were flags flying in front of every house and fluttering in the hands of small children. It was shameful to be without one. Ours, a large one, used to hang from a clothesline stretched tightly between the pillars flanking the front steps. It hung there then, and on the 19th of April, Memorial Day and Armistice Day. It also was hung out when any member of the family returned from far places or later from his war. There were also parades and brass-band concerts and speeches. It was, dammit all, the Fourth of July, the Independence Day of the United States of America. Today the Fourth is silently and inadequately observed. Were George Patton alive he would wildly disapprove. He would note the absence of flags, mutter something about lily-livered bastards and, if need be, buy his own dynamite so that he might resoundingly greet the dawn. He held, and expressed, very firm opinions on this kind of thing.

When the Ayer children were still little, but already destructive pyromaniacs, Uncle George gave them great pleasure in many ways. The best was when he played his role of helpless victim. The rules of this game were simple. He would sit on a wooden chair placed on the gravel of our driveway, attired generally in riding clothes. His position was with arms crossed on his deep chest and his back to us, while he gazed pensively into space. With furtive approach and in semi-silence some child would place a firecracker under the chair, touch punk to the fuse and tiptoe gleefully away. When the detonation finally took place Uncle George would emit a high-pitched scream, clap his hands to his head, then gallop across the driveway to hide behind a rhododendron bush. Several minutes later Major Patton, D.S.C., Silver Star and Purple Heart, would emerge, survey the territory and once more sit down to await the inevitable.

On one never to be forgotten Fourth he arrived in a mood quite new to all of us children. His jaw was grimly set, his step firm and he clutched in his arms a large square box. "I have come to get even with you little stinkers. Stand well back and take cover. I'm about to unveil the biggest most powerful goddam firecracker in the whole world."

Fascinated we watched as he undid the string, removed the top of the box, and began plucking out handfuls of excelsior. I was compelled to edge closer trying to be the first to see the monster itself. "Now dammit, I said this is dangerous, so dammit, get back. And that's an order." And so it was; there was no doubt about it.

At last all the wrappings were gone. Tenderly and using a pair of firetongs, Uncle George extracted the explosive from the box, gingerly set it down about fifty yards away. There it stood, red and huge and menacing with a white fuse nearly three feet long. To this he touched the end of his cigar. For seconds nothing happened. Then there came a small spurt of blue smoke, a slight sizzle of sound. And the man with the cigar sprinted away. Awestruck, we watched the puff of smoke, the line of black edge up the white length of fuse. I stood rooted in place. No, I would not move farther back. I did, however, want to put my hands over my ears. But that was considered the acme of being a sissy. It seemed to take forever, but at last there was no fuse left. We braced ourselves. Here it came at last. And when it did it was with a feeble PIPP as the huge cracker merely twitched slightly as if it had contained a Mexican jumping bean, and nothing more.

I hated Uncle George for a little while that day and two or three of us had to choke back tears of anger and disappointment. He more than made up for it later with a dazzling and reverberating display of night fireworks.

It was a treasured custom in my family, before the law forbade, for Father, my Uncle Keith Merrill, and Uncle George when present, jointly to purchase a large assortment of big rockets, aerial bombs, pinwheels and the rest of the lovely panoply. These were set off from a float at the end of the pier extending into the ocean from "Avalon." It was a beautiful sight. As the leading pyromaniac in the family, Uncle George one unforgettable night was to be fuse-lighter-in-chief.

Uncle Keith was in the foreign service. He was a kind and considerate man who sported an Adolphe Menjou mustache and believed that he could play the trumpet. He did not, however, know much about certain more mundane or technical things. It was a cool, misty night. Therefore he had lit a fire which blazed brightly in his living room, spreading a welcome heat but also from time to time snapping out explosions of gas which tossed small red embers onto the marble apron. Since it was damp the fireworks might be damp, and Uncle Keith had stacked them all directly in front of this fire, enough powder in all to blow the roof from his house. When Uncle George entered the room, he used language. I cannot speak for the others present, but certain it is that I was so interested I forgot to be shocked. In fact, I was delighted.

There will be other references to the Patton vocabulary, but this one more event to me has a certain charm. It took place not long afterward in that other Commonwealth, Virginia. I believe the year was 1934 and the dramatis personae members of the Potomac Hunt Club.

The then Major Patton's blond, pigtailed daughter, Ruth Ellen, was out fox hunting. She had just set her horse, Cimmerian, to a gallop at a solid and forbidding rail fence. This is a very critical moment, much like when an airplane has been committed to its final approach. There is little the pilot can do if anything gets in his path. In this case, something did — a male rider, coattails flying in the breeze, sawing wildly with his reins and bit at his horse's outraged mouth, and totally out of control. He was heading on collision course with Ruth Ellen. At the last second only the greatest luck prevented a very nasty, high-speed accident. Patton was witness to the scene and to the fact that the rider wore somewhat nondescript cavalry uniform. He thereupon galloped up to the offender and began in his high-pitched, carrying voice what he said any well-educated and cultured man should be able to do: that is, curse steadily for three minutes without repeating himself once. Ruth Ellen, as well as disinterested bystanders, told me that he exceeded his norm.

Uncle George was sometimes almost violent in defense of his children, especially his daughters whom he jealously protected against dangers real and imaginary. He was, however, never easy on them. He constantly sought to train them in most of the accomplishments he felt they needed to accompany and keep up with a man. I have often suspected that the reason was that since he had been married for fourteen years before Aunt Bea bore him young George, he had become afraid that he might never have a son. In this instance his protective anger brought repercussions. It was not long before he was informed by his commanding officer that the

War Department had been advised by the State Department that his cursee happened to be the Military Attaché from the Argentine with a rank far more illustrious than he who had cursed. An apology, therefore, was immediately in order, and in writing.

I remember my father later asking, "But George, what in the devil could you say by way of explanation after what you called the man?" We never saw a copy of the communiqué, but we were shown the reply. In essence it stated that the writer had greatly enjoyed in the Estados Unidos the great sport of the hunting of the fox, and that he was complimented that the American major had seen fit to refer to him in Anglo-Saxon sporting terms. Something tells me that Aunt Beatrice had a hand in the drafting of the apology. She was nearly always a great diplomat. There were many times when Uncle George was not.

CHAPTER IV

A very gallant lady

IN ORDER to judge, or even partially to understand a man, it is necessary to know something of those closest to him. In the case of George Patton, the two in question were beyond doubt his wife, née Beatrice Ayer, and her brother, my father, Frederick Ayer, Jr. He gave to each complete reliance; and they gave him complete support from the time of his marriage in 1910 to the day of his death.

Because the background of my aunt and my father was so different from that of the Pattons, it seems useful here to recall just a little of their father, a true Yankee from a very long line of New England Yankees, some of them quite rugged people. For instance, one of these with the wonderful name of Elkhana Fanning made as his dying request that he be buried in a chestnut coffin so that he would assuredly "go snapping and crackling through Hell." In his *Reminiscences* my Grandfather Ayer wrote he rather supposed his late departed relative would do just that.

I never knew Frederick Ayer, since he died in 1917 during his ninety-sixth year. But there are certain facts which bear noting. For instance, this man as an orphan held his first job in a country general store at the age of eleven; and a pallet under the counter was his bed. From that time forward for eighty-four years he worked incredibly hard, amassing during this lifetime a great deal of money. Nowhere, however have I been able to find so much as a hint that he made any of this money through meanness to another, or through any form of dishonesty. His proudest affirmation was, "I have never earned a single dollar of which I was ashamed."

During the apogee of his business life he lived in Lowell, Massachusetts, where still alive today are dozens of citizens bearing names such as Frederick Ayer Dupré, or Arsenault, or Boudreau. They were named by their parents in honor of a man who had acted, where government stood impotent, and had singlehandedly rallied and directed the forces which halted a murderous plague. Later he was a power, in fact the power, in the American Woolen Company, most of whose Lawrence Mill was one night destroyed by fire. Alerted to this fact very early in the morning he was asked, "Do you wish, sir, to be driven down to the mills?"

"Was anyone killed or seriously hurt?"

"No, sir."

"Then what use is served by looking at ruins? No, order my carriage, I will go to the station. I'll take the train into Boston and just borrow the money to build a new and better plant."

His whole approach to life was equally practical. For instance, after the disastrous Chicago fire he went heavily to the financial assistance of that city and asked for this no interest, only title to a downtown business block when it should be rebuilt. It had in those days a worth certainly equal to that of a block in the business district of New York City.

Grandfather Ayer was, however, the first New England businessman to give female employees a monthly day off with pay at a time of their own choosing. Fellow manufacturers told him that he was insane and would ruin business. He was told the same thing when he helped finance Alexander Graham Bell and the New York subway system.

Frederick Ayer rode horseback daily while in his nineties and quite regularly chopped wood for exercise. He sported a wide and snowy beard and resembled not a little an artist's conception of an Old Testament prophet or an old-world patriarch. He never, however, grew old; never fell behind the future. Even during the last years of his life he was sending voluminous correspondence to the British General Staff urging them to use armored tanks against the Germans. I do not know whether his military son-in-law had anything to do with this, but Grandfather no matter what his age was certainly more than capable of thinking and acting for himself.

Frederick Ayer, at the age of sixty-three, married for the second time. His wife was Ellen Banning, a lady of considerable histrionic talent. As a member of a rich and well-known family she was a rarity in the theater of those days; society did not consider her activities quite proper. Accordingly, her manager had the stage directions for the plays of Shakespeare rewritten so that at no time should Miss Banning appear in a scene with a male actor without another woman on the stage. During her portrayal of Juliet, for example, the nurse was kept present in a corner busily knitting throughout the balcony scene.

Grandmother Ayer told her family many times how she first met the man who was to be her husband. She had declined an invitation to a dinner dance, preferring to attend a performance by the great actor Edwin Booth. She said that after it was over she spotted in the lobby the best-looking man she had ever seen. To her surprise he came over, to say, "Of course you don't know me, Miss Banning, but I am Frederick Ayer. When I was told of a lady who had the great good taste to witness Booth instead of attending an ordinary party, I decided that there was no reason why she should not have a chance to do both. My carriage is waiting right outside."

Grandfather may not have been an actor but still he was a man whose talents were not to be minimized. His second marriage produced his fifth, sixth and seventh child, my father, and two sisters each of whom would inherit, to varying degrees, their mother's capacity for dramatic displays of temperament. In all there were seven Ayer children whose birth dates ranged over nearly forty-five years.

Thus, Beatrice Ayer, like her younger brother and sister, was brought up as a daughter of the more than rich in a household dominated by an old, but never aging New England patriarch. They lacked nothing that money could buy, but they learned, by God, to do exactly as they were told.

Aunt Bea did not escape from the parental nest with ease. Her father strongly objected to her marrying a soldier and stated to her that he would not have his "little bird" living in some miserable outpost of dust and tents. His daughter retaliated by retiring to her room on an apparent hunger strike while her sister Katherine smuggled food to her as often as possible. I do not know what tactics finally won the day but have been told that my grandfather, who then also saw that war was coming, wrote to my Uncle George: "From now on I'll take care of making the money. You take care of winning the glory."

George Patton at the time of his marriage did a character-istic thing. He turned over every cent he owned to his sister Anita and signed over to her his prospective share of his fa-ther's estate. And from those very early days, with the ex-ception of the expenses of his house, he spent no money on himself except his Army pay. It was also at this time that he gave to my father a near likeness of his own snake ring made of platinum and gold but lacking the jeweled eyes. Now, however, I will not write more about the relationship between these two men who were so very unlike and yet admired each other so greatly. At this point, rather, it is the time to take a look at Beatrice Ayer Patton.

If Aunt Bea had been even a little spoiled she did not show it even in her early life as the wife of a soldier. She went with her husband to every post to which he was assigned, and some of them were highly unattractive, like Sierra Blanca, Texas, or Fort Clark. This was especially true in the first days before World War I, and shortly after it. Those were the times when people said, "We do not need a standing army," and "The army is a refuge for men who just couldn't earn a living any other way." At each post she and Uncle George lived no more richly than neighboring officers of equal rank. An exception to this rule were George Patton's horses. They lived very well indeed.

At one point, in fact, Uncle George shared the ownership of a racing stable with the famous "Billy" Mitchell and like-wise the services of a talented groom named Kail. This man's abilities were such that, without anyone spending a dime, the stable was always equipped with more tack at the end of each season than at its beginning.

Young memories and old photographs tell me that Aunt Bea was a beautiful woman who often wore her long hair in braids coiled about her head, and that this hair was chestnut color and undone would fall below her hips. Her eyes were the wide-gazing ones of the very nearsighted. She was petite, but had the great endurance and the somewhat grim courage of those who must too often fight fear.

Throughout his life she battled constantly for her husband. She did so with courage, but added to it an essential leaven of diplomacy and finesse. This leaven was necessary since Patton was always a man of views strongly held and more strongly expressed, and his temper was not easily controlled. She had, therefore, often to soothe hurt feelings, effect reconciliations, explain the inexplicable, and pick up all the pieces when he broke things. From this it must not be inferred that she was in any way a meek person. On one occasion she inflicted physical damage upon a man who had unjustly criticized her husband. It happened just after the First World War in the old Wadsworth house, which is now the Sulgrave Club in Washington. Uncle George had parked the automobile and had just come in the door to join his wife who was waiting in the hall. He was, at the time, in full evening dress uniform complete with medals. A somewhat less than sober and quite fat Reserve Colonel spotted him coming and muttered something apparently unpleasant. Aunt Bea asked him to repeat more clearly; the man did. "I said that man's one of those all chicken, chicken on his shoulder and chicken in the heart."

Auntie Bea had already knocked him over and was pounding his head on the oaken floor before Uncle George could pull her off. She told us that about three years later she found herself seated next to her victim at another dinner. She did not at first recognize him, but evidently he could not forget her. Finally, calling on his nerve, he broke the icy silence. "What do we do Mrs. Patton, if we're left alone to talk?" At this point Aunt Bea remembered who he was. "Oh, that'll be easy, Colonel, we shall recite the multiplication tables to each other."

There were other less direct ways in which she helped George Patton's career. For example, she read voluminously and studied intently the histories and cultures of each place the family was assigned. Her acquaintanceship everywhere was vast and varied. I remember traveling in her company about the Hawaiian Islands where she knew, and was liked, by everyone from the Big Four families and the governor to Japanese vegetable growers and native fishermen. She knew and could talk on equal terms with the Curator of the Museum on Oahu and Dr. Jagger, the famed volcanologist of Mauna Loa.

She could play on the piano by ear a song heard once and set it in a key to suit the voices of any assemblage. I remember so many evenings gathered around a piano, the much-traveled grand at "Green Meadows," the Steinway in the echoing living room of Avalon, the little-used and not completely in tune instrument at the home of my parents. Aunt Beatrice, petite but powerful, perched on stool or bench, would smile back over her shoulder and ask, "Now, what does anyone want to sing next?"

It didn't matter what song was named, she could play it. Even if she had never heard it before if someone hummed one stanza with reasonable accuracy she could carry on from there. Some of us could sing on key. Some, such as my father and I, compromised by simply singing loudly. My sister then had a clear soprano voice, as she does now as a concert singer. This very mixed chorus did not bother Bea Patton at all. Somehow she managed to find a key to fit the group as it sang the old songs and the new, hymns, spirituals, or folk songs. It was a wonderful way to spend an evening; and like too many simple yet wonderful things it seems to have passed from our lives.

Aunt Bea not only played music, she could write it and did so, including several accepted marches. Probably the most spectacular of these was "The March of the Armored Force," now the official 2nd Armored Division march. It has certain touches which must have been added by her husband since it is scored to open with the wail of a tank siren and the firing of guns. In addition to an instinctive knowledge of music, she had a fine command of the written word. She was completely bilingual in French and English. For example, she had published a reasonably successful novel, *Blood of the Shark* and also a beautiful volume titled *Légendes Hawaiennes.*

She never did, however, adopt her husband's practice of spelling the same word in several different ways. In spelling she was solidly consistent. In another field she was not. If asked for someone's telephone number or address she would smilingly and graciously invent one on the spot. She felt this was far more friendly than having to say that she really didn't know.

She became an accomplished sailorwoman in craft ranging from small racing sloops in which she won many championships to 60-foot schooners. She did, in fact, accompany her husband, and stand regular watches at the wheel, on both Pacific crossings in the 45-foot *Arcturus.* The westward voyage was done in nearly record time. On the return in 1937,

Grandfather Patton, circa
1860. Killed at the battle of
Winchester, 1863.

Susan Glassell Patton, circa
1860. She had second sight.

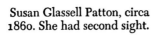

Grandfather
Don Benito Wilson,
circa 1850.

Grandmother Margaret Hereford
Wilson and Hereford child,
circa 1860.

Father, George S. Patton, Jr.
Above: At Virginia Military
Academy in 1873.
At right: circa 1885.

Mother, Mrs. George S.
Patton, Jr., circa 1888.

The second G. S. Patton, Jr., 1891.

G. S. Patton, Jr., and father,
California, 1901.

G. S. Patton, Jr., Santa
Catalina, California, 1905.

West Point, 1909.

Beatrice Ayer Patton, 1909.

George S. Patton, Jr., and
Beatrice Ayer Patton, 1910.

The groom's father
and Beatrice Ayer Patton.

Uncle George, Bea Jr., Aunt Bea, Ruth Ellen, 1914.

however, the winds rose so high and the waves were so terrible that the boat had to heave to for six full days. This means that with only one small headsail the boat must be held constantly into the wind, or risk being swamped and capsized. During this time, each helmsman had to be lashed to the wheelpost so that he or she would not be tossed helpless into the sea.

My cousin George says the fury of that storm is still uncomfortably clear in his memory, but not so much so as one vivid scene in the small stuffy cabin of the *Arcturus*. "You remember that Daddy had an iron-clad digestive system, even if he did go and have his stomach pumped out after every Christmas. But this day was something exceptional. There they sat, my old man, Doc Graves and Joe Ekeland. Sat, hell! They were braced against the bulkheads with backs, both legs and one arm apiece since the boat was literally standing on her beam ends — and they were smoking long black cigars, drinking warm bourbon out of Pyrex glasses and eating cold potatoes and greasy lamb. It made me sick just to look at them, but they were having a wonderful time."

Merely to stand erect during a rough storm is a constant physical effort. Even with "one hand for the ship" one is thrown around and bruised. When a boat's motion is precipitously up and down, cooking in a tiny galley is something like trying to balance a bowl of soup while riding a bucking horse. Trimming or changing sails is an occupation for an acrobat, while wrestling the wheel for a four-hour watch can exhaust a strong man. Often, as in the case of the six-day blow, a hundred or more hours can go by during which neither sun, moon nor stars are visible, and in those days there was no Loran or other electronic aid to small craft navigation. Deep ocean yachting can be in short a very rugged, cold and wet business; and Aunt Beatrice stood up to it all.

One of the Pattons' companions on the first crossing, and a lifetime personal friend, was Gordon C. Prince, one of the bravest men I have known. He was one of the first American combat flyers in the balsawood and bailing wire planes of World War I. He was an intrepid steeplechase rider, and he would say in a booming voice anything that came into his mind. Once, when outraged by the thirty-six dollar price of some lace panties he had selected for his wife for Christmas at Best & Co. in Boston, he announced for all to hear, "Why dammit, I know where I can buy these filled for half that price."

Gordon later became agonizingly crippled by arthritis, yet for several years he continued to ride to hounds. In fact, he was still Master of Foxhounds at the Myopia Hunt Club in Hamilton, Massachusetts, when he quite literally had to be lifted onto and from his horse. During the Second World War he had to be similarly assisted into and out of an airplane. Nevertheless, he flew for the duration as a submarine hunter of the Civil Air Patrol out of Boston. He was once wounded by a stray .22-caliber bullet loosed by some youngster potting at birds and Patton's only word of sympathy was to wire, "Sorry you were shot, for God's sake next time marry the girl." Gordon Prince always met and still meets life head-on. This, and his sense of noblesse oblige made him a natural friend to a man like Uncle George. He too sat in a place of honor at the Patton dinner in Boston in July 1945.

I have talked with Gordon Prince and asked him for his re-membrance of the ocean trip to Hawaii, particularly his recollection of Uncle George during those days. This is what he had to say:

George intended to know his navigation cold, don't you know. Why before we left for the West Coast he used to drive thirty miles to Chesapeake Bay and back nearly every night so that he could practice taking star fixes from the moving platform of another boat. Once on our way aboard the *Arcturus*, he was very serious about his navigation, checked and double-checked himself. It was a damned good job, at that. After all those days at sea we hit Mauna Kea right smack on the nose. There was never any question who was in charge on the schooner. But there was this. George would ask one or more of us he felt knew as much or more than he did about any particular phase of the thing. He'd listen carefully, then put it all together and make his decision. Once he'd made it, don't you know, he'd never have any second thoughts or look back.

There were many hours to kill on the long watches, especially at night, and George would tell some fine stories from his own experiences and from history. I never knew a man who had read and remembered so much in that field. He used to say that this was the most important study in the world since different countries, or rather peoples, tended to behave in the same way they had before and thus history would always repeat itself.

He used to recite poetry, lots of it. You know I have a damned good memory for poems myself, but for every one I could recite, he had a half dozen. He would give us long passages from the *Iliad*, and a huge amount of Kipling. He'd memorized "The Helmet of Navarre," and "The Revenge" —

you know, "At Flores in the Azores Sir Richard Grenville lay" and so on. He knew most of Macaulay by heart, things like "Horatius at the Bridge." He liked poems about heroism and patriotism, things with bugles and flags and drums. But somehow George was very religious. He used to talk with us for hours about the different religions, and of how well he had understood and gotten on with the priests during World War I. He had a great admiration for the Catholic Church. He said he liked its priests because they were so militant in their faith.

There was something almost Japanese or Mohammedan in George's views about war and death. A man just could not be a coward; if he was, why he simply ceased to exist as a human. A brave man falling in battle against the infidel, or whoever, was sure to go to a better heaven.

Do you know, when he came home after the Second War he talked the same way, about people like his friend Cardinal Spellman. He admired the man a lot. But there was a difference in 1945, George was sad and discouraged. Some of the letters and so on he wrote after going back to Germany in the fall damn near made me cry. He was a disillusioned man who felt he had been betrayed by politics, politicians and the press for having done his duty as he saw it. He knew how dangerous the Russians were and talked about it. A lot of times he used to let his hair down and confide his thinking to people because he trusted them. Then someone would break this confidence. He never could understand it.

It's a sad thing maybe, to say about a friend, but I'm glad he died when he did. He was no politician, but he did see things correctly in their long and wide range. He would have been crucified even worse than he was if he'd had to come home and speak his mind. It would have been dramatic

as he had a beautiful way with words; and it would have
been true, but they'd have murdered him. I think that in her
heart Aunt Bea felt this also.

Beatrice Patton was an apparently avid horsewoman, riding in countless shows, and to the hounds when her husband
was stationed in Virginia, or when she was living at their
country place in Massachusetts. She was, as has been said,
quite small and dreadfully nearsighted. I am positive that
she was afraid when she rode. In fact, I feel that she hated
the sport. She carried on with it nonetheless, because
"Georgie" rode and loved it and so, by God, would she. It is
fact, however, that she continued to ride to hounds over tall
fences and rough country even after he died. Her own death
came in a fall while hunting at the age of sixty-seven. She
had just taken a large fence and her horse had floundered on
landing, throwing her heavily to the ground. My father
jumped from his horse and rushed over to her but there was
nothing he could do to help. From the fall, or the unwonted
exertion, her aorta had ruptured, and she died right there in
her brother's arms.

She became over the years a forceful and persuasive public
speaker in two languages and, in fact, took up the torch for
Patton's major belief after death had taken it from his hand.
As early as 1946 she was active in advocacy and debate for
the cause of universal military training. Her argument, as
had been his, was that if it were enacted it would show more
convincingly than in any other way to the men in the Krem-
lin that we meant what we said. She was outspoken in her
belief that the Patton judgment would be proved sound.

Aunt Bea was also a teacher. She could relate events and
explain things in a way which anchored them firmly in the

mind of the listener. Admittedly, she did, upon occasion, re-
sort to very pragmatic measures. For instance, at Fort Myer,
Virginia, where she taught Sunday school she rewarded the
punctual and the diligent by letting them handle the Colonel's revolver and feel with their stubby fingers the notches
in the hardwood grip, telling the delighted youngsters that
each represented an enemy killed in armed combat.

Typical of this great lady was her behavior during her husband's funeral. My father who accompanied her told me
about it. The train carrying Uncle George's body was made
up in Heidelberg, Germany, in the French zone of occupation, and moved slowly toward Luxembourg. It was a bitter
cold cloud-covered December day. Evidently the route had
become known to the French Command. In any event, at
more than a dozen cities and towns detachments of French
troops had gathered as guards of honor along the tracks,
each one with huge sheaves of beautiful flowers which a
spokesman reverently laid in the baggage car containing the
casket of their liberator. How or from where they had managed to find such flowers in the dead-cold of winter, Father
said he had no idea. He told me that to him there was something even more impressive about this cortege. In addition
to the French there were gathered at each stopping point
great crowds of Germans, people whose armies Patton had
worse than decimated no more than six months before. Each
man of them stood bareheaded at the arrival of the funeral
train and so stood until it had chuffed itself away into the
gloom. What Father did not mention has been supplied me
by Van S. Merle-Smith, Jr., the General's last aide. This was
the fact, that all the stops were between 1:00 A.M. and 6:00
A.M. in the morning.

It was fitting, I think, that the man who first went up to meet Aunt Bea's car at the cemetery and to hand her out was General Jean Houdemon, now wearing five stars and, although needing two canes to walk, otherwise as military in bearing as ever. He had, he told her, "Come to say goodbye to the man who saved my life — my oldest and dearest friend in good times and in bad." Talking of his sister, Father said, "And do you know, at every single stop Bea stepped out onto the platform and made a short speech in French, thanking the troops for their tribute to George." It did not seem to surprise Father that she had, even in her exhaustion and grief, done such a thing. Thinking upon it now, neither does it surprise me.

Later, she toured Europe more widely and stopped in England, France, and North Africa to call on many dignitaries, or just ordinary citizens who had been mentioned in her husband's letters as being friends or valued allies. She also visited Moscow and wore the gorgeous Soviet medal awarded to her husband on behalf of his government by the Russian Ambassador to Belgium. It entitled the wearer to travel the subways of Moscow gratis and for life.

In retrospect it is easy to see that the existence of Beatrice Patton must sometimes have been hard. For forty years of it she had to deal with a temperamental and contentious prima donna whose behavior at times was hard to excuse. In fact, her devotion was often so intense that it was almost frightening to others. And it carried literally to the grave. She left instructions that her ashes were to rest beside those of her husband in the American Military Cemetery at Hamm in the Duchy of Luxembourg.

She was, in short, herself capable of drama, unusually talented, quite often stubborn or obstinate, and highly intelligent. But, above all, she was a remarkable wife and a very gallant lady.

CHAPTER V

"An unwritten page"

WHAT did George Patton look like as a younger man? What was actually his basic character? What was he really like before he emerged from the deserts of Indio, California, to strike into Africa and Sicily, then to explode across the lands of Northern Europe? Those who choose to can of course remember what he looked like toward the end: in an almost larger than life-size pose, standing very tall, chin and chest outthrust, pistols at hips on a broad leather, especially made belt cinching in the waist of his Eisenhower jacket. They can remember, possibly, views of him with head emerging from the turret of a tank; or standing dramatically to survey a battlefield through upraised binoculars. Or they may retain a vision of a bright splash of ribbons across the tunic's breast, plus a helmet burnished and lacquered beyond brightness carrying one, two, three, and, finally, four silver stars. Certainly those who remember at all can see an almost arrogantly erect figure, an aura of showmanship, a display of strength, possibly more than a hint of brutality or heartlessness. This was his public image which gave rise to such sobriquets as the "Green Hornet," and "Old Blood and Guts." It also lay behind remarks I have heard often repeated, remarks like "a fine field commander sure, but boastful, unmanageable," "possibly a Nazi-lover," "certainly the man who in a Sicilian hospital slapped a sick soldier in the face."

What I would like to suggest is that George Patton finally succeeded in creating a man in his own image of himself, and that he both profited and suffered from his handiwork. This had to be so since, in the long run, the outward show to too great a degree belied the truth.

Of course, I cannot recall him very clearly until he had reached the age of almost forty. But I have carefully studied his photographs and talked to people of insight who knew him in his late twenties and thirties. The photographs are most revealing. In addition to the tight, high collars, the slicked-down hair, the too formal poses of the day, they show the following: a tall, slender, perhaps posturing young man, light-complexioned, very fair-haired, even to his almost invisible eyebrows; a fairly high forehead, piercing eyes, the somewhat heavy aquiline nose of his maternal grandfather, Don Benito Wilson, above a not yet very strong, slightly petulant mouth.

While discussing early pictures of his father a little while ago my cousin George said to me, "Just wait a minute. There's something I'd like to show you." He left the room to return with a small oval antique silver frame enclosing an old portrait photograph. "That was Daddy during his First Class year at the Point. He gave it to Mother then." It was not a very good picture — formal, stiff and rather empty of expression. "Now turn it over and look at the back." I did so, to find in Aunt Bea's unmistakable script: "An unwritten page. I wonder what will be written on it," and the date, June 1909.

The young Patton did not appear particularly powerful in body. This is not surprising since he was sickly as a little boy. The appearance, however, was becoming deceptive as he was by now driving himself physically. It is no secret that he was a far from spectacular student, failing mathematics and thus requiring five years to graduate from West Point. Nevertheless, later pictures and athletic records show the degree to which he forced his mind as well as his body. The mouth becomes tighter, the brow more furrowed, the chest deeper and the shoulders heavier. These do not seem so much the changes of advancing years as the result of intense and concentrated effort directed solely at self. I have spoken of his "war face," constantly practiced according to his own words before a mirror. Well, there are ample witnesses to the fact that his words were true. Mark Twain's remark is here appropriate: "Anyone who at age 45 does not like his face has only himself to blame."

Even at West Point there became evident traits or opinions from which he was never to deviate. Despite his complete dedication to military service, he never came to trust a Regular Army medical officer. "When I was in my third year," he told me, "I fractured a leg playing football. The poor bastard in the next infirmary bed was suffering from acute dysentery. Somehow the diet orders became mixed up. The medics sent him my heavy training-table meals. To me they gave the boiled skim milk. He died and I damned nearly starved to death."

Likewise, although even as a cadet strongly for the maintenance of tradition and discipline, he early rebelled against anything he considered unfair. I remember his telling of one example which he ever afterwards considered of importance in his life. "There was a tradition, or at least a habit, at West

Point called The Silence. This was: when one officer whom the cadets felt had behaved poorly toward them came into the mess hall, the corps would rise to attention and remain entirely silent at the meal thereafter. One day when I happened to be in command of the battalion and was bringing them into the hall, I sensed that a 'silence' was about to be put on against a young officer. I felt they were wrong about the man and I was opposed in any event to the practice. Therefore, I surprised hell out of them. I called the battalion to attention and marched them right back to quarters — and without lunch. The young officer called me down for breaking tradition; but I think I convinced him I was right. A man knows instinctively, he must know, when he is right."

He had held a vision of himself ever since he was a small boy as a strong leader of men in battle and he strove constantly to mold himself to that vision even to the extent of changing his physical appearance by force of will alone. One thing he could never change: the timbre of his voice. It remained high-pitched, even when his rank commanded four stars. It was never able to achieve resonance, but he did build into it a carrying power and a power of holding attention and of command, even if this were achieved by the shock value of what he said.

He was thus able to put others on the defensive, give himself time to marshal his forces. He did this on the telephone, even in the earliest days of my recollection. I can still hear him: "Major Patton speaking. What do you want?" It was said with such cutting edge to the words that the caller thought he had heard: "This is *General* Patton. How dare you disturb me, and what the hell do you want anyway? Speak up man, dammit, or get off the phone." It is easy to imagine the effect when he did, in fact, become a general. I have heard him often and can understand how some people who knew they were right, and Patton wrong, still felt that they ought to apologize — or slug him. At Fort Benning with the 2nd Armored, at Indio, California, in North Africa, Sicily, France — and in East Germany — he sometimes practiced one of his own precepts of command, "Put yourself in the shoes of your subordinate," by taking over, at unannounced intervals, the telephone of the Duty Officer or Officer of the Day at his headquarters. Some I know who, calling him unforewarned, still shudder today at the memory.

Concerning this practice, Uncle George had this to tell us at Nancy in 1944: "I don't really do it to scare anybody. I strongly believe that whenever he can, especially during busy times, a General should answer his own telephone — that is, except the very few hours when he has to sleep. Sometimes even minutes are important. A deputy commander wants an answer. The commander himself must know the exact situation at all times. But," and here he grinned, "I must admit, I managed to keep some of my Juniors on their god-damned toes."

Whatever the process, whatever the sequence of development through his life, the end result was evident, and probably inevitable. There was never the slightest doubt who was in charge when George Patton was around. But I am still certain that this was not so true when he was a very young officer, and I think he himself was generally aware of the fact.

It has often been written and repeated that he was a great natural athlete. He was not a natural athlete, except insofar as he had excellent reflexes and perfect eyesight. Actually he

drove himself without mercy toward the perfection which
was his goal, and in this way achieved, at least in his chosen
fields of athletics, more than a measure of greatness. I know
from what he told me, and from having watched him in action, that running came hard to him and that he hated swimming and was quite lacking in ease and gracefulness in the
water. Nevertheless, he was chosen as the first American
officer to represent his country in the military pentathlon of
the 1912 Olympic games at Stockholm.

The pentathlon demands a variety of skills, and great
stamina. It consists of a long steeplechase, pistol shooting,
fencing, a grueling swimming race, and a cross-country foot
race of 5000 meters. Riding a borrowed horse he finished
third in the steeplechase. In the practice round on the pistol
range he broke the existing Olympic record, but dropped to
twenty-seventh place in the actual competition. Although
nine shots were beautifully centered, one had, apparently,
missed the target completely. It seems hard to believe that
one so expert could have thrown one shot that wild. This, at
least, was the opinion of the Swedes and others who competed against him. Some of them claimed that one bullet
must have passed exactly through the hole already made by
an earlier round. This could have happened since use was
not made in those days of the micrometered gauge to test the
exact size of a bullet hole. Be that as it may, the scorers had
to accept the evidence of their eyes.

In the fencing competition he placed first, defeating the
champion of the French army and upsetting what had been
a European monopoly. He had trained for the swimming
race in a water-filled wooden tank aboard ship, tying himself to its side by a rope attached to his waist and thrashing

endlessly against its pull. With this for practice, he placed third.

In the cross-country race he punished himself mercilessly and was staggering when he entered the stadium for the final lap. Somehow he completed the course, falling in a dead faint just over the finish line and in front of the King's box — but still barely in third place. He told me fifteen years later that he still had no recollection whatever of running the last four hundred meters or of anything else until he was be ing revived five minutes or so after the finish. In his own written account he recalls that the first cheering words he heard were, "Do you think he's going to live?" He did, and his overall performance, even with the twenty-seventh place in shooting, put him fourth among the military athletes of the world.

Thirty-three years later, at the conclusion of the Second World War, the entire membership of the 1912 Swedish team invited him to a return engagement in Stockholm. There, after so much time — so many battles, cigars, and bottles later — he fired for the record a better pistol target than he had posted in 1912.

This did not surprise me. I had often shot pistol with Uncle George and can testify to the steadiness of his hand and the accuracy of his aim. He had nearly perfect eyesight but told me very early in my life, "Bowser, it doesn't matter how bad your eyesight may be" (and mine was very bad) "if it's anywhere near correctible with glasses and you practice enough, you can end up as good or better than most." Here I have to confess to a horrid truth. Uncle George did indeed, in the younger years of my life call me "Bowser" which, as mentioned was also the name of the white bull terrier he had

given to me. For a long time I feared that he had named the
dog first. A check with my mother brought out the truth that
he named my dog after his name for me. I'm sure I don't
know which order could be considered worse. I am not certain I approve of either.

In discussing the proper use of guns he often told me,
"Never draw a gun on a man unless you intend to kill him.
And believe me if you intend to kill him he will already know
it. Then he will feel the cold breath of the tomb." He gave
me other useful advice. "If you're just trying to scare people
with the noise, use an automatic. If you're trying to kill them
use a revolver, so practice with that." I followed his instruction until eventually, at a distance of thirty feet, I could,
with a .38 Colt, cut in half four out of five cigarettes.

I can remember another pistol range. It belonged to a
neighbor and close friend of Uncle George's, a Reserve
Colonel named Francis Throope Colby of Hamilton, Massachusetts. He had fought in the French, British and U.S.
Armies in World War I, was a noted and courageous big game
hunter, and was, although well overage, to serve again in Africa and in uniform during the war to come. He was, possibly
a more remarkable shot than Uncle George since his skill ran
from heavy elephant guns through deer rifles and shotguns
to small-caliber pistols. He sported a mustache, a glorious
Colonel Blimp British accent, and both harrumphed and
snorted through his nose. Once when a feminine acquaintance, Katherine Wellman of our neighboring town Topsfield,
observed, "Francis, when you snort like that you scare me,"
he answered, "You know, by God, sometimes I scare myself."
Colby was likewise a raconteur and a fine two-fisted drinker. I
once, at my Uncle James Proctor's house in Ipswich, watched

in awe as he consumed eleven stiff scotches and soda, and then broke fifty clay pigeons straight; that is, without a miss.

One evening in 1932 I was invited to his house amid elephant hides, rhinoceros heads, poisoned-tipped Bantu spears and George Patton. Afterwards, with brandy and cigars for the adults, among whom I was not, we went down to his cellar. We also brought pistols. Colby turned on a movie projector, turned off the overhead lights and threw onto a white-painted metal screen his pictures of charging big game and spear-waving natives. The .22-caliber pistols were loaded with explosive-tipped bullets and the evening sport began as each marksman named aloud and fired at his target of choice. Patton and Colby in such a setting were a combination hard to forget. So was some of their language.

Uncle George was a skilled horseman. But here also he drove himself unmercifully, and the same applied to his mounts. I can remember that he encased his 190 pound, over six-foot frame in heavy clothes and forced his legs day after day to run mile on aching mile. He would then drink citrate of magnesia and spend many of his nights in a Turkish bath until he had sweated and starved himself to below 155 pounds to make the weight for a steeplechase. Believe me, it was as pleasant around Uncle George at those times as near a tiger from whose jaws a haunch of game has just been snatched.

He did not tolerate disobedience from horses any more than he did from subordinates or from his own mind and body. I will never forget a hair-raising performance he once put on to teach a horse not to rear onto its hind legs. The horse was a gray belonging to my mother and was named Gun Metal. He was strong, quick moving, and very stubborn. The scene was a mown-over hayfield in Wenham, Massachusetts. The other participants were Mother, our groom John Dixon, myself, and Uncle George. He said to Mother, "Goddammit, Hilda, I can stop the bastard from rearing. If I take some bottles, fill them with water and every time he rears, smash one between his ears. It'll hurt like hell and he'll think he's pouring blood. A couple of times and there'll be no more rearing."

"Maybe so, but you're not doing it to my horse."

"All right, dammit, there's another way." So saying, he vaulted into the saddle and yanked upward at the horse's reins, then did it again. Gun Metal, thus goaded, reared up, front feet well clear of the ground; Uncle George, keeping pressure on the reins, threw his full weight backward. The horse came upright on his hind legs and began then to lose his balance. The rider yanked once more, then kicked his feet out of the stirrups and threw his body clear as Gun Metal came crashing down on his back, all four legs in the air, and perilously close to Uncle George. Before the horse could recover, Patton jumped forward and sat heavily on its head. He stayed there for some time, refusing to allow the thrashing animal to rise. "I guess that'll teach the dirty son-of-a-bitch a lesson." Mother was not pleased, and Gun Metal reared again the very next time he felt so inclined. In fact for some weeks he was dangerously nervous; he was what horsemen call "spooky" and I couldn't blame him.

George Patton dearly loved the game of polo. He likened it to "a good war" and felt it was an essential part of the training of a combat commander. This was because the game moves at such a fierce rate of speed and demands near perfection of teamwork and split-second tactical decisions. It is also an extremely dangerous pastime. From no more than two dozen of my acquaintances with whom I played polo, all have been injured: four of them killed.

Uncle George was never one of the great, or even of the highly skilled polo players. He did, however, make up for most of his deficiencies by the drive and energy he put into its every minute. I have watched him play many times and think it possible that he overdid this and so lost some of the coolness and concentration necessary for true effectiveness. It is certain that his general behavior, and especially his use of language, was not that of a temperate player. This did not, however, hurt his reputation among those who believed a modicum of flamboyant language essential to so hot-blooded a sport.

There is nothing genteel about polo. It is not played on so-called "ponies." Four men to a team are mounted on horses bred for racing, but trained for quick handling. These weigh from 1000 to 1300 pounds each and at top speed reach just under forty miles an hour. They play on a 300-yard field, generally baked hard by summer sun, under rules which permit riding into the other player in bruising contact in order to drive him off the line of the ball.

A match consists of eight periods of seven and one half minutes each, with rest periods long enough only to change mounts. It is nothing less than spectacular when eight well-mounted players stream at top speed down the field on attack or defense. It is spectacular to watch, but to play is damned hard work. I have seen a player in near-perfect physical condition lose as much as twelve pounds during one hot hour of play.

Polo is a fine spectator sport, and in a community such as prewar Hawaii, drew a notable gallery of personalities, both military and civilian. Picture, therefore, as I saw it, such an assemblage dressed in its best under an August sky, lining a field which crowds close against the base of towering Diamond Head. The match being played was for the 1935 Inter-Island Championship, and the teams were: Oahu, captained by Walter Dillingham, and Army, captained by George S. Patton, Jr.

Play entered the fourth period with a tie score. Temperatures, blood pressures and tempers had risen and were still rising. Walter Dillingham had just crashed his horse into Patton at what the Colonel considered a dangerous angle. Rich, varied and high-pitched profanity carried clearly to the ears of all present including General Hugh Drum. The General took official umbrage and at the period's end publicly relieved Patton of his captaincy of his team and forbade him further play in the tournament. There followed then a long delay in the start of the next period during which the Oahu team failed to take the field. Dillingham and Frank Baldwin, captain of the Maui team, at last approached General Drum to ask if it was true that Patton had been banished. They were told it was. I cannot remember which man gave the answer, but cannot forget what it was.

"Well, General, we did not hear any unseemly language, and if George does not play, neither will we, and we will cancel the whole tournament."

Drum recognized *force majeure* when he faced it, but he never forgave Uncle George.

As a matter of fact the General, at the end of Patton's Hawaiian tour of duty, gave him by far the poorest efficiency report of his whole military career. His son George told me, "Daddy brought the report home, not in the least upset. As a matter of fact he thought it was a great joke. He told us,

'The old poop doesn't know it but he's paid me quite a compliment.' Then he read us the concluding section which summed up in just about these words: 'This officer could be of great value in time of war. He is, however, most disruptive to a command in time of peace.'" No one today can say that Hugh Drum was very far wrong.

The degree to which Uncle George threw himself into the heat of polo's battle was well illustrated on a day at the Myopia Hunt Club in Massachusetts, when his scalp was laid open by a blow from a mallet. He simply washed off the blood, soaked a wad of cotton in the overstrength iodine used for cuts on horses, and jammed it down onto the wound under the helmet. At the end of the game the entire top of his head had become one enormous throbbing blister. He had ignored the pain; possibly he had not even felt it.

It was during the early days when Uncle George played polo at Myopia that he became very much attached to another member of our family, my maternal grandmother, Mrs. Charles G. Rice of "Turner Hill" in Ipswich, Massachusetts. She was a most remarkable woman who stood just a few inches more than five feet and weighed about ninety-five pounds; she was possessed of indomitable courage, was a very great hostess, and delighted to spoil her grandchildren. During her lifetime she managed to break nearly every bone in her body in horseback accidents; both legs, both arms, her neck once, her lower spine once, and countless times her ribs and collarbone, finally she suffered a frightful fracture of her pelvis. She died in 1933 as a result of a fall sustained while trying to subdue a vicious horse. And at one time in 1914 by prompt action she quite literally saved George Patton's life.

It came about in this way. Robert Reece, a frequent guest

of the Rice household, came upon an overturned Ford nearby in the Ipswich road. From beneath it projected a pair of booted legs. Reece, although short in stature, was very strong and so managed to lift up the car and drag out a strange man in polo clothes. He was unrecognizable as his face had been ground into the gravel and was masked in dirty crank-case oil. The only action which seemed to him appropriate was to take the unconscious body to Turner Hill.

My grandmother was at work in her study when Roberts, the butler, announced that Mr. Reece was outside on an urgent errand. Grandmother told him, "Roberts, I quite distinctly told you that I was not to be disturbed." "But, Mrs. Rice, Mr. Reece is outside with a dead man." This was almost true, so Grandmother ordered the body placed on a bed and with Reece's help pried open its jaws, and reached down the throat with her fingers to remove the sludge of gravel and oil which was slowly strangling him. She had no idea who the man was and in undressing him found that his undershirt bore the label "Frederick Ayer, Jr." This seemed unreasonable since her new son-in-law was at that time on his honeymoon on a schooner off the coast of Maine. So, after scrubbing the black from what was left of the face she concluded correctly that the still half-dead horseman was Uncle George. Not until she had finished her ministrations and wrapped the man up in blankets did she call a doctor.

Patton was ever thereafter grateful and all during Grandmother's life wrote her letters and sent her small gifts. And he was present at her funeral service in the main living room of Turner Hill. He had come from only as far away as Virginia but told me then that had he been halfway around the world he would have somehow managed to be there since she was such a very gallant lady.

Among the gifts Uncle George sent her was, in 1920, a notebook containing copies of some of his poems and with it a letter. I believe this worth reproducing in full:

My dear Mrs. Rice:

Ever since you so foolishly prevented my untimely departure to another world I have taken occasion to remind you of your error. Yet since you still seem friendly towards me I have decided to expose to you in all its horror the full enormity of your action. To do this I am sending you an expurgated edition of some of my so-called poems. They give a better index to my utter depravity than anything else that I know of. Having read one or two you are at liberty to destroy them lest they infect the minds of the young and gently nurtured.

Should your friendship for me survive this outrage, I hope that for many years I shall have the pleasure of reminding you of what you did for me. The only other person who ever saved my life, Joe Angelo, my orderly, I gave a gold watch. Shall I get you one next year?

Please excuse the fact that this is written on the typewriter but it is the only way I can be sure you will know who wrote the letter.

Give our love to all the family.

Very affectionately,
G. S. PATTON, JR.

Among these poems was the one called "Memories" quoted later herein and a long one, "The End of War," also written at Langres in France in 1917. The second concludes with these stanzas:

The folly of the slogan
Down all the ages rings

The ruin of republics
The funeral dirge of Kings.

At last all strife is ended
Battles shall rage no more
The time of perfect peace has come
There can be no more war.

Still like the foolish revellers
In Bab'lon's banquet hall
They'll take their ease while mocking
The writing on the wall.

They will disband their armies
When THIS great strife is won
And trust again to pacifists
To guard for them their home.

They will return to futileness
As quickly as before
Though truth and history vainly shout
"THERE IS NO END TO WAR."

It was at Turner Hill among other places that Uncle George demonstrated his remarkable memory. Mother told me that after a long family weekend lunch someone had questioned that he was a regular churchgoer. By way of answer, he mounted the sliding stepladder of the library and recited from memory the entire Episcopal Sunday church service including a Lesson of the Day from the Bible, a Responsive Reading, the Twenty-third Psalm, the Doxology and the Benediction. Once more some of his hearers may have been shocked, but I can testify that they were not un-impressed.

CHAPTER VI

No diplomat

★ ★ ★ ★

IT IS possible that polo, and the way Patton played it, served to burn up some of his deep resentments and various angers. His most active years with this game coincided with the years of his bitterest frustration. Having been a full colonel and having held a command in 1918 with responsibilities equal to those of a brigadier general, he was to wait until 1934 again to achieve the actual rank of Lieutenant Colonel. These were also the years during which the Army existed on a financial shoestring — unable, sometimes even unwilling, to develop and purchase the modern tanks which Patton felt would determine the outcome of the next war. He felt this war inevitably must come, either because of the resurgence of the German military under the Nazis or the growing ambitions of the Japanese. He often told us so.

He had a particularly trying time during his second tour of duty in the Hawaiian Islands. He was a desk-bound officer with the duties on the Staff of G–2 and G–3. As was then almost universal in our armed services, there was no money available to man and operate an adequate intelligence section. Accordingly, he financed one out of his own pocket and was generally ridiculed for doing so. He should not have been. His personal network of informants was effective, his own evaluations sound even if disturbing. In 1936 and 1937 he drew up a detailed estimate of how he believed the Japanese attack would eventually come against Pearl Harbor and other installations, including the sneak dawn attack on a day when ships and planes would be closely packed together and largely unmanned. The facts about his study have been confirmed in other accounts, including that of General Harry Semmes in *Portrait of Patton*, but I wish to give them as Uncle George told them to me in the summer of 1937 when he returned from Hawaii for leave in Massachusetts prior to reassignment. "That was no idle exercise on my part, and not just to amuse myself. I had plenty of damned other things to do. An attack like that is perfectly feasible if we're off-guard, and it's within the Jap mentality. You'll remember that's how they began their war with Russia. They haven't forgotten how well it worked. It did no good to write that report. I turned it in to the ranking naval officer of the command and he just put it in his safe. Nobody else had the combination except his own houseboy and he was, of course, a good loyal Japanese. Nobody ever saw the report again — not on our side, anyway."

There was another more personal thing which disturbed him. During those days, and thereafter, it was clear to his family and even to me that Uncle George had an overpowering fear of growing old or losing any of his physical powers. This was obvious from his conversation and behavior, as well as constant attention to his waistline and the spectacular fit of his uniforms. Sometimes this feeling on his part resulted in behavior which fell far short of correct. I can bear witness, however, that his worries were groundless. Ten more years did not age him or noticeably diminish his powers.

It has been written that George Patton was fearless. Such a statement is an obvious absurdity since no man is fearless. Uncle George often said this to me: "Any man who tells you he has never been scared in battle is either a damned liar or completely insane." The truth is, I think, that Patton had no expressed fear of death, since he could not permit himself to have. His constantly repeated view of dying was, "A man simply goes back out the same door by which he came in — and I have never heard anyone complain about where he came from." In a way talk of death was part of this man's stock in trade, but he did not particularly like to have anyone talk of it to him.

I remember a lighter example of this reaction which took place that 1935 summer in Hawaii. Uncle George had just purchased a long black Packard. It was, even brand-new, a real pile of rattling junk. He himself said so, and that it was nowhere near as good a car as the Cadillac. I, of course, asked him, "Then why didn't you buy a Cadillac?"

"I'll tell you why. The salesman drove one up for me to inspect, proudly showed off each piece of chromium and patted the thing on the hood like a horse. Then he opened a door and closed it solidly. 'Please to notice, Colonel,' the God-damned fool said, 'how the doors shut with a fine, heavy "klunk" just like the gate of a vault in a graveyard.'"

Yes, the Colonel was, in those days, an angry, frustrated and sometimes bitter man. His house was not a happy place, nor were the lives of his wife and children easy. A racehorse in top condition, especially if a stallion, behaves very badly when pent up day after day in a narrow corral. It is not pleasant, not even safe, to be closed in with him, particularly if there are young mares in close vicinity. Also, horses do not drink hard liquor. There were, therefore, quite a few fence rails kicked to pieces during those years in Hawaii.

George Patton sometimes took strange paths toward his twin goals of promotion and of convincing top brass and Congress that his theories of armament and warfare were correct. He might be passed over, his ideas might be pigeonholed, but, by God, he himself was not going to be ignored; he would be personally noticed. Such an attitude can at times serve a useful purpose during war. It is nearly always professionally disastrous during days of peace. Senior officers, also stuck in the ruts they hate, but lacking sufficient imagination to break out, take offense; and offense shows up in fitness reports even though disguised in military officialese.

Patton did not conform in uniform any more than he did in language. He often appeared wearing nonregulation belt and pistol, particularly the Sunday school adjunct with its storied notches. The acquiring of the first two of these had been under circumstances sufficiently spectacular in themselves. This is the story in one of the forms in which it became legend. During the Pancho Villa hunt in Mexico, young Patton, then aide to "Black Jack" Pershing, had jumped his cavalry mount over an adobe wall into an enclosure. There were two of Villa's lieutenants with rifles aimed in his direction. Neither lived long enough to wound either the American or his horse. He proved at that time that he was a world expert with the revolver, and deadly fast. The facts were, however, that Patton and his companions arrived at the scene in touring cars and entered the fray on foot. It was the Villistas who were mounted, with the exception of Cárdenas who was the most important bandit killed. Up to his last bullet Cárdenas had fought very well and, quite typically, Patton admired him for it; "the man had nerve," he said.

There is no controversy concerning his next action, however. It was to strap the two bodies, deer-hunter fashion, to fenders of an old open touring car and return with his trophies to the tent of his General Pershing. Perhaps Uncle George had, in doing this simply taken an atavistic leaf from the journal of Don Benito Wilson, his flamboyant grandfather.

A dozen years later he told me of the immediate sequel. "Why, in that temperature it wouldn't have taken long for a couple of Mexican stiffs to drive a buzzard off a gut-wagon. So we decided to hold a quick funeral. Digging the graves was simple, but no one of us knew the burial service. Finally, a tough old sergeant said, "Don't worry, sir, I know what to do." So we let him. It was short and sweet. He raised one hand and recited:

> Ashes to ashes and dust to dust,
> If Villa won't bury you, Uncle Sam must.

I have no way of knowing if the tale was apocryphal. But somehow, I don't think that it was.

One legend, however, which was and is totally incorrect and nonfactual was that Uncle George then or at any time thereafter carried a pearl-handled pistol, either revolver or automatic. He took great care to point this out to me. "Goddammit, Bowser, my guns are ivory-handled. Nobody but a pimp for a cheap New Orleans whorehouse would carry one with pearl grips."

It was not just a sometimes inclination with George Patton to say exactly what he thought about any subject or person. To do so was his almost invariable habit. Beyond this, however, he sometimes had an urge to state loudly and with clarity some things he did not really believe in at all, or believed only in part, for the sole purpose of testing the reaction of his audience; nor did he believe in suppressing these urges. This was quite consistent with his early written advice to me on the use of profanity and obscenity. Nevertheless, there were occasions when his listeners may have been interested, but not to the extent where they failed to be shocked, or even damned angry.

Father has told me, for example, about the dinner after a polo match at Narragansett, Rhode Island, against a visiting team of youthful British officers. Patton had somehow developed an aversion to the captain of the English team whom he outranked. When the brandy, Fourteenth Amendment or not, was being served, Uncle George rapped for attention and delivered himself of a short, but pithy, speech. In substance he said that there had been current long enough a serious historical misconception. This was to the effect that the Germans were responsible for the outbreak of the 1914 World War. The facts, however, were, and after careful research he had assembled the documentation to prove them, that England, and England alone, was the guilty party. He then sat down to horrid silence.

Uncle George, as mentioned, had been badly wounded during the Battle of the Argonne, the last important, and the most vicious engagement to be fought by our troops during World War I. On the first day of the battle against the then elite of the German army, the 1st Prussian Guard, he was on foot directing tanks. The infantry, supposed to move forward with them, was pinned down by machine-gun fire. Patton was among them, and it was then that he said he actually saw his grandfather and great-uncles looking down from the clouds and telling him to get up and fight. In any event he did so, leading a nearly suicidal charge. It was for this action that he and his runner Sergeant Joe Angelo each received the Distinguished Service Cross, and it was at this time that a bullet smashed into his upper thigh and resulted, as he wrote Aunt Bea from the hospital, in his "missing half of my bottom, but otherwise all right."

It produced, in fact, quite a dreadful wound which left a long angry scar. Mother has told me of several instances, especially in this season of his greatest discontent when he made unusual use of his affliction. At tea parties, as they were then called during prohibition's dark hours, especially on Boston's North Shore, he would tend to become bored with certain stuffy females. He found that he could liven things considerably if he walked up to one of them, leaned over as though in confidence, unbuckled his belt, and confided, "I know, my dear Mrs. ———, you want to see where I was shot by the Hun during the war. Here, I'll turn around and you can help me." Not surprisingly, he was officially banished from the main beach at Narragansett for wearing bikini-like trunks designed deliberately to reveal at least a portion of this honorable scar.

Among the places in which he behaved worst was the home of my Uncle Keith Merrill, the one with the mustache, the one who was with the State Department. Outstanding was one dinner party at the Merrills' house on Belmont Road in Washington. Around the beautifully appointed table sat foreign dignitaries, formally clad and wearing their decorations. Also present were their ladies. There ensued one of those dreadful silences which sometimes punctuate even the most carefully planned soirée. The steak had been passed around the table and had reached as far as the then Major Patton, gorgeously attired in formal dress blues. He served himself, carefully, then picked up the large steak bone, silently wrapped it in his napkin, rose and left the room. The silence, if possible, grew more complete.

It was broken as Patton returned to announce loudly, "I've never in my life had enough to eat in this house. But I'm generous. If any of you would like to join me in gnawing on a bone in front of the fire later, you're certainly welcome."

This was almost one of the times when people were so interested they failed to be shocked — almost but not quite. It was really inexcusable of Uncle George and my Aunt Katherine was just barely tolerant in a tight-lipped sort of way. Then later came incidents and remarks which went beyond the pale of kindness and propriety. In fact, Patton made observations about Uncle Keith which no man's wife could pardon. So, for a while he was forbidden the hospitality of his own sister-in-law.

When Uncle George was angry at his superiors, the world, or himself, he would show off more flamboyantly than usual; and he could be quite needlessly cruel to others, especially those who were close to him. And every time he was cruel, or thoughtless, or indiscreet, Aunt Bea was forced to repair the damage, make apologies, and soothe hurt feelings. Sometimes she must have been very angry with her husband. But in public she hid it well.

CHAPTER VII

Of friends and horses

UNCLE GEORGE, as noted, was a deep student of history
and her constant handmaiden, warfare. He was a geopolitician, but never, or hardly ever, a politician in the narrower
domestic sense. He had ideas and he delighted in expressing
them, however outrageous they might seem. I remember,
one instance. I believe it was in early 1937, when more than
a few people had begun to recognize the potential of the
Mexican threat to expropriate United States oil interests in
that country. Patton, therefore, publicly delivered himself
of some less than diplomatic remarks. These were to the effect that the Mexicans were no damned good anyhow. They
were preparing to steal our properties. The U.S. Army was
getting too soft and out of training. Ergo, we should kill several birds with one stone and invade, conquer and occupy
the country. The Russians, Italians, and Germans were training their troops in Spain. We should do the same south of the
border.

Later that year he horrified another audience with a modest proposal. The only nations of the world worth a damn in
his opinion were the United States, Great Britain and Ger-

many. They should, therefore, form a political and military alliance eventually to fight the rest of the world, and most especially all Tartars, Mongols and Chinese before it was too late. The fact that there was sometimes more than a grain of reason and logic in the sayings of this military enfant terrible did not, however, speed his promotion; nor make any easier the role of his wife.

One brief but dramatic scene still today comes to mind. It may help a little to explain why George Patton sometimes acted the way he did. The locale was at Fort Myer, Virginia, the time early in April of 1932. Present were the military and the Military Affairs Committees of the Congress. Major Patton's family and I were also there. The purpose of the gathering was to watch a demonstration of the toughness, speed and maneuverability of a light tank. It was then called, after its inventor, the "Christie Crawler."

It was an impressive demonstration. Over very rough terrain in and out of deep tank trap ditches, through water and over steep bunkers this tank ran at high speed. Nothing like it had yet been seen in this country, or anywhere else for that matter. Further to demonstrate its safety, Patton strapped goggles and helmet on his wife and let her ride the beast on a second run through its paces. She emerged from the iron turret afterwards grinning broadly, masked in dust, but unbruised. A Congressman, whose name slips memory, finally came over to congratulate everyone concerned, particularly Uncle George. "It's a beautiful tank, Georgie. Certainly the best we've ever seen. But we're not going to buy it, you know. I doubt we would even if it were driven up the steps of the Capitol, and loaded with votes."

Christie had a similar experience with the British and

French authorities; but not with the Nazis or the Russians. It was most galling for Patton later to learn that his iron-clad protégé was to participate in the Red invasion of Finland, and later that its more advanced Nazi descendants had spear-headed the Panzer sweep through the Low Countries and into France. There is precious little comfort under such circumstances in being able to say, "I told you so."

The evening of the tank demonstration day did, however, witness a happier scene, a costume dance given for Uncle George's eldest daughter, Beatrice. I attended, no more than sixteen, and still fairly pudgy. I had, with great pride, and great effort, squeezed myself into a Baron Scarpia costume which had belonged to my father. It was complete with satin knee breeches, buckle shoes and white-powdered wig. Uncle George had similarly squeezed himself into his 1909 West Point cadet uniform, surmounted by its plumed shako. There is a picture of the two of us and seven-year-old G. S. Patton IV, standing at rigid attention. It is difficult to tell who is holding in his stomach with the greatest muscular effort. I do not remember much else about this party except our costumes and the fact that that night too, Uncle George used language about some young college man whose behavior, in addition to his basic crime of being a civilian, was offensive to him.

Looking back over these years in the early 1930's, I believe, on the whole, that Uncle George had certain justification for bitterness, and for expressing it. Reconnaissance as well as combat cavalry units, the early darlings of Patton's heart, were being phased out. Swift, heavy armor, his old love and his new, was not being placed on the tables of organization, at least not in near sufficient quantity. War was coming and he knew it; knew now, also, that his country would face it for a crucial period unable adequately to aid in arming her allies and would remain herself, for desperate protracted months, disgracefully poorly prepared.

Whether or not he was in those days bitter, he could when he chose be charming and most vitally interesting to those around him.

There come to mind, therefore, other and pleasant scenes featuring Uncle George which took place before the last days of peace and the first days of his ultimate war — the one for which he had trained all of his life. The time of the first of these is also early April 1932. I remember this because it was then I asked Ruth Ellen Patton to come to the Fifth Form spring dance at the Hill School. This I did despite the fact that I had known her since we were both three years old and indulged in hair-pulling contests. She still has the long golden hair of her mother, while I am only a little short of bald.

I had been spending part of my vacation with the Pattons and had been taken on tours of historic interest by Aunt Bea all the way from the Smithsonian Institute in Washington through Annapolis and up to the beautiful old section of Dover, Delaware. Now it had come Uncle George's turn and he had driven us to the area around Gettysburg, the mark of the high tide of the Confederacy, site of the battle in which his grandfather's brother, Waller Tazewell Patton, fell. Uncle George carried no map or ground plans, and no notes; he did not need them, for he was on familiar ground. As he strode along, the tweed jacket and flannel pants he wore seemed to become a uniform of gray, and the straight peeled branch he carried in his hand a sword. Almost yard-by-yard he

took us over the hallowed battleground pointing out where
each battery of artillery had been placed; where the various
units had been mustered and where they had been moved.
Little by little for his listeners the lush, green fields turned
sered and dirty in the stifling July heat of 1863. Gradually
the quiet of early spring was broken by the rattle of musketry,
the crash of cannon, the cries and groans of soldiers, the
screams of gutted horses. Then, there came alive for us, or
for me at least, the unfurling of flags and the ring of bugles
and finally the high-pitched Rebel yell heralding the hopeless gallantry of Pickett's charge across the plain, up the slope
up to the crest of Cemetery Ridge.

When Uncle George stood, stick upraised, at that mark of
the high tide, the few big scattered stones on the ground at
his feet became the solid, high granite wall from behind
which had blasted the Union cannon and over which
swarmed the heroes in gray, only to be mowed down by
Yankee lead and bayonets. When I looked at Uncle George
then, standing head thrown back and with arm outstretched,
I shivered, as I do a little now in memory. He *was* a proud
son of Virginia, defender of her honor. He *was* Waller Tazewell Patton, or George S. Patton of Winchester, and he was
about to die for a glorious cause.

On the way back to Washington we stopped, probably at
Aunt Bea's suggestion, at some rural antique shop to look for
something; I cannot recall what it was. No matter. We had
been there for a few minutes when Uncle George cried,
"Goddammit Bea, all of you, come here and look at this."
We did so. "This" was an ancient six-chambered revolver
with the ejector rod on the side, rather than directly beneath
the barrel. "Now where have any of you seen one exactly like

this before?" For a minute no one answered. Then Ruth Ellen spoke up — "I think I know, Daddy, on the grave of the young Benét." He told her with pride that she was absolutely right.

I didn't have the slightest idea as to who the young Benét was, but later that day found out. Before we returned to the Patton house we were driven to the cemetery at Fort Myer, Virginia, where by the red of the setting sun we looked down on the beautiful marble likeness of William Benét who also had fallen in the War between the States. There, by his hand, lay the carved replica of the old pistol Uncle George had purchased a little while before. He was, I was told, some ancestor to Stephen Vincent Benét who wrote the magnificent poetry of *John Brown's Body* which was another of George Patton's favorite works.

After a family dinner that evening Uncle George was still in his Confederate mood. I cannot forget one last thing he said. "Maybe you don't remember who General Bee was, but certainly you will all recognize what he said. It was at the first battle of Manassas where he stood up tall in his stirrups with saber upraised and shouted, 'There stands Jackson like a stone wall. Rally behind the Virginians.' At that very instant a bullet struck him square in the forehead and he dropped dead. You know, you have to have been a hell of a good man all your life for the gods to grant you that you die like that."

I detail this day because it showed to me something which I now understand so much more clearly. To George Patton war, however terrible, was a romantic thing; battle was man's apotheosis to his best, and ancestors were men who were inescapably always with one. I feel that the contrast between this belief — or will to believe — that battle was romantic and chivalrous and brave, and the realization that it was dirty, gut-wrenching, and very dreadful was part of the inner conflict which tormented him. Of course, he must have known there had been nothing pretty about Gettysburg. Nor had Uncle George ever laid claim to an incarnation as a Confederate officer. Still, he *had* been there through his father's stories of his ancestors and his own yearning toward their gallantry. Also, his studies of history had been always so complete that he could not fail ever to be able to identify himself with that history.

He had another quite unrelated talent. He was a very good carpenter, although lacking the patience and meticulousness to be the near-perfect cabinetmaker that my father became. In 1933, Uncle George decided that anything anyone else could build he could build better; and this included a boat. He began it and, much profanity and more amateur help later, finished it in his Washington garage. It was homely and offensive to Father, who firmly believed that a boat was not a boat unless it carried sail. Nevertheless, Father helped greatly, and I a little, even in the face of Uncle George's repeated loud assertion that he himself and none other had discovered the coarse rasp file, a tool quite possibly used by Noah — the greatest invention since the wheel. The end product was christened the *Menehune*, a Hawaiian word at whose meaning today I cannot even guess. I do remember, however, that with what his great friend Joe Ekeland, who sailed with him on the *Arcturus*, would not have called "Good Yudgment" he piloted his unlikely craft along the Atlantic coast northward all the way to Boston.

Other scenes from those leisurely days of peace are still

strong in memory; and some of them also involve horses as
well as people. One takes place on a rock-strewn, tree-bor-
dered path running precipitately down the crest of a hill in
the Blue Ridge country of Virginia. We are on horseback,
riding to baying hounds on the scent of some invisible fox.
At the head of the charge rides the Master of Foxhounds of
the Cobler Hunt. From time to time he raises the coppered
horn to his lips to blow the notes of "Follow Along."

"Following along" is rough, jolting and perilous. One fox
out of the thousands which depredate the hen runs of Virginia is in truth a useless quarry. What is more, the chances
of catching him are not as good as one in fifty. Nevertheless,
when the Master turns to look over his broad and firm-set
back it is clear from his face that he is at the height of enjoy-
ment. He is driving his horse, he is driving himself, and he
is leading on the rest of the mounted field. He is using his
muscles, and his balance and testing the quickness of his reactions. Perhaps above all he is, and knows he is, never very
far from danger. It makes him smile a little.

As mentioned, Uncle George was very fond of Mother, who
was herself a magnificent rider, and she of him although
sometimes it was hard to see why. Once in the Warrenton
country of Virginia they were trying by automobile to locate
the horse vans. Abruptly the dirt road they were following
came to an end at the bank of a swollen creek. Patton got
out of the car and waded across in order to ask directions of
a man driving horses and plow along the hillside beyond. He
instructed Mother, "You just sit here and don't do a damned
thing." Mother did not do as she was told since she felt the
car slowly, but steadily sinking beneath her into the rich, red
mud. Trying to back it out she mired the back wheels help-

lessly deep. When Patton returned he used language, then stalked away to ask the plowman for help in pulling out the car. He then turned back, reached into his coat pocket and drew out a packet of soggy sandwiches. These he tossed to Mother with the endearing comment, "There's no reason that even a damned fool should starve." He later more than made up for this gallantry. When he left in 1927 for his first tour of duty in the Hawaiian Islands he presented Mother with "Allemonde" his beautiful thoroughbred chestnut hunter. This gift was not an unmixed blessing. I had personal experience with one of Allemonde's habits. One endearing trait was, while at a gallop, to drop his head and one shoulder and then rapidly change direction. Only extreme vigilance and a tight grip could keep the rider from being projected from his saddle to make jarring contact with the ground.

Patton always tried to do, and have others do, more than the ordinary. For instance, he taught himself from scratch two separate and technically distinct systems of celestial navigation for his small craft Pacific crossings and used what he called "a sort of bastard mixture of both plus some damned fine dead-reckoning." And this was a man who had had to repeat a West Point year for failing in mathematics. What is more, on the gale-swept return crossing he took along his twelve-year-old son.

To me, however, he always looked more natural on a horse than at the tiller of a sailboat. It was more in character, the character of a somewhat ruthless knight in armor or an officer of dragoons; in short, always a cavalryman. One day on horseback stands out most vividly. My parents and I had ridden the three miles to his place, "Green Meadows." Uncle George galloped up to us and reined to a halt. He was grinning happily. To my father he announced, "By God, Fred, I've got something new to show you. It's the biggest god-damned thing you've ever seen, just come along with me."

We did, down to a lower pasture, to find an enormous brand-new Aiken jump. This is an obstacle consisting of a post and solid split-rail fence with brush and evergreen branches mounded against both sides. The average height of such a jump encountered in a horseshow or steeplechase is about three feet ten inches. This monster was five feet two inches high, completely rigid, and eighteen feet wide.

Uncle George was told it was a beautiful fence, but whatever was it for, standing alone beside a line of trees?

"It's my qualifying jump, that's what it is."

" 'Qualifying' for what, for heaven's sake?"

"Just plain qualifying, dammit! By God, this will separate the men from the boys and the horses from the crowbait."

It soon very nearly separated me from my saddle, but my horse and I somehow qualified. We would not have dared to do otherwise.

George Patton's head groom in those days was typical of the people he attracted. He was a tall, pantherlike Oklahoman whom I never knew by any more name than Kent. He was a man of strong opinions. In the winter of 1936 my parents had taken four horses to Middleburg, Virginia, for part of the fox-hunting season. Their head groom, John Dixon, was a mulatto. Obviously housing problems developed in that highly segregated area. So did something else. On the morning after Dixon's arrival four white grooms looked much as though they had passed some time in the ring with Joe Louis. Patton asked Kent, "What in hell happened around here last night?"

The drawled answer, "Why Colonel, it was just that some

of those no-account bastards tried to claim that John Dixon wasn't white."

I can easily understand how Kent could have caused such carnage. I once saw him in action even after he had wholly lost the use of one arm in an accident. The matter he handled was a vicious fight between two eighty-pound dogs. He simply waded into the middle of it and one-handed snatched up by its scruff first one animal, then the other, and smashed them heavily to the ground.

Kent, unfortunately, was forced to leave the Patton employ because of certain complex marital difficulties which eventually resolved themselves. He later became one of the leading trainers at the William Randolph Hearst stables in Ajo, California; but he did not forget his eastern friends. His two children were christened George Patton Kent and Ruth Ellen Patton Kent, and he continues to exchange cards with his daughter's namesake.

Patton, ever since his early career, had attracted men of rare character and unswerving loyalty, and, as in the case of Kent, they were by no means limited to members of the officer corps. He knew what any commander must learn, that he is totally helpless without the aid and respect of the most important man in the Army, the experienced noncom.

Uncle George was to have many fine sergeants, but I doubt that any were as useful or as spectacular as Master Sergeant "Tommy" Thompson. He was a tough, wiry, sometimes alcoholic redhead who had at one time served as enlisted man under Patton at Fort Riley, Kansas. Uncle George told me of what happened later.

When I was assigned in France in 1917 to take over command of the newly formed tank unit, things were in their

usual god-awful mess — supply situation fouled up, equipment missing, nobody knowing what in hell was going on.
I'd been there only a few hours when I saw a familiar-look-
ing soldier sort of strolling along. I yelled, "Hey Corporal,
god dammit, aren't you Thompson?"

He saluted and "Yes, sir, Colonel Patton, I am."

"Well from now on it's Sergeant Thompson and you are attached to my headquarters, to me personally, Thompson.
I've been over our equipment list and we're three touring
cars and four motorcycles short." Thompson just saluted
again and left on his errands. Early the next morning he reported to me in these words: "The Colonel will, I hope, be
glad to know that he is now one touring car and two motorcycles ahead."

Later on we had a lot of trouble with our tanks breaking
down. They were sort of jerry-built in those days, you see.
Well, at one point nearly all of them had collapsed right up
at the front. The trouble was our mechanics were some
damned civilians from Detroit and it said in their contracts
that they need not go closer to danger than two miles from
the front lines. I complained about this to Thompson, and a
day later all tanks had been repaired. I asked him how this
had been accomplished.

"If the Colonel does not mind, Sergeant Thompson would
prefer not to tell him until after the war."

I told him he'd better tell me right then.

"Well, in that case, the Colonel will understand that those
Detroit civilians were pretty sleepy at 4:00 A.M. when me
and the Corporal woke them up and herded them into a couple of trucks. We drove them to the front and shoved them
out again. Then me, I took out my gun while the Corporal

read the roll call. Then I said, real loud, 'If there's any son-of-a-bitch here who think's he's not two miles back of the line, let him step forward.' You know, Colonel, not a one of them did."

Thompson did a lot of things like that for me. So when at the end of the war he asked, "Would the Colonel object if Sergeant Thompson got himself a little shack to live in. He's tired of tents," I just told him to go ahead. Even I didn't expect what happened. Very shortly Thompson was installed in a handsome small white house I'd never seen before. It was fully furnished, including plumbing, except that there was nothing to which the plumbing could be connected. I asked Thompson how in hell he had acquired the house.

He asked, "Is the Colonel certain he wishes to know?"

I told him, god-dammit yes.

"The Colonel doesn't think too highly of the Red Cross, does he?"

I admitted that I did not.

"Well, perhaps the Colonel knows that there is a Red Cross unit about two miles down the road, a particularly low class of unit if the Sergeant may say so. Well I was down there the other day and this fat-assed civilian asked me, 'Sergeant, can you move this house with one or two of your tanks?' I said, of course, and here it is."

A few years after the war Thompson showed up again in the same dust-swept post as the Pattons at Fort Meade. Aunt Bea told me about it. Thompson deplored that she, in her overcrowded quarters, did not have even room for a kitchen. Furthermore, he did something about it. Using familiar tactics he arrived at her quarters in a tornado of dust — a small house dragging on rollers behind his tank. He dismounted, saluted smartly and announced, "Your new kitchen, Mrs. Colonel Patton, ma'am."

Aunt Bea told me that this was almost the last she saw of her larcenous knight. The facts of his marriages to three different ladies at the same time had finally come to light. A distinguished career was brought to an end. He did, however, make a comeback of sorts.

Ruth Ellen, however, remembers the last time she and her family did see the fabulous Sergeant. It was in 1927 in Hawaii. Uncle George had, on seeing him on a street corner, impulsively invited him to dinner with them. He came, bringing with him still another Mrs. Thompson. The meal was to be veal cutlets and artichokes and there was not quite enough to go around. The Pattons' cook, Togo, said to Aunt Bea, "Missy Patton no worry. All is take care of, please." It was. The hostess's plate, she discovered, contained a veal cutlet made of bread crumbs packed together and disguised by some thick sauce. The vegetable was the extra artichoke leaves molded together in the shape of the real thing and drenched in Hollandaise. At this time the wily Thompson, who had been a notorious drunk, had a job as a prohibition agent on Honolulu. *Sic Transit* . . .

CHAPTER VIII

Déjà vu

★ ★ ★ ★

UNCLE GEORGE perforce lived in many places, but this Virginian from California chose for his ultimate home a site in Massachusetts, a Yankee house in a rural Yankee country-side. "Green Meadows" is quite an old house, having been built in approximately 1839. It is two-storied and of the typical New England, early clapboard construction in which no one window is exactly the same size as the other. The plank-ing of the several ground floor rooms are not precisely at the same level and, if you should drop a marble on any one it would roll slowly until stopped by a wall. The main stairway is narrow and precipitate. Building it this way saved space. The biggest room, the parlor, looks as if it might originally have been the connecting barn, since it is high-studded with sharply slanting eaves held apart by old exposed beams. There is also a new section added by Uncle George and Aunt Bea consisting of a living room, a den and an upstairs bed-room. In short, it is an unpretentious house which wanders across the crest of a low hillside. The total effect, however, is quite beautiful since the building is framed by some splen-did trees, particularly three huge elms, a fine boxwood hedge and a grape arbor.

The salient feature of the place, however, is the lovely vista of fields stretching down and away toward the Ipswich River on the right and to the left upward to another hill which carries its split-rail fence and trees outlined against the sky. On this side the house faces southwest, and anyone sitting on the terrace can feel that nothing stands between him and the sunset. On the other side, too, there can often occur a startling effect. The setting sun in springtime casts its searchlight at eye level through the house in such a way that from the street it seems as if the whole inside were on fire. There is a stable big enough to house twelve horses, a corral, two large paddocks, a farm barn and a garage, and a small boathouse for canoes at the edge of the river.

Most of Uncle George's important trophies from two world wars are, of course, today in the Patton Museum at West Point and at other military posts. There are, however, in and about the house at "Green Meadows" some fine souvenirs. Many of them are quite typical, German helmets, Nazi daggers, and so on. Two, however, are in no way usual. On the terrace facing forever to the river is a fine bronze Spanish cannon bearing the arms of Charles XII and taken from the French Fort Lyautey in Africa, which makes, as such guns always do, a fine perching place for the very young visitor and the inquisitive bird. Also on the terrace of the house is bronze of quite another sort. It is a copy of the bust of Adolf Hitler sculptured, I believe, by Arno Brucker, and "liberated" by the Third Army. Uncle George sent it home together with a square metal plaque which carries the inscription: "This is for my dogs to piss on — G.S.P. Jr." According to my friend George C. Murnane, Jr., of New York, and then of Patton's personal staff, this bronze was taken from the summer villa of

Max Amman on the Tergensee south of Munich. This man was editor of the *Volkischer Beobachter* and the publisher of *Mein Kampf*.

Hitler's bust apart, "Green Meadows" suggests a reasonable degree of affluence and a leisurely form of life which may have gone forever. It suggests to some that since George Patton and his wife both came of wealthy parents, the General dared to act as he did because he had no financial fears. Some people have said that, of course, he could dare professional risks and speak his mind since the worst that could happen to him would be to be cashiered from the Army. I propose that such an analysis is completely wrong. George Patton would have acted as he did no matter what his circumstances. Furthermore, he never had, and could not, conceive of himself in any role other than a military leader of men. He would have been lost, helpless and desperate in the business world. It would have been a prison camp with practices and practitioners he would have never understood. He might choose to resign, but to have been cashiered from the Army would have been to him the ultimate and irremediable disgrace.

It was at "Green Meadows" that Uncle George talked to his children and to me of many things. I can see him now standing tall before the fireplace, or sitting relaxed beside it, highly polished boots stretched before him, generally with the foot of one crossed upon the ankle of the other. I remember how he used to tell us of earlier battles by those he felt had been the bravest of the brave, the ancient Greeks before Troy, at Plataea, on the seas of Salamis and at Marathon, and I remember a book he gave me so many years before — *The Spartan*, to him "another of the world's greatest books." It was written by Caroline Dale Snedeker, the Mary Renault of her day.

It is the story of the one lonely survivor of the heroic three hundred of Leonidas at Thermopylae. He is stoned and abused and hounded as a coward, although in fact he had been smitten by fever and snow-blindness while on an espionage mission within the enemy Persian lines. He pays long penance to the gods, saves the life of a little child, and is because of this, at the last, purged of his curse and returns to war.

When all seems lost at Plataea, when the Grecian ranks are melting under a rain of heavy spearlike Persian arrows, when the priests have consulted the omens in the steaming entrails of a sheep and still delay, the Spartan, Aristodemos, can stand inaction no longer. In a soaring battle cry he damns the oracles and charges the enemy. The Athenians follow, and the last big battle of the war is won. The Spartan is killed, but is laid out on a prince's crimson cloak, shield on chest and bronze sword by his side. Condemned and rejected in life, he is in death a hero for the ages.

I think that there were many times when George Patton must have seen himself in such a role. Given his frustrations, his certainty that often he alone was right, above all, given his basic conflict between sensitivity and toughness and his self-dramatizing nature, this could not have been otherwise.

On one of those days before his fire he spoke of the distant past; read aloud some of his favorite passages from the *Iliad*. And it was then I had asked, "Uncle George, do you really believe in reincarnation?"

This was his answer: "I don't know about other people; but for myself there has never been any question. I just don't think it, I damn well know there are places I've been before, and not in this life. For instance, when I took over my first command in France, at Langres, a young French liaison officer met me and offered to show me around since I had never been there before. For some reason I said, "You don't have to. I know this place. I know it well. Of course he didn't believe me. But to make a long story short, I told the driver where to go in the small, typical French city — almost as if someone were at my ear, whispering the directions. I took him to what had been the Roman Amphitheater, the drill ground, the Forum, and the Temples of Mars and Apollo. Of course, some had been built over, or almost totally torn down to use the marble and granite blocks somewhere else. I even showed him correctly the spot where Caesar had earlier pitched his tent. But I never made a wrong turn. You see, I had been there before."

In one of his "so-called poems" he wrote of this while still in Langres, in the mid-war year of 1917.

Memories

I sat in my throbbing char d'assaut
In the shade of the ruins of Rome,
And I knew that despite the dimming years
The place had once been home.

Yes, more than once I have seen these walls
Rise sharp on the brow of the hill
And more than once I have trod that road
That winds, like a snake, from the rill.

First it was in the brass of Rome
With the white dust on my brow

And the second time, 'neath the flag of a duke
Whose name is legend now.

. . . .

Later I passed in rattling plate
When time had crumbled the walls
And the laurel thicket covered the slopes
That once were watchers' stalls.

'Twas here they brought us after the fight
We'd had in the field out there
And underneath that pile of stones
Is the place where our corpses are.

And now again I am here for war
Where as Roman and knight I have been.
Again I practice to fight the Hun
And attack him by machine.

So; the three old hags still play their game
Still men the counters are;
And many peg out in the game of peace
Pray God, my count shall be war.

I know he believed this; in fact, was sure of it. In his letters, most of which were very good, and in his poems, most
of which were obviously very bad, he again and again
stressed the point. There is another long poem written in
1944 and called "Through a Glass Darkly," concluding with
these three stanzas, which re-emphasizes the point stressed
twenty-eight years earlier.

So as through a glass and darkly
The age long strife I see

Where I fought in many guises,
Many names — but always me.

And I see not in my blindness
What the objects were I wrought
But as God rules o'er our bickerings
It was through His will I fought.

So forever in the future,
Shall I battle as of yore
Dying to be born a fighter,
But to die again once more.

There was more to his belief. In the same conversation he put it in these words. "And that wasn't all. I mean that's not all I know. I am sure your ancestors are always with you. They are watching you. They expect a hell of a lot out of you."

I asked, "How do you mean?"

"Well, it's something you know, or you don't. But sometimes you can even see. Once in France we were pinned down by German fire, especially some heavy machine guns. I was lying flat on my belly and scared to death, hardly daring to lift my head. But finally I did, and looked up to a bank of clouds glowing reddish in the almost setting sun. And then, just as clear as clear can be, I saw their heads, the heads of my grandfather and his brothers. Their mouths weren't moving; they weren't saying anything to me. But they were looking, looking with not so much in anger as with unhappy scowls. I could read their eyes and they said to me, 'Georgie, Georgie, you're a disappointment to us lying low down there. Just remember lots of Pattons have been killed, but there never was one who was a coward.'

"So I got up, drew my gun, and gave commands. And at the last Colonel George and the others were still there, but smiling. Of course, we won that particular battle."

As a matter of fact Patton rallied some three hundred infantrymen at revolver point — and then, on foot, led a tank attack.

"And something else used to happen quite regularly, especially in the earlier days of my war in France. Father used to come to me in the evenings to my tent and sit down to talk and assure me that I would do all right and act bravely in the battle coming the next day. He was just as real as in his study at home at 'Lake Vineyard.'"

My friend James P. Nolan, now an investment banker of Washington, has recollection of the Patton of those early days which also helps to show that soldier's other, or strictly military face.

I certainly remember the first time I ever saw George Patton. It was at Langres, when the American Armored Corps was being formed. I was a very new Lieutenant in charge of a work gang of troops trying to make a roadway out of a sea of mud. Two freshly arrived young officers had just walked up to me, looking lost and most unmilitary with bags of dirty laundry slung over their shoulders. They were searching for the officers' club. Just then Colonel Patton came striding into view around the corner, belted, booted and polished to a fine gleam. We officers saluted, the muddy enlisted men leaned on their shovels and stared. The Colonel snapped out, "Who's in charge of this god-damned detail?" I answered, "I am, sir." He then proceeded to tear into me in a most unnerving fashion about my men not being at attention.

I stood my ground just barely, and finally answered, "Yes sir, it was just because they were looking at you, sir."

Then I saw him again that evening at our so-called officers' club. I remember it was furnished with rather shaggy wicker chairs. We hardly dared sit in them because the broken ends might scratch our Sam Brown belts and if Patton saw any scratches like that or unshined buttons, the victim could not sit down to dinner until those in immaculate uniforms had finished.

The next day I was summoned to appear before a Colonel Wyche who had been the disciplinarian at West Point. I was, therefore, not happy. He said to me from behind his desk, "Nolan, Colonel Patton reports that yesterday your detail was slovenly in appearance and leaning on their shovels. Is that correct?" "Yes sir, it is in a way. But we were working in mud above our ankles." "So I understand, Nolan. Well, Colonel Patton wants you to report to his tank outfit at Neuf-châtel."

I must say I was surprised at this, and was more so when I was given a new command, replacing a tank officer who had been killed. Later I saw quite a lot of George Patton and we became good friends. I finally summoned up nerve to ask him why he had picked me for his outfit after the semi-public bawling out he had given me. He answered, "Perfectly simple. I wanted to see how you reacted under pressure — just or unjust. I get most of my best men that way."

Yes, Patton was tough, he was a stickler for regulations and a disciplinarian. But no one will ever be able to calculate the number of lives, particularly lives belonging to us untrained civilian soldiers, he saved in 1917-18 by being the way he was. And another thing: I never knew him to be unfair. Even when it was only he himself who felt he had been he always apologized to the man concerned.

Uncle George was a firm believer in the power of extra-sensory perception, although he probably would never have called it that. He accepted the reality of certain ghosts and told us of some amazing corroborative incidents. He felt sure that powers of telepathy, *déjà vu,* even prophecy were somehow parts of a whole which included a belief in rein-carnation and of the living continuation of everything past. He told us also that some of these somehow mystical abilities were inherited and that he had himself received them from his grandmother, Susan Glassell Patton. That lady, as attested by letters to and from her sister Sally, obviously seems to have had certain telepathic powers. Each time that her husband, George Patton, was wounded during the Civil War, she knew it before being told. On the occasion of his last and fatal wound, she had already packed and gone to the station before a messenger brought the news. She told Sally, "This time George is dying and I am going to him."

Inevitably, therefore, George Patton believed in a God of Battles who was, if properly served, ever on the side of the just, that is to say, Patton's side. He believed in his ancestors and that he must live up to them. And he believed, no matter how dark his prospects, and even when he himself had made them darker, in his own inevitable destiny. He believed, and said so in speeches to his troops, that there was a second and better Heaven for the fallen soldier.

He did not change in his beliefs. Before the crucial actions in the Battle of the Bulge, it seemed wholly natural that he should order a prayer recited to the God of Battles asking for clear skies. It read as follows:

Almighty and most merciful Father, we humbly beseech thee, of great Thy goodness, to restrain these immoderate rains with which we have had to contend. Grant us fair weather for Battle. Graciously harken to us as soldiers who call upon Thee that armed with Thy power we may advance from victory to victory, and crush the oppression and wickedness of our enemies, and establish true justice among men and nations. Amen.

I know that he was not surprised when the fogs lifted and the sun shone clear, and just in time.

He meant it also when later in Luxembourg he said to me, "Freddy, a man must know his own destiny, because he must know what he was meant to be. But if he does not recognize it, then he is lost. He is also lost if — and it will happen only two or three times in his life — if he does not recognize Fate. By this I mean once, or twice, or at the very most, three times, fate will reach out and tap a man on the shoulder. He usually says, 'Go away, I'm busy,' or 'I don't know you so don't bother me.' But if he has the imagination he will turn around and Fate will point out to him what fork in the road he should take. If he has the guts, he will take it."

CHAPTER IX

"It is my destiny to lead"

IN MOST things Uncle George was an individualist, if that be not too mild a term. He felt always, for example, that the existing army field uniform, particularly for tank corpsmen, was impractical, archaic and above all colorless. He, therefore, continually designed new ones and submitted the samples to the War Department. That they would not be accepted was a foregone conclusion. Some of them were, however, extremely practical and comfortable, and most certainly did not lack in color. One of them, in fact, was sufficiently spectacular to earn him with the press the nickname of "The Green Hornet" a comic strip character of that time.

Picture if you can a tall, lanky, unmuscular young caller on Patton's daughter Bea being used as a tailor's dummy for one of the newest uniform creations. The unfortunate victim was not only thin, he sported a reddish-gold mustache, used a genuine Oxford accent and, worst of all, was a civilian and a member of the Foreign Service at that. The combination made Bill Lacy beneath contempt. He later became a highly talented career ambassador, then an Assistant Secretary of State, but tells me that the scene still makes him shudder. I don't blame him. He told me how it was.

"Your uncle stood me up right there in his living room and started in, 'Now, dammit, get out of those pants and jacket — certainly right here. Where else? Now get into this uniform; stand still, dammit, and I'll do up the buttons. Yes, those buttons! Now, goddammit, stand straight — chest out; and suck in that gut. Now, by God, that's better, but you can be thankful you're not in my regiment — I'd build some muscle onto that skinny frame and teach you how to march like a man.'"

Despite this treatment, Lacy feels today as he has for many years. "Your uncle was the greatest soldier and gentleman this country has produced since Robert E. Lee, but he should have been a Virginia dragoon, mounted on a big black horse and with a saber in his hand. He was the modern J. E. B. Stuart, the eternal cavalryman." And this from William Sterling Byrd Lacy of Leesburg, Virginia.

In the late summer of 1937, it was, ironically enough, a horse which very nearly ended Patton's career forever. It kicked him in the leg, breaking the shinbone. The injury was serious enough to release blood clots into the circulatory system, causing thrombophlebitis. From this an embolism came within seconds of killing him. His surgeon told me that a weaker man would never have survived.

The surgeon, too, is worth noting as one of the close friends and admirers in Patton's life. He was a magnificent big man named Peer P. Johnson, who lived to the age of eighty-four and was until three years ago still Chief of Staff and a practicing surgeon in the large hospital of Beverly, Massachusetts. He lived by a principle he often expounded to us: "I've just been listening to a lot of nonsense about poor so-and-so having worked himself to death. That just doesn't happen to a real man. What happens too often is that men stop looking forward, stop learning new things and then they rust to death."

He practiced what he preached, in his work and in his time away from work. During his late seventies, for example, he taught himself the language of France, then later that of Spain and by himself took extended trips in those countries. He remained to the end an avid yachtsman and was another man of strong opinions. It was inevitable that he and Uncle George should have been kindred spirits and that he should have been seated at a place of honor at the General's triumphant dinner in Boston in June of 1945.

Uncle George himself told me about his illness, "I know that I passed out — and then was aware that I was lying on some battlefield on a big Norse shield. After a while two armored Vikings came and started to lift me up on that shield to carry me to Valhalla. Then one of them shook his head, and they gently put me down again, and I came to, here in bed. I guess they're not ready to take me yet. I still have a job to do."

During his period of convalescence he kept his wing of the Beverly Hospital in uproar. Friends decorated his room with festoons of varicolored toilet paper and provided a seemingly inexhaustible liquor supply. There came an endless stream of visitors, one of whom fondly tacked a cardboard sign above the door which read, in bold red letters, "Hula-Hula Night Club: G. S. Patton, Prop."

When he became partially ambulatory, he was even more of a menace to tranquillity. He was restless and roamed the corridor visiting other patients, dispensing ribaldry and cheer. In a neighboring room was an old friend, "Bo" Amory, who had just recently given birth to a son. To Uncle George she remarked, "Golly, it's wonderful to be able to roll over and lie on my stomach again." In a carrying voice he announced for the benefit of nearby doctors, interns, nurses and patients, "Why, my dear young lady, had you retained that position in the first place, you would probably not have been in your recent unenviable condition." Those were, according to Bo, his exact words.

It was during his convalescence that he also found time to give me some more advice. "Come back tomorrow morning when you're sure your parents won't be around. They'll never tell you what I'm going to."

He was certainly right in part. The advice was: "So you're now out of college and you're taking a trip to Europe. That's wonderful. But stay as long as you can, see as much as possible because there is going to be one hell of a war — and they're going to blow all kinds of places off the map.

"Now most Americans, Freddy, behave like Elks when they get abroad. They talk too much and they boast too much, and they don't learn a damned thing. No matter what country you're in, keep your eyes open for what the people are doing, and try to do the same. Watch to see if someone else is smoking at the table before you light up. If no one else pulls out a lady's chair for her, don't you go doing so; same way with taking off hats in elevators and so on.

"No matter how true it may be, don't ever say 'Well, the Empire State is taller . . . or a Cadillac bigger . . . or a Texas steak thicker. Always compliment people on what they have which pleases you. You'll surprise most of them if you ask 'Isn't that little landscape a Corot?' Even if it isn't, they'll be delighted you asked. If you have spotted it correctly, they'll be amazed.

"Ask all kinds of questions. Be intelligently curious. Your hosts will consider you gracious and well educated even if you haven't volunteered a thing. Also you'll learn a hell of a lot. By God, I wish some of our so-called diplomats could teach themselves this lesson.

"Now, about women. In Europe you'll find all kinds of good-looking ones that can be slept with. You'll think that you must be one hell of a man because of this. Well, you won't be. You'll be just another young American, still wet behind the ears. So always remember this. If you can take her to bed it means that somebody else — and maybe a whole parade of somebody elses — have done so already. So now listen and I'll give you some good practical advice about precautions to take."

This he did — in detail, then scowled at me. "But I'll be damned annoyed with you if you go messing around like that. You hear me?"

I meekly said, "Yes, Uncle George."

"Now go and get me my wallet out of the dresser drawer."

I brought it and he leafed through it to extract a $100 bill. "Here now, don't look so surprised, take it. I want you to take it and spend it on the two best-looking girls that you can find. But one at a time, that is. Now goodbye, and when you get back, tell me what you learned."

It was also during this period of convalescence that Uncle George commissioned Alden's shipyard to build him a schooner. Into her was to go every improvement for comfort and safety on the high seas which half a lifetime of sailing experience had taught him. She was to be, and is today, called by the name he gave her — *When and If.* "*When* the next war is over, *and if* I live through it, Bea and I are going to sail her around the world."

The man who rigged this ship; every rope, lanyard, stay, wire, plate and cable, alone and unassisted, was another of the men attracted in mutual friendship and loyalty to George Patton. This was the wonderful Swede named Joe Ekeland mentioned earlier who had been Uncle George's paid right hand on both Pacific crossings.

Joe was all Swede — and had been before the mast since the age of ten. He was a master rigger of ships. He knew all the major harbors of the seven seas and was the living canvas for a signed masterpiece — a tattooed dragon named Moo Fat which extended from nape nearly to coccyx on his incredible back. The strength of his upper body was almost shocking. One 1935 summer day at dockside in Pearl Harbor I saw him break a bronze turnbuckle by turning it with his bare hands while trying to tauten the mainstay of a Star Boat. This is a thing normally done, and with some difficulty, by the use of a ten-inch metal spanner.

Aunt Bea at this point asked, "Joe, how did you ever become so strong in the arms?"

"By God, Mrs. Patton, since I vas leedle boy I never vent nowhere on my legs." Joe had a wonderful way with words. I once heard him describing his feminine ideal, Greta Garbo, thus: "You know she has a lovely clean mouth yust like a healthy dog."

Joe was a loyal friend and a man of high principles. He detested above all else the hypocritical and the false. Mother often said, "I'd rather turn over a youngster to be trained by Joe than almost anyone else I know." He was also somewhat of a philosopher without portfolio. He once praised my father for an unusual, for him, piece of very cautious sailing. "By God, Mr. Ayer, dot vas goot yudgment. Goot yudgment comes from experience; and experience it comes from bad yudgment." Still later he greatly cheered my young son, then thirteen, who had been unbelievably sloppy aboard ship and constantly underfoot, in these words, accompanied by a massive arm across the shoulders: "By God, Rickie, soonest you remember as youngest member of crew every focking thing goes wrong on this boat is your fault better you get on."

Concerning George Patton, Joe asked me this: "You remember, Yunior, when the General he go back to Sveden to see old friends and get his gold medal and say hello to the King?"

I said I did.

"Vell, by God, Yunior, I tell you vat the General did. He sent vay out in the country to my leedle house for me to come to the hotel where they vere. Snotty fellow at desk he vould not let me go up until the General send down a young Colonel to take me in with important fellers and the King and all. He vas a grand man, a lovely man, vas the General. They vill make no more like him again — not never."

After he had made full recovery from his horse-inflicted wound, Uncle George's star began once more to rise. In July of 1938 he was given command of the 5th Cavalry at Fort Clark, Texas, an unlovely location it is true, but with it a promotion to full colonel. This was almost exactly twenty-one years since he had first commanded his own regiment and held the equivalent of so much rank. Perhaps some in the high command could hear the rising rumble of Nazi armor. Perhaps there was at least the seed of thought somewhere in the land that we might need an army again. In any event, six months later he was again transferred. This time to Fort Myer, Virginia, and to command of his old regiment, the 3rd Cavalry. It was here that I had the pleasure of seeing him

Pershing's aide—Mexico, 1915.

"There's life in the old man yet."
Riding off Walter Dillingham, Hawaii, 1927.

Fort Meyer, Virginia, 1920.

"My war face," 1927.

Above: With son George S. Patton IV, Hamilton, Massachusetts, 1929. *Below:* National Capitol Horse Show, same year.

Honolulu, 1939, just prior to departure for California. Left
to right: G. S. Patton, Jr., Francis Graves, Beatrice Ayer Patton,
Joe Ekeland, G. S. Patton IV, and Suzuki.

G. S. Patton, Jr., with
Beatrice Ayer Patton, Jr.,
Hamilton, Massachusetts.

Below: G. S. Patton, Jr.,
James W. Totten,
Ruth Ellen Patton Totten.

At daughter Ruth Ellen's
"Gone With the Wind"
birthday party, 1940.

"Green Hornet."

Night before leaving for North Africa.

again, in the rough hunting country already described, on the parade ground, and in his own quarters on the Post.

In July of 1940 Uncle George's second daughter, my blond friend Ruth Ellen, was married to Lieutenant, now General, James W. Totten in Massachusetts. The reception at their summer place, "Green Meadows," was held out of doors on the great sloping lawn. This reception welcomed about two hundred family members and friends, from four years of age to eighty, and was courtly and dignified, even if some of the individual guests were not.

It was an amazing agglomeration of people. In addition to brothers and sisters and their cousins and their uncles and their aunts, there was Dr. Peer P. Johnson, Gordon Prince, Kent, Alice Holmes, who had been the Pattons' nurse for uncounted years, Mary Crowley, who had nursed my Grandfather Ayer during World War I and was to live until 1962; ancient Cousin Annie Ruggles, who preferred leather upholstery in her car "because it's so much easier to clean when people throw up," all the employees of my father's office, various family chauffeurs, Colonel Francis T. Colby, still snorting through his nose, and a small squad of young new and bewildered lieutenants who had come to stand up for the groom.

These ushers had already suffered two hard days of exposure to our long-tailed family, especially at cocktails in my parent's house when my two brothers and I walked down the stairs and into the gloomy front hall. We had each put on a dark suit and reversed our stiff collars in order impartially to bestow our dubious but solemn blessings on one and all.

At last everybody at the reception had been kissed several

times each and drunk as much as he could, should, or wanted
to. The cake had been cut, the bouquet thrown and caught,
and the bride dressed for travel. I was standing with the
more active members of the wedding a few yards away from
the front door with a traditional bag of rice. On schedule,
Jimmie and Ruth Ellen ran the gauntlet and scrambled into
the front seat of the getaway car. As it began to move away,
there rose a high, horrible yell as Uncle George leaped from a
stone wall onto the roof of the moving automobile. Kneeling
precariously on this top, he then emptied the chambers of
two revolvers resoundingly into the atmosphere. Only most
restrained driving on the part of the family chauffeur, Reggie
Maidment, prevented serious damage to Totten's new father-
in-law, who soon came sauntering back up the road, looking
very pleased with himself.

In September 1940 Uncle George was made a temporary
Brigadier General, a rapid promotion indeed. Hardly two
months later he was transferred from cavalry to the other
branch he had so long fought for, armor. And now it was not
merely an adjunct to infantry. We had belatedly learned at
least something from Adolf Hitler. We were creating the Armored Force, and Patton was a Brigade Commander of the
2nd Armored Division. His success in this job was spectacular. On April 14, 1941, he was elevated to temporary Major
General and given command of the Division.

Many stories were written concerning Patton tactics, observations, leadership and so on during the Fort Benning
period. There is one occurrence, however, which has not
been reported and, although essentially nonmilitary in nature, was wholly typical. My friend J. Hunter Drum of
Washington, D.C., a nephew of the General Hugh Drum of

Patton's Hawaiian days, was an officer of Military Police with the 4th Infantry Division at Benning. He told me about his first view there of Uncle George. "He used to go driving through our area like a bat out of Hell, way over the posted speed limit. Our General, Lloyd Fredendall, had very little use for your uncle and I'm told the feeling was mutual. He ordered me to have my men arrest Patton if he came roaring through again. I carried out my orders and one of my M.P.'s chased him, right on his tail, clear through the 4th Division area and into that of the 2nd Armored where he finally caught him. There he said, 'General, I am sorry but I have to arrest you for speeding in our division area. General Fredendall —' Patton turned on the poor youngster, '—— General Fredendall, Corporal. You and I are now both in 2nd Armored territory, and you can go to hell.'

"The next thing Patton did, since he knew he was in the wrong and in potential trouble, was to call up Fredendall and say 'Lloyd, I just wanted to take this chance to compliment you on the great efficiency of your Military Police Unit.'

"He then got hold of me and said he'd like to have me in his Headquarters. I told him I would enjoy this also, but that I was assigned to infantry and was not a tanker. He said to that, 'Makes no difference. Just apply to your Uncle Hughie and ask for a transfer.' I leave you to imagine how far I succeeded with that one. There was zero love lost between those two generals; but I'm sure they respected each other."

It was in 1940 or a little later that Patton designed the uniform which as I have mentioned earned for him the nickname of the "Green Hornet." It had Robin Hood green pants with black stripes down the side, a diagonally buttoned jacket of the same color and as headgear a gilded pro football helmet. He sent mother and father an 8 x 10 glossy of himself so arrayed, with the addition of tanker's goggles and a gas mask. He looked in this a little as did those days' concept of the space traveler. It bore the inscription "This is me. Merry Christmas."

In March 1942 he was placed in command of the First Armored Corps then already slated for use in the Desert of Africa. Being a realist he wanted to train his men in similar evil terrain. He needed a desert, and found it and mapped out the area from a plane, fifteen thousand acres of it, mostly in California. I have driven through some of it by jeep and can see why. Although the gilded oasis of Palm Springs lies only sixty miles to the north, it is a terrifying terrain. During the summer months the heat is blazing and direct, soaring to 120° on many days. There is no shade of any kind and there are blinding dust storms. When it rains heavily the waters roar down from the mountains through the sunken washes of the desert in devastating flash floods.

During the months in this desert Patton drove himself as mercilessly as his men and when they came out they were tough, dehydrated and leanly stripped of all excess flesh. They were as nearly combat-trained as is possible for troops who have not yet been fired upon in anger. When he went to London in August 1942 to discuss the planning of the North African invasion he knew that he was ready for the job and had forged the striking tool with which to do it. To the rest of the world it was perfectly evident that Old Blood and Guts had been picked to smash somewhere, and soon, at Hitler. The as yet unanswered questions were only, When? and Where?

Early in September I was recalled from my enforced association with the criminal elements of Cincinnati to attend a period of retraining at F.B.I. Headquarters in Washington, D.C. On my second night in the city I was given more than an inkling of the answers to the two key questions. Uncle George had called me with an invitation to dinner at the Metropolitan Club. We had finished dinner and coffee and talked only of family and sports and horses. Then we walked the two flights down to the second floor where he took me by the arm and steered me to the door of the library. It was totally deserted at that hour. "Now go in and sit down. I'm going to order us some brandy and we're going to have a talk." After the brandy was brought and we were comfortably settled in the deep leather chairs, it was he who talked, and I who listened.

He never told me exactly where, but let me know that the landing would be in French North Africa. I begged him to take me as an aide, interpreter, personal gunman, or in any other capacity, pointing out that I was bilingual and thought I was just as fast and almost as accurate with a pistol as he.

He shook his head over that one and pointed his cigar at me. His golden snake ring caught the lamplight. "No, goddammit Freddy, I'm not going to do it. We have plenty of officers who can talk at least adequate French, and so do I, and they've all supposedly been taught to shoot. A lot of us are going to be killed off and I don't want this to happen to you."

"Well, why the hell not? I want to get into this war, but they say I'm too nearsighted. If you asked for me, that would do it."

"No, that's not the point. I know you're as brave as the next man, so relax. Hoover's trained you to do a job here at home. You've got to stay here and keep an eye on all these subversive bastards, and I don't mean any silly native Nazis. There are all kinds of low-class slime who are trying, and will try, to wreck this country from inside. Most of them don't know it, but a few of them do, that what they are actually doing is working for the Russians. It doesn't matter whether they call themselves Communists, or Socialists, or are just plain foolish liberals, that's what they're doing."

As mentioned earlier, Uncle George had little or no use for civilians as a class. He considered, moreover, that the very lowest form of life among them was the politician. He often said to me, and to others, that he had a modest proposal for congressmen. Anyone who voted for an appropriation bill would go to jail if he failed to vote the tax measure to pay for it. Among all others, he felt the lowest type of politician to be the liberal Democrat. This in the 1940's put him in a dichotomous position, since it was the Roosevelt Administration and a Democratic Congress which had once again armed the country and involved it in the war which Patton had been somehow hoping for, or at least expecting, ever since the 1920's. He still, however, had little faith that the Administration or the Joint Chiefs of Staff knew what they were doing.

Be that as it may, his approach to a solution of anything he considered internal subversion was drastic and direct. "What you ought to do when you have the ringleaders tagged is not to intern them. Hell no. They ought to be taken out, lined up against a wall and shot. They're just plain traitors." I did not argue the legal niceties, but agreed in principle. J. Edgar Hoover had consistently believed, and so instructed us, that the most dangerous and possibly ultimate enemy was not Germany or Japan, but Soviet Russia and her international network. I repeated these observations to Uncle George.

"That is a very smart man, Freddy; that is why I want you to keep working for him. He has studied a lot and knows what will happen. Now, let me tell you something else. You're reading today a lot of bull about the masses of Germans encircling heroic Stalingrad, etc. Well, I'm not one bit impressed. Anyone will fight for his homeland. But there are masses more of the Russians than there are Germans; and for their numbers they're doing a damned poor job. You see we've been fed a lot of propaganda by our Red friends and believed it."

"How do you mean?"

"Well, take the German troops occupying France, Norway, Belgium and other places, then take the ones fighting in Africa, the ones in reserve training centers in Germany, and the ones that must be elsewhere on the Russian front, add them all up and subtract the total from the maximum number of military age males in a country of seventy-five million. Even assuming that not a single man of fighting age is a factory worker, you'll see what I mean. There just cannot possibly be the number of Nazi troops in Russia that our Red friends claim; and there can't be that many facing Montgomery either. We're doing it again. We're taking counsel of our fears, and scaring hell out of ourselves. You shouldn't underestimate an enemy, but it's just as fatal to overestimate him. Believe me we're going to whip hell out of the Germans once we get bloodied in battle, and get rolling."

He poured us each another brandy, laced his fingers across one knee and leaned back, seeming to look off into nothing.

"I'll tell you something else that's going to happen. Some day I'm going to bust loose across Europe and be heading hell-bent for Berlin. Then either some coward or some dirty politician is going to get worried and order me to stop. So you know what? If I ever break loose, I mean when I do, I'm going to smash my command radio receivers or else send back no position reports and keep going. Then nobody can say I didn't follow orders."

His own records show that on at least one occasion during August 1945 in his race across France, and again in Germany, he indeed did stop sending position reports. About smashing his radio, I do not know. Sometimes Uncle George was inclined to exaggerate just a little.

The last thing he said that night before the firm handshake of goodbye was "Don't you worry about me, Freddy. I'm not going to be killed, not now anyway. It is my destiny to lead the biggest army ever assembled under one flag and to smash the Germans with it. And so God isn't going to let me be killed before I do."

Then, as though the two ideas were indissolubly connected, "You know, I went out to Walter Reed this afternoon to see General Pershing. He was the greatest man I have ever known. And I told him that I was going to the wars once more and had come to see him as I had promised and to ask for his blessing. Right there in the hospital room he laid his old hand on my shoulder and said, "Of course I give it to you, George. I know that you are going over again. You'll do fine. You'll be all right."

I remember that Uncle George's voice then choked up a little and that with the back of his hand, the one with the snake ring, he wiped at his eyes.

Four days later, just three before he left to fight his last war, Uncle George told my father that he was one of the few people on earth that he trusted completely, that there would be those who now and later would attempt to vilify and mis-represent him, and that, therefore, he would write my fathe1 as much as was permitted by censorship and would late1 entrust to him his personal papers, and written account of all that would happen both in and out of battle. This he did. Many of these letters have been printed in his own *War As 1 Knew It,* and a few in Harvey Semmes' *Portrait of Patton.* None of the diary material has been published except certain excerpts from Semmes' book and a first installment in the Hearst press obtained from a carbon copy of the diaries which had been stolen and peddled by the technical sergeant who typed them. Immediate legal action at my father's in-stance prevented further depredation.

Out of consideration for the feelings or reputations of cer-tain men still living, the Patton children have so far refrained from publishing this material. Ruth Ellen and George have both told me, however, that someday not so far distant this situation will change. Dead men have no feelings and, for better or worse, their reputations should by then be made.

Be that as it may, George Patton trusted Frederick Ayer, who in turn believed in him and stood up for him, even at times when the soldier's conduct must have caused a certain amount of distress to my father's sister.

It still seems remarkable to me that two men so disparate in personality should have been so close. Father was brought up in the rich patriarchal household I have already described. There were two things he wanted always to be: a surgeon or the editor of a newspaper. His father's death and his own sense of duty blocked him, however, from these paths; and he picked up the reins of the family business. Early in his life, he adopted certain unshakable ethical beliefs, and even a few prejudices, which he has seen no reason even today to change. Although he spent over a year traveling the world after graduation from college, even including some highly hazardous rhinocerous hunting in Africa, his outlook became, or remained, a little parochial in some aspects. He worked extremely hard in service to the public, at business and at sports — in that order of importance. The planning for, charity-financing of, and management of hospitals became his major interest. His particular joy and pride was and is the Beverly Hospital in Massachusetts, almost wholly his and Peer Johnson's personal creation. It will be Father's most fitting monument. Father did not have, so far as I know, any of his sister's love of music, verbal ability, and interest in literature, or history for that matter. There was nothing whatever flamboyant in his personality. He lacked as he does now, any true vividness of imagination and he never had a roving eye.

He was and is a man of tremendous courage both physical and moral. I have seen him take a terrible beating, both in body and in spirit, through the destruction by political change of cherished beliefs. I have seen him then rise each time to fight again.

Once, playing polo, he was hit on the point of the jaw so hard that his teeth almost severed his tongue. After downing one big slug of whiskey, he simply stuck out his tongue and sat stoically while his friend Dr. Johnson sewed it together again without benefit of anesthetic. I have also seen him, at the age of seventy-one, knocked to the ground and

trampled by a horse, dislocating a hip and cracking several
ribs. Forty-eight hours later he was at the helm of the *When
and If,* now his schooner, firm in his assertion that there was
nothing which good New England rum and salt sea air could
not cure.

He was strong and kept himself in fine condition. He
eventually taught himself to ride very well, to hunt, play polo
and race in steeplechases. In his fiftieth year he rode, in one
day, winners in three events: a 3½-mile race over fences, another 2½-mile steeplechase, and a flat race. Even for a
much younger man, a feat of magnificent conditioning and
great stamina. Father is today seventy-five years old and still
rides horseback, sails his schooner and tramps into the Maine
ducklands in the fall. He has, thank God, at last given up
trying to ski.

He has always been the only completely honest man I have
known. Quite literally, I have never known him to tell a lie.
He has, therefore, often been disappointed to the point of
outrage not to have found this same honesty in other men
with whom he has had to deal. High on the list he found
politicians, whether appointed or elected.

Perhaps, deep inside, Father and Uncle George were somewhat alike after all. Each was very brave, but Father's was a
quiet, steady courage. Each held strong and unalterable
convictions. In his own way, each was intensely patriotic,
both were devoted family men with a sense of identification
with and loyalty to other members of his family. Undoubt-
edly these deeply rooted qualities were the common bonds
which subconsciously drew these men together. Still, I believe that it was the characteristics in which they differed
that each admired, even possibly envied, in the other.

Regardless of my personal opinion, the fact is, Father fought for and defended Uncle George during all the time he knew him. Even at the end, when the auto accident occurred, he managed, along with Dr. Franc Ingraham, to locate and dispatch two great neurosurgeons to the General's bedside.

He, himself, took all the required inoculations, including all three typhoid shots, at one time, and as a result, boarded the plane for Germany with a fever of 104°. He was with George Patton at the very last, and ever since has fought with every resource at his command against the press, publishers, politicians, knaves and fools to protect his friend's reputation after death.

One man was a soldier by profession, the other was not; yet, I am still not sure who was the better fighter.

On the next to last night before the sailing, Father and Mother were to see a less attractive facet of this soldier's personal vision of the future. It was after dinner in their living room in Wenham, Massachusetts. Patton became overdramatic, almost hysterical and ranting in his conversation. There were tears in his eyes. "It's god-awful. It's terrible, that's what it is. I can see it in a vision. It comes to haunt me at night. I am standing there knee-deep in the water and all around as far as the eye can see are dead men, floating like a school of dynamited fish. And they're all floating face up with their eyes wide open and their skins a ghastly white. And they're all looking at me as they float by and saying, 'Patton, you bastard, it's your fault. You did this to me. You killed me.' I can't stand it, I tell you. By God, I won't go. I won't go."

But of course he did.

CHAPTER X

A commander's mission

THE history of the North African and Sicilian campaigns has been reported many times. George Patton has written of both as he saw them from his vantage point in *War As I Knew It,* which was published posthumously. General Harry Semmes has recounted them in *Portrait of Patton.* General Omar N. Bradley has detailed them in *A Soldier's Story.* I still, however, feel today that there are a few incidents which should be recalled to help fill out this brief portrait of a soldier.

Uncle George's own account of the action of November 9, the second day ashore for him and for his troops, should come first. It is short and, for him, not painted in dramatic words. It does, however, show him re-establishing a principle of command which he had always held and by which he abided until the very end of the war.

On the morning of November 9, I went to the beach at Fedhala accompanied by Lieutenant Stiller, my aide. The situation we found was very bad. Boats were coming in and not being pushed off after unloading. There was shell-fire, and French aviators were strafing the beach. Although they missed it by a considerable distance whenever they strafed, our men would take cover and delay unloading operations, and particularly the unloading of ammunition, which was vitally necessary as we were fighting a major engagement, not more than fifteen hundred yards to the south.

By remaining on the beach and personally helping to push off boats and by not taking shelter when enemy planes flew over, I believe I had considerable influence in quieting the nerves of the troops and on making the initial landing a success. I stayed on the beach for nearly eighteen hours and was wet all over all of that time. People say that army commanders should not indulge in such practices. My theory is that an army commander does what is necessary to accomplish his mission, and that nearly eighty percent of his mission is to arouse morale in his men.

The North African landings in November of 1942, although highly successful, held more of heartbreak than the innate tragedy of most battles. Fighting men of France and the United States, two nations which had always been friends in peace and allies in war, were forced, each by his own orders and his duty, to kill one another. Such bloodshed could not help but leave emotional scars and be a threat to future co-operation.

George Patton's sense of the dramatic and of the fitness of things came at least partly to the rescue. After the surrender, he staged a full-dress military funeral. An American and a French soldier, chosen from among the dead to symbolize the first to fall in action, were interred in a common grave.

Before this, the coffins had stood together, draped in a great flag made of the joined banners; the Tricolor and the Stars and Stripes.

After this Uncle George made a more than ceremonial call on General Noguès, Commander in Chief of the French Forces in Africa. Our government had handed to Patton a long and complex set of surrender terms which the French General was to sign. Uncle George felt that they were humiliating and needlessly harsh. Accordingly, he observed the event by tearing up these papers in the presence of Noguès, saying, in effect, "We are both officers and gentlemen. I respect your valor and that of your men. We have worked and fought together in an earlier war. If you will give me your hand and your word that there will be no trouble between your people and mine, this will be surrender terms enough."

It was enough — and the pledge was not broken. This action helped greatly not only to salvage French pride, but assured that thousands of our troops (Patton estimated the number at 60,000) could be released from potential occupation duty to fight the real enemy.

Shortly after the official surrender of the French, the Sultan of Morocco paid a visit to Patton's headquarters in Casablanca. After an appropriate military review he presented to the General a decoration which he told him carried a most appropriate inscription. The medal was the Order of the Grand Cross of Ouissam Alaouite, a huge silver star bearing the words "Les lions dans leurs tanières tremblent à son approche."

Some six weeks later on the 1st of February Uncle George paid a ceremonial call upon the Berber Pasha of Marrakesh and later joined him on a wild boar hunt. It is clear that Pat-

ton greatly enjoyed this visit; and I think part of his letter
about it worth reproducing here.

We left the palace in the pitch dark about seven
o'clock. I rode with the Pasha and his personal body-
guard in a Rolls-Royce. The others followed in two other
cars accompanied by the sons of the Pasha. We drove
for about two hundred miles through desert gradually
changing into the foothills of the Atlas Mountains. This
was the country in which as a young man the Pasha had
fought, and it was very interesting to hear him describe
the fights which had taken place. He is a Berber, and for
three hundred years his family has ruled this part of the
country as absolute chiefs. I have never met a man in
whom the hereditary qualities of leadership are so apparent. The idea of his superiority is so inbred that he
does not have to show it. Wherever he passes, the Arabs
bow and give a modified Hitler salute. So far as he is
concerned they do not exist, and yet at the table he will
help clear off a course and pick up the crumbs. In profile
he looks very much like an Egyptian mummy with a
café-au-lait complexion on the dark side. His hands are
beautiful.

He said that Arabs would never fight against Berbers
except in buildings; and in his early days they had very
few weapons except muskets, so the only way he could
kill Arabs — of whom we had destroyed many hundreds
— was by sneaking up to a defended house at night and
putting a bomb under it. In this operation they would
make a fuse out of hairs from their whiskers and threads
from their coats, impregnating them with powder; and
when the sun came up, they would tell the Arabs they
would blow up the house if they did not come out. If

they came out, they shot them, which the Pasha described with appropriate gestures. If they refused to come out, they blew a hole in the wall and stormed it and killed them with swords. We described one fight in which he had attacked with two platoons for about twelve hours against a thousand Arabs.

The road we drove along was the one where he had had this fight. Apparently this time the Arabs were not in the houses. He had one platoon attack by fire, and he led the other one in a mounted charge from the flank. He said it was very gay, and that nearly all his men were killed as well as the Arabs. He also showed me an olive grove where he said there were so many dead Arabs that the jackals got sick eating them.

When we reached the place for the drive, the Pasha personally placed the important guests. I was on his left in unquestionably the best place. Wilbur was next beyond me, and on the Pasha's right were Colonels Gay and Williams. Each post was in a blind made of cut brush about three feet high. I could see to the front about forty feet.

When everyone was in position, the beaters, of whom there were about a thousand, started to work. First, jackals and foxes came running very fast through the trees, and I missed three shots, but so did everyone else. Then a very large boar charged immediately in front of the Pasha, who missed him, and then turned with his Mannlicher rifle and opened fire at the boar and the retainers, who were all getting out of his way. Fortunately, no one, including the boar, was hit.

About this time the largest and blackest boar I have ever seen came straight at me over rocks, and downhill.

I hit him in the left eye with a slug at about fifteen feet, and his momentum carried him so that he fell close enough to splash blood on me. It was really quite exciting, because, had I failed to stop him, he would probably have hit me, and he had very fine teeth.

Another boar came whom the Pasha shot through the body, but failed to stop until he had pursued a number of Arabs. Everybody except me turned and shot at this one, and again no one was hit except the boar.

It has always been my ambition to meet a robber Chief in his own country, and also to have an exciting hunt with little danger. The Pasha and my wild boar, which was the largest killed, satisfied my ambitions.

Meanwhile, the real enemy, the German Army, was still very tough. Its backbone was the battle-seasoned lean and hungry Afrika Korps of General Erwin Rommel. Furthermore, at this time there was still an experienced and active Luftwaffe in the skies overhead. Opposed to this enemy were our own largely green troops and, in most cases, inexperienced generals — or at least generals who, since the last war was twenty-four years past, had never been under enemy fire.

One of these generals did not suit Patton. He must still today go nameless because of the words in which his commander wrote of him. In the first instance these were, "General Blank has twice failed to take hill so-and-so. I believe that he is a coward. Therefore, I have ordered him to ride in the lead attack vehicle tomorrow. This will make him either a corpse or a man." The second entry, dated twenty-four hours later, was "General Blank took hill so-and-so with a minimum of casualties. I feel I can now put full confidence in this officer."

Even during the hectic days of battle in Tunisia Uncle George never lost his sense of history or his powers of description. On June 9 he wrote to Aunt Bea about the Arabs.

It took me a long time to realize how much a student of medieval history can gain from observing the Arabs.

All members of our oil-daubed civilization think of roads as long slabs of concrete or black-top, or at least as dragged and graded thoroughfares full of wheel ruts. As a matter of fact, roads, or perhaps it is better to call them trails, existed thousands of years before the earthshaking invention of the wheel was even dreamed of, and it was along such roads that our sandaled or barefoot progenitors moved from place to place just as the Arabs do today.

Viewed from the air, the Arab road is a gently meandering tracery of individual footpaths. Where the going is good, this collection of paths may spread to a width of twenty to forty yards, while, where rocky outcroppings must be circumvented or defiles pass through the wandering tendrils, they come into focus and form a single path, only again to spread out when the going improves. Nowhere is a wheel track or a heelmark, because the Arabs wear heelless slippers or go barefooted; their animals are unshod — there are no vehicles.

In the waterless districts, the roads are generally straight, but not in the brutal mathematical meaning of the term. They are straight only as a man would walk from one point to another, or as the dried slime path where a snail has crossed the sidewalk.

In the coastal lands where there is rain, we have alternative roads. The principal track follows the ridges for the same reason that, in our West, the Indian trails and buffalo paths, and even the highways made by the pioneers, stick to the high ground. In the dry season, the meanderings of the crestlined road are short-circuited at times by trails leading across low ground which would be useless in the rainy season.

In the forest, the roads are even more sinuous. The men who made them could not see very far, so the trail wanders largely and keeps only a general direction.

It takes little imagination to translate the Arab on his white stallion and the men and women on donkeys into the Canterbury pilgrims, while the footman, equipped with a large staff and poniard, can easily be mistaken for Friar Tuck, Little John, or Robin Hood. This similarity not only applies to their dress, save the turban, but also to their whiskers, filth, and probably to their morals; and they are all talking, always talking. They have no other recourse. Few can read, there are no books, no newspapers, no radios, to distract them. Only the spoken word, and truly they are "winged words" with a daily rate of from forty to sixty miles, as we learned during the battles in Tunisia by checking the known origin of a rumor against the time we heard it.

There were two events which took place in North Africa that closely involved Patton's personal feelings, and which weighed heavily on his mind. One of them was not the property of the press, since it concerned a man of relatively unimportant rank. The second did cause certain public comment. The first was the death on April 1, 1943, of his junior aide, Captain Richard Jensen, of Pasadena, California, killed by a bomb fragment while his chief was visiting a forward command post in Tunisia. Patton seemed to feel that somehow it was his fault; and even months later mentioned this to me. I here quote Patton's own letter concerning the event since I feel it gives a better view of a less-known side of Uncle George than any words an author could use.

Twelve Junker 88's bombed them with 500-pound bombs with instantaneous fuses. They fell right in the command post. All jumped into slit trenches, of which there were plenty. One bomb hit right at the edge of the trench Jensen was in, killing him instantly. His watch stopped at 10:12. I am terribly sorry, as he was a fine boy, loyal, unselfish and efficient. As soon as he was brought in, I went to the cemetery with Gaffey. He was on a stretcher rolled up in a shelter half. We uncovered his face and I got on my knees to say a prayer, and all the men did the same. There was some blood from his mouth, but he was not mangled and I doubt if he was hit. There was a small stone bruise on his forehead. I kissed him on the brow and covered him up.

At 1600 Stiller, Sergeant Meeks, Sergeant Mims and I went to the cemetery. Dick was on a stretcher wrapped in a white mattress cover. We had a squad and a trumpeter, but did not fire the volley, as it would make people think an air raid was on. The Corps Chaplain read the Episcopal Service and he was lowered in. There are no coffins here, as there is no wood. Captain Stiller, Lieutenant Craig, Sergeant Meeks and Sergeant Mims carried the stretcher. They were all his friends.

I enclosed a lock of his hair in a letter to his mother. I radioed to Bea, through Beedle Smith, to notify the Jensen family. He was a fine man and officer. He had no vices. I can't see the reason that such fine young men get killed. I shall miss him a lot. *"C'est la guerre."*

General Bradley confirms the details of this story quite vividly since he was under the shelling: The General next to him was grievously wounded, a driver blown into a red mist, and his own jeep riddled and immobilized.

The second occurrence was the capture by the Germans of Patton's eldest and perhaps favorite son-in-law, John K. Waters, then a Colonel. Waters is very handsome, completely courageous and a dedicated soldier. He won nearly every honor available at West Point and lived almost too rigidly, if that be possible, to the code, "A point of honor is never debatable." At the disastrous battle and subsequent retreat at Kasserine Pass in Tunisia, the only serious land defeat suffered by the United States since Bataan and Corregidor, his outfit was cut off and forced to retreat. True to his code, Waters, as commanding officer, remained behind with a few men to cover the withdrawal. This they successfully did, but at the end the small group was betrayed by some Arabs they had trusted and were taken prisoner. It was to be months before his family learned where he was and more than two years until he was released. The story of that event would, however, become a plaything of the press and will be recounted later in these pages.

CHAPTER XI

"I just slapped a soldier"

★ ★ ★ ★

PATTON's strategy and tactics in the lightning conquest of Sicily, his personal bravery as on the beach at Gela, have probably been largely forgotten by the American public. Even his own written version of the battle on the beach is laconic.

> While we were on the beach at Gela, waiting for a boat to take us out to the *Monrovia*, I saw the most stupid thing I have ever seen soldiers do. There were about three hundred 500-pound bombs and seven tons of 20 mm. high-explosive shell piled on the sand, and, in between the bombs and boxes of ammunition, the soldiers were digging foxholes. I told them that if they wanted to save the Graves Registration burials that was a fine thing to do, but otherwise, they'd better dig somewhere else.
>
> About the time we got through explaining this to them, two Hurricane Bombers came over and strafed the beach, and all the soldiers jumped right back into the same holes they had dug. I continued to walk up and down and soon shamed them into getting up.

We got back to the *Monrovia* at 1900, completely wet. This is the first day in this campaign that I think I earned my pay.

The American public has not, however, forgotten that Patton once slapped a hospitalized soldier. Some people seem unwilling that the event ever be forgotten. It seems to me, therefore, that some attempt should be made here to place the incident in its true perspective, that is, in the setting of a shooting war. Before trying to do this, however, I would like to set down two eyewitness views of George Patton in Sicily.

A law associate of mine in Washington is General Jess Larson (Ret.). He was a Lieutenant Colonel of artillery during the campaign in Sicily and has told me the following: "We had pushed through to the North Coast of the island and were trying to drive along it to Messina. There was only one road, running between steep hills, and the Germans, naturally, had concentrated everything they had, and it was plenty, in this area to block us off. I had gone up a ravine about two hundred yards to the left of the main road which was being hit with horrid regularity by those damned 88's. Believe me, I was doing all I could, even to inch my guns forward a little at a time, and was scared as hell.

"Suddenly, I see coming in our direction up the road a cloud of dust, and damned if it isn't Patton in that open command car of his, accompanied by outriders and staff. He stops, steps down into the road and looks around as if he were looking for a seat at a baseball game. Then, almost as if on a parade ground, he starts striding up the ravine toward my position where I'm sitting sweating in clothes I haven't changed in eleven days. Shells are still dropping all over the place, but they don't seem to bother him. Anyway, he said to me, 'Goddammit, Colonel, get a move on, get off your behind. We've got a war to fight.' Then he went and did the same to the other commanders, and a little later, I had a talk with some of the other boys and one of them summed it up, 'Jesus Christ, Larson, that old son-of-a-bitch is going to get some of us killed.' He did, but he got his army moving."

The second Sicilian incident is not only typical of Patton, it also underscores his personal feelings for Sir Bernard Law Montgomery. The first hand witness is George C. Murnane, Jr., an old friend of mine, then a First Lieutenant on Uncle George's personal staff, now a partner of Lazard Frères in New York City. Here are the words in which he told it to me:

You'll remember, that during the North African campaign, Monty, almost like a senior prefect in school, used to call in various commanders, including some of ours and deliver lectures. He used to call this a "military critique." This one was even more high, mighty and objectionable than the usual. In it, he said that whereas American equipment was magnificent, our troops were inadequately trained and rather poorly led. He made the modest proposal, therefore, that these troops should be taken out of Africa for more training, and that our equipment be turned over to him, so that he could get on with the war.

I leave you to imagine the steam which was coming out of Patton's ears. He managed to obtain a sort of half-baked apology; but it was far from satisfactory, and he did not forgive.

When we hit Sicily the plan was for Patton to move up the

center a certain distance and then hold, while Monty drove from the south all the way to the north coast at Messina. That was the plan, but your uncle had another: He told us we were going to reach Messina before Monty, if it killed him and all of us. It didn't and we did. In fact, Monty had hardly moved at all. Of course, he was facing mostly Germans, and we had fought mostly Italians, but victory was no less sweet. I remember it very well. We were in some olive grove, or other, hoping it would be a nice camouflage against bombers. Your uncle and "Hap" Gay were off to one side. Suddenly, Patton yelled "Hey, Murnane." I hurried over. He pointed at a five-gallon jerry can.

"You see that can, Murnane?"

"Yes, sir, of course."

"Well, I want you to take it to Monty, down at Taormina and give him a message from me. Now listen."

"Yes, sir."

"The message is as follows: 'Although sadly short of gasoline myself, I know of your admiration for our equipment and can spare you this five gallons. It will be more than enough to take you as far as you will probably advance in the next two days.'"

"But, my God, General, I can't do that."

"Yes you can, dammit, because that's an order. You hear?"

"Yes, sir."

Well, there I was, a first lieutenant, ordered on an errand to insult a Field Marshal, but I took off by jeep anyway. I managed to reach "Pete" de Guinguand, Monty's Chief of Staff, who, thank heavens, had a sense of humor, and explained the thing to him. He told me that insofar as my boss was concerned, the can and message had been delivered.

There was a sequel to this Messina business much later when we were, if memory serves me right, at Nancy in France. Air Marshal Parks, who had been in charge during the battle of Britain showed up at headquarters and told me he wanted to see the General. I delivered the message to your uncle, who was not pleased. He didn't want to see "any of Monty's damned friends," then said, "Oh well, send him in, I suppose I have to see him."

The very first words from Parks were, "I'm on my way to a command in the Far East, but wanted to come in to say hello and thank you for the hundred pounds I won. I bet it that you'd reach Messina before Monty."

Well, that was the open sesame. Patton was grinning all over, and the two men spent a very pleasant evening. You could almost say that to be an enemy of Monty's, was to be a friend of your uncle's.

Here then, is George Patton's written version of the notorious slapping incident.

During the attack on Troina, I drove to the headquarters of General Bradley, who was conducting the attack, accompanied by General Lucas. Just before we got there, I saw a field hospital in a valley and stopped to inspect it. There were some three hundred and fifty badly wounded men in the hospital, all of whom were very heroic under their sufferings, and all of whom were interested in the success of the operation.

Just as I was leaving the hospital, I saw a soldier sitting on a box near the dressing station. I stopped and said to him, "What is the matter with you, boy?" He said, "Nothing, I just can't take it." I asked what he meant. He said, "I just can't stand being shot at." I said, "You mean that you are malingering here?" He burst into tears and I immediately saw that he was an hysterical case. I, therefore, slapped him across the face with my glove and told him to get up, join his unit, and make a man of himself, which he did. Actually, at the time, he was absent without leave.

I am convinced that my action in this case was entirely correct, and that, had other officers had the courage to do likewise, the shameful use of "battle fatigue" as an excuse for cowardice would have been infinitely reduced.

George Patton believed what he believed. Throughout his career he wrote, and told to all who would listen, that there was no excuse for what was once called "shell-shock" and later on "battle fatigue." He said that a man who was out of action because of this condition was little better than a traitor, since he was leaving a gap in the line next to a fellow soldier and thereby increasing that man's risk of death. It was his stated belief that the best way to handle a battle fatigue case was to ridicule the man and so shame him into return to active duty. These things he said; but behind his action were certainly two basic factors. First, Patton was so highly emotional that he was sometimes too quick to violently expressed anger. Second, he believed that any man who was not a fool should be somewhat afraid in battle since it heightened his instincts for self-preservation; but, as Gordon Prince has suggested, he was quite literally constitutionally incapable of recognizing that a real man could have any capacity to act the coward, never mind hold any conceivable excuse for doing so.

Whatever the case, the General made a complete round of

all the major units in the area; and, however galling it may have been to him, made at each a handsome speech of apology. In his own way he was an accomplished actor and lived to the hilt each role he chose to play.

For added light on the slapping incident here is an eyewitness account from Daniel Currier, who was on duty as a medic in the field hospital at the time:

"The General had been visiting each ward of the hospital. He hated hospitals, but forced himself always to do this. The last ward through which he had passed, contained some of the most terribly wounded: Men missing legs, men with no arms, men blinded or with faces sickeningly smashed. With each he had chatted, handed out cigarettes, took names and addresses so that letters home could be written. The men had done their best to be cheerful. Patton's eyes, however, were filled with tears and his face quivered.

"Then he came across a soldier, unwounded, sitting on a packing case, still wearing his helmet. He was weeping and acting in a hysterical manner. This was more than Patton could stand. He did slap him across the face with a glove and tell him to act like a man and go back to his outfit. It was a perfectly normal method of handling a hysterical person according to me, one that many a doctor has used himself."

It may well have been a perfectly normal action for a doctor to take and as such acceptable. Evidently, on the part of an army commander it was not — not this time in any case.

I have asked General Omar N. Bradley about the incident. Here is what he wished to add: "As a matter of fact, George was on his way to my headquarters, when he stopped off to visit the hospital. When he did arrive, he told me that he had, with his gloves, slapped a malingering soldier, who was just a coward and that it would maybe make a man out of him. He seemed absolutely certain that he had done the right thing.

"The next day, however, General Kean came to me with a very rough report from the hospital commandant, addressed through channels to Eisenhower. After reading it, I decided it was a very damaging thing, so I sealed it in an envelope marked 'To be opened only by Bradley or Kean.' A funny thing happened long afterwards, when I was back in the Pentagon. Someone had been sorting my files for me and brought me the envelope. I think I had completely forgotten its existence. Anyway, I burned it."

This was to be one of the first of many times that Omar Bradley would go to bat for George Patton, a demonstration of confidence Patton was to prove was far from misplaced.

Every correspondent in the theater came to know of the incident. No one reported it, either because he felt it so basically unimportant, or because he thought it would be damaging to reputation and disruptive of morale. Drew Pearson was the only newspaperman to report the event. If it be unfair to suggest that he acted as the tool of other interests in doing what he did, there remain but two alternative explanations: one, he thought his story would be good for the national war effort and the morale of troops — a patent absurdity; two, he placed a very high value on having a "scoop" — a sense of values which seems to me hideously distorted. The result, however, was nearly lethal to Patton; nearly but not quite.

George Patton had been decorated in 1918 for his part in an action where he threatened to shoot men who hesitated to advance. In 1943 he was nearly cashiered for slapping a soldier who showed cowardice, or at least hysteria.

There was another quite different happening, during the Sicilian campaign, perhaps small in itself, but interesting in the interpretation Uncle George placed upon it. A field artillery shell landed flat, a few feet away from where the General was standing on a road, and lay spinning and smoking on its side for a second or so. Somehow, it did not detonate. He told me later, "I knew then, once more for certain, that I was destined to live to do great things." Patton continued with this theme of destiny in a related story.

"General Allenby told me once of how he had gone to capture two notorious armed bandits in India and had instead been trapped by them, one with a shotgun, the other with an automatic. He thought he was dead for sure, but the shotgun shells were wet and the pistol misfired. He said of the event: 'My dear Patton, nature creates certain men to handle crises. Most of them never know it, because they are never told. Something, such as happened that day, told me that I was one of the men destined to do some very important job, because I had been given a seventh sense — that of luck. But luck is just like a sum of gold in the bank which must be spent. There is only so much, and the gold of a combat infantryman is spent much more rapidly than that of a rear echelon cook.'" Uncle George added, "Well, that dud shell was the second time I had been told. The first was in the Argonne in the First World War. Now I know I have been marked to do great things, but, of course, I don't know how much luck I may have left."

There has also been much said about Patton's activities in England prior to the invasion — especially of how he moved

from place to place along the coast in order to make the enemy believe that the cross-channel invasion would strike elsewhere than was actually planned. He was the one Allied
general the Germans most feared, and most respected. They
had met him before. This evaluation is confirmed in the
memoirs of two such generals as Hans Speidel and Gerd von
Rundstedt.

Of course, in England, as elsewhere, Patton also made
speeches. One did no harm and possibly more than a little
good. It most certainly will remain in happy memory for
those who heard it. This was a speech to his own troops prior
to invasion. In its original form, it is almost unprintable, although dozens of typed copies are in existence. In condensed
form and not much more printable, however, its peroration
was this: "Of course, some of us are going to die, but if you
remember your training and use properly the weapons you
have been issued, the number can be very small. I hope that
if there are any cowards among you, that all of them will be
killed, thus we will save the —— for the brave. Then, long
after this is all over, and your grandchildren gather around
your knees to ask, 'Grandpa, what did you do during the war?'
you won't have to answer, 'I spent it shovelling mule dung in
Louisiana.' "

The second speech was just as typical, but it did no good
at all, since it caused an unhappy stir in political quarters.
He made it at Wooford at the opening of a combined Services
Club. In it he, among other comments, lauded the fighting
qualities of the British soldiers, outlined the purposes for
which we were both at war, and then bluntly stated, "Obviously, it is and will be the manifest destiny of Britain and the
United States to rule the postwar world."

General Omar Bradley had this to say about the event: "It would have passed as a local boner coming from anybody less than George, but believe me, it exploded into a world crisis, when it reached the press wires. All kinds of nasty editorials were written and George's nomination for promotion to permanent Major General was tabled by the Senate. Furthermore, Ike was just about at the end of his rope as far as George was concerned."

Evidently Uncle George had committed the sin of too pointedly failing to include the Russians among the rulers of the postwar world. A little later, he expressed his own view. "Anybody, Freddy, who wants the Russians to rule any part of this world is a God-damned fool. What's more, do you think they're going to stop fighting to get the Nazis off their soil just because one American hurt their feelings? Would we, if the Nazis had invaded across the Rio Grande and the Russians did not give us battle credits in a news release? I told you before, there are some people you should have stayed at home to take out and shoot."

George Patton, while still in England, was most fearful that he would not get into the war before it ended. His reputation had been, he felt, unjustly smirched by the slapping incident and he was under an almost desperate compulsion to prove that he was still a great General.

General Bradley told me this about it. "When we received the report of the July 20th assassination attempt on Hitler, we were greatly cheered. Not so with George Patton. He came to me and said, 'For God's sake, Brad, you've got to get me into this fight before the war is over. You know I'm in the doghouse, and I'm very apt to die there, unless I have a chance to do something spectacular.' He certainly did something spectacular, when he got going. In his dash across France, no other commander could have matched him in boldness. I still think today, that the fact he had to humble himself, and had a long time to think after the slapping business helped make him the great soldier he was on the Continent."

General Bradley may be right. It is, however, hard to think of George Patton, other than at prayer, as being in any way humble or, for any reason, changing his approach to strategy, tactics or leadership. But, whatever the case, he was not long to be denied the opportunity toward which he had driven all of his life.

During his period away from battle, however, George Patton did as he had always done. He studied the maps of Europe and read history, and from there made predictions for the future. In his own recollections he had this to say:

Thinking over the probable course of events, I picked out certain points which I felt sure would be the scenes of battles or else be very critical in the operation. In fact, I told Mr. J. J. McCloy, the Assistant Secretary of War, when he visited Peover, that the first big battle of the Third Army would be at Rennes. Actually it was the second big battle.

I also picked Laval, Chateaubriant, Nantes, Angers, Tours, Orléans, and Bourges and Nevers, because at the time I felt we should go south of the bend of the Loire. I am still not sure that we should not have done so.

Many other points, at most of which we subsequently fought, were selected; but since I have not my map here, I cannot name them all. I do remember that Chartres and Troyes and, strange to say, Worms and Mainz, were marked. It is of interest to note that this study was made on a road map of France, scale 1:1,000,000, and if "The greatest study of mankind is man," surely the greatest study of war is the road net . . .

I also read *The Norman Conquest* by Freeman, paying particular attention to the roads William the Conqueror used in his operations in Normandy and Brittany. The roads used in those days had to be on ground which was always practicable. Therefore, using these roads, even in modern times, permits easy by-passing when the enemy resorts, as he always does, to demolition.

Here was a general who admittedly horrified the stodgy and unimaginative and scared hell out of others. However, the coach of the Green Bay Packers will not bench his best ground-gainer for the title game, merely because his language in the locker room has been a little crude or his attitude toward the front office less than respectful. From the record this general was the Army's greatest ground-gainer. The coaches knew it. Dwight D. Eisenhower and Omar Bradley recognized Patton's worth, and gave him to do the job he knew best, and then backed him up: Eisenhower, occasionally and perhaps, understandably, with dragging feet; Bradley, most generally, wholeheartedly.

A historical fact, which is often forgotten, is that General Omar Bradley had been, earlier in the war, under Patton's command. In fact, he and General Lucian Truscott had been in charge of the second hazardous, but spectacularly successful, leapfrogging amphibious operations along the coast of Sicily. Concerning this reversal in roles, General Bradley had this to tell me: "I had some genuine reservations at the thought of having George in my command. Knowing his temperament, I was afraid that he would be terribly disappointed and thus bitter and resentful. Instead, he acted like a real soldier. When he joined my command in August 1944 he came eagerly and as a friend, and with no grievance. My association with your uncle in Europe remains one of the brightest memories of my military career."

CHAPTER XII

Not even the Red Army

EVEN before Patton was unshackled, there was an immense pressure upon General Eisenhower which, in his difficult position as Supreme Commander of Combined Armies, it was not possible for him to ignore. This was the British demand for a spectacular victory on the part of their own armies and their then hero Field Marshal Montgomery. Later the pressure increased. Even as the U.S. forces broke crashingly out of the Normandy perimeter, Patton was fully aware of the situation. Even Sergeant George Meeks, his colored orderly, said to him, " 'Fore God, General, that Montgomery is going to grow grass and limpets on his left foot, if he don't pull it out of the water." As it was, Patton's divisions rampaged westward to St. Lô; eastward to Brest toward Rennes; then northward through Avranches and Argentan in an attempt to seal off the escape route of the German Seventh Army at Falaise. At a crucial moment, however, his XV Corps was ordered by SHAEF to halt at Argentan to await the arrival of Montgomery's army from the north. This force did not arrive in time. As a result, nearly half of the enemy escaped, mauled and with a huge loss of armor, it is true, but alive and thus able eventually to regroup and re-equip, to fight again most effectively in the Battle of the Bulge. George Patton was angry.

General Bradley was almost as angry but in a more moderate way. He told me that he was very critical of Montgomery's dilatory and cautious tactics at the time and, in retrospect, still feels the same way. I did not, however, ask him why he halted the Third Army at Argentan. In his book *A Soldier's Story* he explained that he was afraid that if Patton kept on going north he and the British might accidentally engage each other. Also, he was afraid that Patton's forces would be stretched too thin to prevent the Germans from breaking out. The SHAEF claim was that the British had sown the Falaise area with land mines and thus it would have been perilous for the Third Army to move in. Robert S. Allen, then a Colonel of Intelligence, in his book *Lucky Forward*, flatly denied the SHAEF claim, stating that the real and only reason Patton had been halted was that Montgomery had insisted that it was he who should close the gap.

I cannot say who was most accurate in this matter, but do know how Uncle George felt about it.

I make no claim as military analyst or historian, but have read, observed and been told enough to know that there was, to put it midly, a marked difference in the approach of Uncle George and Montgomery to battle. Montgomery was far more cautious and believed in building up a marked superiority in numbers, and artillery firepower, all along the line, before he moved forward. Patton, on the other hand, believed in a smashing blow on a narrower front with his power lined up more in depth. He often struck at the enemy's strongest point and then fanned out behind their lines as he did, for instance, with the 26th Division with the crossing of the Moselle. He preferred to risk heavy casualties over a relatively brief time. A war of attrition was alien to his nature and beliefs. He had tremendous enthusiasm and no matter what his personal fears, which he admitted were often great, exuded complete confidence that each operation he had planned would succeed. These feelings communicated themselves to his staff, his commanders down the line and to his troops. His approach was that of Henry of Navarre, who went into battle at Crécy at the head of his troops, crying "Suivez mon panache blanc." Patton wore no white plume, but when he gave orders to strike forward and follow, the Third Army did. He was considered rash by some, but he achieved spectacular results.

Again to use the football analogy, it is obvious that the coach of the New York Giants must be classed as an expert witness on the offensive strength of the Green Bay Packers; so likewise must have been the German Army High Command on the merits of the armies facing their own. A captured Oberkommando Herres analysis had this to say: "General Patton is clearly the number one. He is the most modern, and the only master of offensive. Patton is the most dangerous General on all fronts. The tactics of other generals are well known and countermeasures can be effected against them. Patton's tactics are daring and unpredictable. He fights not only the troops opposing him, but the German Reich."

Likewise, as Giant linebacker Sam Huff should be an expert on the offensive drive of wingback Jim Taylor, so should have been Major General Richard Schimpf of the 3rd Paratroop Division on the methods of Patton. He said, after cap-

ture, "We can always rely on Allied hesitancy to exploit successes to give us the time to withdraw and regroup in order
to slow up the next thrust. But with your General Patton it
was different. He was very aggressive in exploiting penetra-
tion. His breakthrough at Avranches was an example of this.
So was his phenomenal campaign in the Palatinate."

My associate Jess Larson, to whom I have referred earlier,
recently tried to describe to me the capacity of George Patton to inspire:

This was at the time the Combined Chiefs had thought up
a great idea. Two United States, one British, and one Cana-
dian division, after the Dieppe raid had done its reconnaissance, were to invade France. The time would have been
late 1942, and the purpose, to cover our real intent of invad-
ing North Africa. Also, it was conceded beforehand that it
would be suicidal to the divisions involved, and I was an
artillery officer with one of them, the 45th. Our Navy declined to have anything to do with such a scheme, so the
Army decided to acquire its own fleet of transports and train
us for amphibious operations. We had just completed this
training on the beaches of Cape Cod and had returned to
Fort Devens and had been assured we were ready to go. It
was an unpleasant idea.

In any event, there we were, lined up in rows on the drill
ground, waiting to be addressed by your uncle. Suddenly he
appeared out of nowhere, polished boots, pistol and all, and
marched like a one-man parade up to the stand, then trotted
up its steps. Before any protocol could be observed, he bel-
lowed into the microphone, "Is there any man here among
you, who's afraid to die?"

Believe me there were plenty of us, and the following silence grew more silent still: then he launched into one of those speeches of his. He talked about the enemy and how we must hate him; he told us never to forget that our job was to kill and keep on killing. Then he changed pitch and soared up into his firm belief in the god of battles and to his certainty that the only sure best heaven was for the soldier fallen in action. When he finished every man present, was on his feet, or standing on a bench cheering his damned head off. They were ready to invade Hell, then. I personally, had never been so moved in my life.

George Murnane, previously mentioned, recently gave me his own analysis of the Patton approach to leadership.

As you know, I was with his headquarters right from the beginning in Indio, when he commanded the I Armored Corps, right on through the war and until September 1945. He commanded absolute loyalty, because he himself gave it, not only to his superiors but what is even more important, to his subordinates. Even to me, as a lieutenant and then as a captain, he entrusted some of the damnedest tasks, always telling me "I ordered you to do it, Murnane. So if anything goes wrong, I'll take the blame," and this he did. Also, as you know, we on his staff, especially early in the war, often felt and sometimes stated to him that Eisenhower was not backing him up sufficiently, giving him a free enough rein, or supplies enough, etc. Let me tell you that every time one of us said something like that he tore the Hell out of us. He really simply would not tolerate such talk on our part. Of course, he'd argue hammer and tongues with Ike in person, but that was a different matter.

Just after we had broken out of the Normandy beachhead, your uncle was notified that a general who shall go nameless had been assigned to command one of his divisions. He really blew up and rushed over to Ike's headquarters to protest that he, by God, wouldn't have such a miserable incompetent under him. Ike assured him that he certainly would, that it was a fait accompli, and to pipe down.

Patton's fears were justified. Not far from Chartres, the general in question really made a terrible mess of things. It was so bad, in fact, that Ike came to Patton to protest in turn. I was there and heard every word. "George, you'll just have to relieve General So-and-so. He's dreadful."

"No, I'm not going to do that, not now."

"But, just a little while ago, you told me you wouldn't have him on a bet."

"True, but he was one of your spare generals, then. Now he's one of my generals. I'll straighten him out myself."

That was that.

On another occasion, Patton had directed that a certain operation take place. The subordinate commander objected, saying he did not believe it could succeed. Words became heated, and I tried to move discreetly out of earshot. Lieutenants belong in the far background when generals are having a row, but I couldn't help hearing your uncle's final words: "All right, God damn it, I am sending the following dispatch to the War Department: 'Over the objections of such-and-such a commander I have ordered the following operation. I take full responsibility for the outcome whether success or failure.' Does that satisfy you?" It did, and the operation was a smashing success.

Uncle George himself told me something which bears directly on this matter of leadership: "General Pershing, during

1918 was asked by his commander in chief, Marshal Foch, to subordinate his American Divisions to the wishes of the overall high command and to amalgamate them operationally with the French division. Pershing refused point-blank and said, 'You can relieve me of my command, but until that time, although my Army is under your orders, my divisions are under mine.' In North Africa I faced the same problem. Alexander [Field Marshal, Sir Harold Alexander whom Patton considered the finest British field commander alive] one evening called me up to say, 'George, in the next operation I want you to take your 2nd Division and move it up to ——.' I interrupted him to say, 'As my commander, you can order me to march my army into the sea, and I will. But no one, including the Lord Almighty, has the right to tell the commander of an army how he shall dispose of his divisions.' You know, he didn't even boggle at that; he just said, 'You know, George, you're absolutely right.' "

General Dwight D. Eisenhower, at the war's end, summed up the whole situation in a brief handful of words: "No one but Patton could exert such an extraordinary and ruthless driving power at critical moments or demonstrated the ability of getting the utmost out of soldiers in offensive operation."

After the mopping-up operations at St. Lô, and other Nazi bastions, Patton's already feared and famous 3rd Army broke loose, and drove irresistibly and almost unchecked across Northern France. He told me that during part of this advance, he did in fact stop sending back any position reports, because otherwise, "some directive-reading S.O.B. would tell me, 'Patton, you've already reached your designated objective, so stop there and await further orders.' Why hell, the only thing for an army to do when it has the enemy on the run is to keep going until it runs out of gas, and then continue on foot, to keep killing until it runs out of ammunition and then go on killing with bayonets and rifle butts."

Employing most if not all of these tactics, he actually reached the German frontier the first week in September, finding before him little but disorganized and demoralized troops, even discovering that the famous Siegfried Line was virtually untenanted. He felt that with fresh logistical support, he could race on and reach Berlin in a very few weeks. To this end, he is reported to have sent a wire back to Commanding General ComZone in Paris: "Have just pissed in Rhine, for God's sake send gasoline." I have a photograph on which he has inscribed, for my father, that it shows him having just completed such action. This picture was taken, however, on the second occasion that he reached the Rhine; in the spring of 1945 when he actually crossed the river.

I asked General Bradley if he believed that Uncle George could that fall have driven on into Germany. He answered, "You know, he might have. On the first of September [1944] George crashed into the headquarters of Tactical Air Command and pleaded with me. He had recently requisitioned 400,000 gallons of gasoline, but received only 31,000. 'Dammit, Brad,' he said to me, 'get me the 400,000 gallons and I'll have you inside Germany in two days.' Well, you know your uncle was inclined to exaggerate, but this time, I couldn't dispute him. He had already roared through Verdun, and was barely seventy miles from the Saar River with nothing in front of him but the empty fortification of the Siegfried Line."

In his own account of the days following September 15 Patton had opinions to express on this and other subjects.

Next day we had a visitation of Russians, whom I avoided by going to the front, but I retaliated for their treatment of our observers by fixing them a G–2 map which showed exactly nothing. On visiting the XII Corps, I found General Eddy quite nervous. I told him to go to bed early and take a large drink, as I wished him to be in position to rush the Siegfried Line.

I was certainly very full of hopes that day and saw myself crossing the Rhine. I even advised Eddy that, in the advance, he should form a column of divisions and, after securing the gap in the Siegfried Line, he should send some armor, backed by a mounted combat team, straight on with the hope of securing a bridge at Worms, while, with the remainder of his command, he pushed back the shoulders of the hole and mopped up the area between the Saar and the Moselle. "The best-laid plans of mice and men gang aft agley."

In driving to the XII Corps via Toul, Pannes, and Essey, I went over the same places I had lived in and attacked twenty-six years and four days before. Some of the landmarks were very clear, but a wall behind which I had lain while directing an attack was made of cement, whereas in my memory it had been stone. Possibly they had built a new one. In any event, I must have walked a terribly long way on that twelfth of September, 1918 . . .

Bradley called to say that Monty wanted all the American troops to stop so that he, Monty, could make a "dagger thrust with the Twenty-First Army Group at the heart of Germany." Bradley said he thought it would be more like a "butter-knife thrust." In order to avoid such an eventuality, it was evident that the Third Army should get deeply involved at once, so I asked Bradley not to call me until after dark on the nineteenth.

But four days later, the Bradley-Patton offensive ground to a halt, not because of enemy resistance, but because of orders from above.

It must have come as rather cold comfort when Averell Harriman later told Uncle George what Stalin had said to him in the presence of the Red Army's Chief of Staff: "The Red Army could not even have conceived, never mind have executed the Third Army's incredible dash across France."

In his summing up, writing less than one month after the end of hostilities, Patton recapitulated his feelings as follows.

> In every case, practically throughout the campaign, I was under wraps from the Higher Command. This may have been a good thing, as perhaps I am too impetuous. However, I do not believe that I was, and feel that had I been permitted to go all out, the war would have ended sooner and more lives would have been saved. Particularly I think this statement applies to the time when, early in September, we were halted, owing to the desire, or the necessity, on the part of General Eisenhower in backing Montgomery's move to the north. At that time there was no question of doubt that we could have gone through and on across the Rhine within ten days. This would have saved a great many thousand men.
>
> (As the Church says "Here endeth the Second Lesson.")

Since the witness in this case might be accused of prejudice, we should look to one who was forced to be professionally objective such as General Schimpf above referred to. In his evaluation of the strategic situation in question he wrote:

There is no question that if your Third Army had not been halted [by orders from SHAEF] before Metz in September, it would have penetrated the Siegfried Line very quickly and been across the Rhine in a short time. At that time we were powerless to cope with the situation in that portion of the front. But when your Third Army was halted, we obtained the time to regroup and we used that opportunity to the utmost.

Supreme Headquarters Allied Expeditionary Forces had, however, its own plans, and they did not involve Patton's doing much more than mounting a holding operation. All available supplies were now to be diverted northward for a drive into and through Holland, for the now infamous Nijmegen–Arnhem push. The spearhead of this attack was to be a great force of British and U.S. paratroops and glider-borne infantry; the sledgehammer to follow would be the British armor. Given the existing logistics situation — including the fact that only one cross-channel gasoline pipeline was completed, with its terminus at Alençon, still two hundred miles behind the front — it was obvious that all other Allied forces in France had to be stripped of fuel and air cover, and thus immobilized.

The plan to drive through Holland had as its strategic intention the complete securing of the vital Port of Antwerp. This was a most desirable objective, but the plan had certain fatal flaws. I have asked General Bradley for his own evaluation of this proposal. Here is his answer: "For the first time in his life Monty came forward with a daring plan involving himself and it was one of the worst ideas I ever heard. I did not believe it would succeed and said so. I thought it was a terrible mistake then, and I still think so today."

The Third Army, as well as the First, were, as a result, later bogged down in the face of powerful German forces which had had a chance to regroup and resupply themselves. This was in the second week of September 1944. Except for the Von Rundstedt offensive in the Ardennes, the situation would remain far too static from then until February of the next year. The cost in casualties, in material, can today be exactly calculated. The cost to the free world of the loss of time which permitted the Soviets so many more months to grind ahead, can never be reckoned with accuracy.

Patton was fully aware of this situation, because Colonel Oscar Koch had told him about it; and Koch was, in his opinion, the best Assistant Chief of Staff, Intelligence, in the American forces. From what I was able to hear and read in my position on the staff of Colonel A. Gordon Sheen, Chief of Counter-Intelligence for Eisenhower's Headquarters, I felt there was ample evidence to support such an evaluation of the man. Patton also had available to him, through the Intelligence Services of the British, decodes of certain German top-level operational orders transmitted by radio. It is easy, therefore, to imagine his frame of mind as he sat in command of a huge, battle-tested, and eager army, without air cover, and without fuel for his tanks. He did manage to steal a certain amount of gasoline by having some of his own officers and white-helmeted Military Police divert fuel trucks from their appointed destination, along the Red Ball Route, and thus to his own dumps. There is a story that he himself stood at a major highway junction and personally ordered the drivers to change routes. I do not know whether the tale is true. If it is, many people who knew Patton would not be much surprised. He was always a practical man who believed in direct action.

He wrote at the time to Aunt Bea, "There is current a hor-
rid rumor which officially, of course, I must hope is not true.
It is that some 3rd Army men disguised themselves as 1st
Army personnel and diverted a battalion of gas trucks to
their own dumps. To reverse the statement about the Light
Brigade, 'This is not war, but it is magnificent.' "

During the following period of only comparative inaction,
Uncle George did, however, manage to revisit some scenes of
his earlier war. He wrote of these and showed that his feeling for continuity and the nature of his humor had scarcely
changed after twenty-seven years.

On the twenty-sixth, Colonel Codman, Colonel Campanole, and I drove to Gondrecourt for the purpose of
locating a Madame Jouatte, who had been General Marshall's landlady in 1917. Gondrecourt had not changed
at all since I had last seen it, but the family we were in
search of had gone to Southern France. However, the
mayor, who had two charming daughters, gave us some
wine, and one of the girls played the piano.

From Gondrecourt we drove, via Neufchâteau, to
Chaumont and had lunch at the Hôtel de France, where
General Pershing, General Harbord, de Chambrun, and
I lunched in the fall of 1917 when we visited Chaumont
for the first time and selected it as Headquarters for the
AEF. The same people were running the hotel — only
one generation younger. They offered us some of the
same kind of meat we had had in 1917. After lunch we
visited General Pershing's house in town and also the
barracks which had housed our Headquarters for two
years.

Some fifteen days before, the XV Corps, Third Army,
recaptured Chaumont, our Air Force had attacked and

ruined the barracks. However, my little office by the gate was intact. I rather like it, as it was the seat of my first considerable command as Commandant of General Pershing's Headquarters, American Expeditionary Force.

While at the barracks, Colonel Campanole received a horrible shock. All the way down he had been telling us of a beautiful French girl he had known in 1917 and 1918, and whom he had high hopes of again meeting. This lady was connected with the police in some manner, so at the barracks I asked a policeman if he knew her, explaining that she was a great friend of Colonel Campanole's. The policeman, with more candor than politeness, turned to Campy and said, "Oh, yes, I know her well, but she is too old even for you."

After receiving this shock, we drove to Val des Ecoliers, where General Pershing lived during the latter part of the war and where I was Aide to the Prince of Wales, danced with him and taught him to shoot craps. Unfortunately, the place had been very much looted.

We then drove through Langres, where we had no time to stop, and on to Bourg, my Tank Brigade Headquarters in 1918. The first man I saw in the street was standing on the same manure pile whereon I am sure he had perched in 1918. I asked if he had been there during the last war, to which he replied, "Oh, yes, General Patton, and you were here then as a Colonel." He then formed a triumphal procession of all the village armed with pitchforks, scythes, and rakes, and we proceeded to rediscover my old haunts, including my office, and my billet in the château of Madame de Vaux.

The grave of that national hero, "Abandoned Rear," was still maintained by the natives. It originated in this manner. In 1917, the Mayor, who lived in the "new house" at Bourg, bearing the date 1760, came to me, weeping copiously, to say that we had failed to tell him of the death of one of my soldiers. Being unaware of this sad fact and not liking to admit it to a stranger, I stalled until I found out that no one was dead. However, he insisted that we visit the "grave" so we went together and found a newly closed latrine pit with the earth properly banked and a stick at one end to which was affixed crosswise a sign saying, "Abandoned Rear." This the French had taken for a cross. I never told them the truth.

CHAPTER XIII

"I have studied the German all my life"

It was about two weeks after the Arnhem–Nijmegan operations that I first visited Uncle George at his headquarters in
Nancy. I had arrived by jeep with a friend and neighbor,
Colonel Edward H. Osgood, Jr., Deputy G–3 of SHAEF, and
we were dusty, dirty and tired. I am sure my appearance
made me quite out of place in the surroundings of this particular headquarters where every man I saw was clean-
shaven, all boots polished, and everyone wore his necktie
and helmet. There was great efficiency and complete discipline and, therefore, fine *esprit de corps.*

In my own experience, if I asked a soldier what was his
outfit he would almost invariably answer by Regiment or at
most, by Division. He scarcely ever answered by Army, except in the case of the Third. Then the almost invariable reply was, "I'm with Patton." My first encounter with this form
of pride had been over coffee at the snowbound Stephensville
Airport in Newfoundland. The sergeant seated next to me
wore the blue "A" shoulder patch of the Third and a splendid shiner. I asked him what had happened. "Very simple,
sir. Some ignorant bastard of a soldier told me Patton was no

damned good. You ought to see what's left of his face." Since that day to this, it has been my experience across this country, in talking to lawyers and bank presidents, stevedores and bartenders, to have them reply with prideful memory of loyalty: "I was with Patton." Even at a butcher shop in Bayeux, France, in 1961, I complimented the proprietor Henri Tardieu on the cleanliness of his establishment and the quality of his meat. He commented, "But it is only natural. During the war, this was my job, for your greatest soldier, *le grand* General Patton. Ah, there was a man!"

Osgood and I had arrived from SHAEF in Versailles, with only two stops, one to heat up the coffee on the motor block of our jeep and the second, to check in with several officers of General Bradley's Headquarters at 12th Army Group. That day I encountered coincidences which somehow in wartime seem to become not the exception but the rule. Since I was in the counterintelligence business I had been told to check in with a Major Saxe at 12th Army Group and a Captain Hallett at Third Army, each officer to me no more than a name. Yet, Edward Saxe turned out to be an old friend from Law School and James B. Hallett was a Harvard classmate next to whom I had played briefly in the football line.

When I arrived in Nancy, I confronted the immaculate guards at the entrance to the old château which served as the Patton Headquarters. Personally, I presented rather a sorry sight. This was not surprising, since only shortly before I had been placed in charge of the F.B.I. agents operating in the European Theater, furnished with a simulated commission of Lieutenant Colonel, and instructed to go out and buy myself the needed uniforms. This I had done at the quartermaster store in Washington. By now, I had only barely learned the proper way to lace my own canvas leggings and the rest of my clothing fell far short of proper fit. The only gear which did not feel unfamiliar was the .38-caliber Colt revolver, quick-draw holster and belt which had been standard to me since entering on duty with the Bureau.

In any event, after proving my identity almost to the satisfaction of the entrance guard, I was escorted along the echoing wooden corridors of the château and presented to one of the staff aides. Here was another coincidence. The officer in question was the George Murnane, Jr., I have previously mentioned. His friendly manner did not, however, prepare me for what happened next once I had been ushered into the presence. There stood not Uncle George but General George S. Patton, Jr., tall, broad of shoulder, immaculate in ribbon-splashed jacket above salmon-pink officer's trousers, and flanked by his country's and his Army's flags. His posture was as erect as ever. This I noticed at once. Then, on studying his face closely, I saw that the lines had deepened and that there was a little puffiness about the eyes. He looked tired, or at least discouraged. Of course, he had been in almost continuous battle for two years and had just been halted in his dash for the heart of Germany. He still had his cigar, however, holding it between the long fingers of his right hand on which the gold rings shone. Somehow, they now looked less adornment than brass knuckles.

Uncle George did not move forward at first or even smile. His high-pitched voice had not changed at all. It was wholly familiar to me as he barked out, "What in hell are you doing over here? I thought I told you to stay home and catch Commies?" He then looked me up and down with apparent distaste. "And that's the God-damnedest poorest excuse for a uniform I've ever seen. If you're going to have dinner with me tonight, you'll have to do better than that."

"But it's the only kind of uniform I have."

"Well, it won't do. How tall are you?"

"Six feet even."

"What do you weight?"

"One eighty-three."

"O.K. Then you'll wear one of mine."

That was how it worked out. Sergeant Meeks, the General's orderly, took charge and outfitted me with Eisenhower jacket, beautifully pressed pants and polished shoes. Other than the shoes, the fit was just about perfect. I was, nevertheless, somewhat nervous when I again made my appearance. Patton, however, was delighted. He was then fifty-nine years of age and I was twenty-nine, and as nearly as possible in perfect physical condition. His waistline tautened visibly, and his shoulders went back a little more squarely as he examined his visiting nephew. "Now, by God, wait till I explain this to that God-damned pill-roller." The pill-roller in question was Colonel Charles Odom, Chief Medical Officer of the Staff. To him, and every other member, Uncle George pointed me out with appropriate explanation. Until the time that a good stiff drink was placed in my hand, I felt only the embarrassment of being much too visibly a tailor's live dummy.

After completing a no more than mediocre dinner with the staff, I had finally a chance to talk with Uncle George alone. We were seated in the corner of a sort of large den or small library from which all the owner's books had been stripped, either by the Nazis or earlier to save them from such theft. I, of course, asked him the day's most obvious question. In answer, he had this to say: "Of course, I'm disappointed and damned angry and it's going to cost us like hell before we're through. But someday, by God, I'm going to beg, borrow or steal enough gasoline, ammunition and aircover to get a big attack going. I've already stolen enough gas to put me in jail for life, but it's nowhere near enough to keep us rolling. Someday I may even steal a whole damned division of armor and bust the hell out of here. Come on with me, and I'll show you exactly just what I'm going to do."

We then went down the hall to the sentry-guarded "war room" which was still busy at that time in the evening. This was one of the great prides of Third Army staff. In the peacetime commands of today it would not draw much attention. Then, however, it was quite extraordinary. Mounted on sliding panels along the walls were detailed small-scale maps of all territory, Allied as well as enemy, held of immediate or future tactical and strategic interest. Each map was covered with an acetate overlay on which was marked, as it was received, every new piece of intelligence relative to troop, armor, transport, supply depot, rail, artillery and air disposition likewise both Allied and enemy. Also there were, as there had been ever since the Third's landing in France, table-mounted contour models of terrain being fought and to be fought over. These models had often been difficult to build under battle conditions, but great ingenuity in both theft and improvisation had somehow supplied the materials. The commanding general believed that terrain determined the plans of battle more than any other factor; and his staff had provided him these visual presentations of such terrain.

This evening Uncle George had Colonel Koch slide back wooden panels on one of the walls to reveal a detailed large-scale map of the area comprising the eastern border area of France and a large strip of Western Germany. The General stood before this, long pointer in hand, almost like a lecturer in a high school classroom. He tapped the map with the pointer's tip. "Now listen carefully. What is important is where a roadway exists, or where you can build one. If there is no possibility of either you can't move heavy supplies, or even light ones in sufficient quantity to support a major attack. That was true in Caesar's day and it's true now. Once the supplies are there, big hills, forests, or rivers won't stop a determined army; there is no obstacle that can't be breached if hit hard enough and in depth.

"So now look here. When the day comes, I'm going to move this outfit twenty-six kilometers in the first twenty-four hours to this point here, and this group here." For the next fifteen minutes he detailed, almost regiment by regiment, what he intended someday to do.

He did not get his chance for another five months, but when it came to him, he carried out almost to the kilometer what he had so early planned. Also, to give himself sufficient striking force, he did not actually steal, but did, however in February 1945, first beg and then somewhat illegally retain a full division of armor, the 10th. He did this as he told it to me by asking its commanding general one simple question, "How would you like to join me in one damned fine war?"

After leaving the "war room" we rejoined his staff. To us then, Patton had something to say which no one who was present should ever forget: "I have studied the German all my life. I have read the memoirs of his generals and political leaders. I have even read his philosophers and listened to his music. I have studied in detail the accounts of every damned one of his battles. I know exactly how he will react under any given set of circumstances. He hasn't the slightest idea what I'm going to do. Therefore, when the day comes, I'm going to whip hell out of him."

In twenty years of intelligence work, I have still to hear a better or a more succinct and accurate definition of total intelligence concerning a national enemy, potential or all too real.

A few other incidents stand out from that first visit.

The main railroad bridge across the river at Nancy had been heavily bombed, and its center span had dropped into the Moselle. There were a great number of the badly wounded who had to be evacuated by train to a bigger and more adequately equipped base hospital. To save lives and limbs this had to be done in a hurry. Patton asked his Chief of Engineers how long it would take to repair the bridge.

"Two to three days, sir."

"Too damned long, you'll work around the clock if necessary, and do it in twenty-four hours."

"But my God, sir. If we do that we'll be under floodlights and be like sitting ducks for their bombers."

"So we would — and I'll tell you what I'm going to do. I'm going to pull in every damned A.A. gun in this area and we'll have us a damned fine Heinkel shoot."

That is how it worked out. The Luftwaffe fell for the bait. Some dozen bombers were knocked from the sky; and the first chock-full hospital train rolled across the bridge on schedule.

The next night, apparently undeterred, more planes returned to attack. We were seated at dinner in the General's mess when what seemed like all the guns in town from 90-

mm. rifles to side arms began firing, all at once. Patton suggested that we go outside and watch the fireworks. This we did — for a little while. Then much of what had gone up began to come down in tiny, but nonetheless lethal pieces. Several smacked onto the slate roofs around us, and against the flagstones of our courtyard.

The General removed his cigar from his mouth, turned to us. "I don't know about you gentlemen, but this night air is too cold for my old bald head. I think I'll go in and put on my helmet, before I come out again."

Quietly, and in order of rank, we followed to do the same.

Next morning at the staff briefing, Colonel Oscar Koch presented the intelligence picture — disposition of enemy troops, new materiel brought into the line, expected German reactions and so forth. He then came to the air raid. "The anti-aircraft people," he summarized, "say that forty-five German bombers came over last night and that they shot down fifteen. Allowing for the slight percentage error occasionally present in such reports, we conclude that fifteen planes came over and that they shot down three." I could see why Uncle George considered this man to be the best in the business.

Later that same day occurred an incident which illustrated part of the reason why Patton was sometime the bane, as well as the delight, of the press corps. He, or someone on his staff, had determined that the 90-mm. anti-aircraft gun, fed with armor-piercing shells and used as a rifle, should prove effective against the reinforced concrete of the German blockhouses. Therefore, he staged a demonstration against some of the old French World War I fortifications. At a range of over fifteen hundred yards the big rifles were amaz-

ingly accurate, hitting regularly within two or three feet of
the large white target crosses which had been painted on the
concrete. Furthermore, their shells ripped right on through
the thick French concrete. Afterward, I watched a reporter,
notebook in hand, come eagerly up to Uncle George. "General Patton, sir, what do you conclude from the test firing
done today?"

Both hands on hips, the General gave him his answer: "I
conclude, young man, that if we had been fighting the
French with this gun in 1917, we would have beaten hell out
of them."

Two dreary, costly months of slow slogging forward in the
mud were what followed. The fortress city of Metz was reduced and Driant, the largest German fort, bypassed. This
last was a typical Patton maneuver. His staff study of the
problem recommended a frontal attack, although it noted
that Fort Driant was virtually impregnable and that attacking it would cost heavily in casualties. His answer after this
briefing was — "Well, damn it, we won't attack, we'll just
go around. The bastards will have to come out someday,
when they run out of food and water — and they can't hurt
us with their big guns if we're behind them." This, of course,
was pretty much how it actually worked out.

During the bypassing of Metz there was, however, some
very heavy fighting, particularly at Pont-à-Mousson on the
Moselle River. The right bank was heavily held by SS troops
and the bridges had been destroyed. Thus Third Army forces
were driven back twice after unsuccessful attacks; and Patton
had decided to wipe out the town by artillery fire so that it
could not serve as enemy cover. It was then he received a
phone call from General MacBride's forward command post.
"There's a beat-up old French civilian here who claims to be

a General Houdemon and an old friend of yours. He rowed across the river under shellfire and says it's not necessary to shell the town. He says there are passable fords about a mile away both upstream and down."

Uncle George told MacBride, "He's right. Houdemon is my dearest French friend. Hold off the artillery fire and obey his instructions about using the fords just as if they came from me." The Third Army tanks crossed successfully and attacked the SS troops from the rear, thus clearing the area of German resistance.

Mme. Jacqueline Rethoré, daughter of General Houdemon, told me more about this. "My father was allowed to cross on his pretext that he was looking for a surgeon to care for the wounded who had been evacuated to our cellar from the destroyed hospital. My sister also rowed across under shelling and saved the lives of eight GI's who had been lying wounded and unable to move in the cold mud. Father knew about the fords in the river because he had taken his regiment of mounted dragoons across them in the old days. After he had turned over the information to the Third Army, however, the SS people became suspicious. You know he had been an Air Force General who flew combat himself until the surrender of 1940. So they arrested him and sent him off to a concentration camp. We, of course, did not know this then and did not know whether he had been wounded or killed or captured. I know that Uncle Georgie had him searched for everywhere: in hospitals even and in the forest, since that is where my father used to hide out from the Nazis. I know also that General Patton went searching for Father personally. He was never found until two days before V-E Day, having just escaped again from prison camp.

"Then the officer who found him drove him to my husband,

Jean, at Third Army headquarters and both of them went to Uncle Georgie at Regensburg where he gave them a great dinner at the castle of Thurm und Taxis. The next morning Uncle Georgie gave his own plane, complete with M.P. guard, to my father to take him and Jean back to Paris in time for V-E day. He told the pilot, 'Let General Houdemon fly this thing if he wants to.' And he did."

CHAPTER XIV

God of battles

JUST before Christmas lightning struck, the massive Panzer thrust of Gerd von Rundstedt westward by Bastogne. It came as a tactical surprise to Supreme Headquarters, Allied Expeditionary Forces; however, it was not only a surprise but deadly to the unprepared troops who bore the brunt of the attack. It should not have come as a surprise to anyone. To my personal knowledge, four high-ranking intelligence officers accurately called the shots. They were Colonel Kenneth Dixon, G–2 of First Army, Colonel Jean Rethoré, O.S.S., Colonel Oscar Koch, G–2 of Third Army, Colonel A. Gordon Sheen, Chief of Counter Intelligence, SHAEF, to whose staff I was at the time attached.

On the basis of positive intelligence acquired by both conventional and highly unconventional means, Dixon and Koch believed the Germans would strike through the Ardennes. This showed them a heavy concentration of movement along the road and rail nets behind the suspected take-off point. Koch was convinced, as was his chief, George Patton, for several added reasons. It was within the known German and Nazi mentality at the moment to demand a spectacular and demoralizing counter attack in one of the few areas where the Allied line was held by comparatively untried troops, and the whole fitted what Patton had earlier described as the classic pattern of war from Roman days to the present.

Uncle George had also a personal and dramatic reason for crediting reports of a German buildup. Jean Rethoré, son-in-law to General Houdemon, was the chief of the O.S.S. unit attached to Third Army. During the Nazi occupation of France he had led a large resistance group under the name of "Colonel Bilbane," and had kept most of his people working for him thereafter. Many of them worked as line-crossers: both men and girls, to provide much valued information. In Jacqueline Rethoré's own words, "One of the girls swam two times across the Moselle River to get information and many others did the like, and Jean gave warnings about the Von Rundstedt attack three times before it occurred. These warnings went from the Third Army but were not taken into consideration by the Army group [12th] chief. Jean could give you details: but I know Uncle Georgie 'served it hot' to those responsible afterward."

I'll bet he did just that.

Colonel Sheen also had good reasons for his belief. Allied counterintelligence personnel had been capturing enemy parachute and line-crossing agents of various nationalities — many in U.S. and British uniforms, in locations back of the Bastogne area. Some of these men had admitted, under what can politely be described as intensive interrogation, that their assigned tasks were to cut the gasoline pipeline and land phone lines, also to commit high-level military and political assassinations. Others were equipped with a shortwave radio transmitter to report disposition and movements of Allied troops and supplies into and within the area.

I was present at one of these interrogations. This happened by accident rather than by intent as a result of my paying an official call on one of the most interesting officers I have ever met, Colonel Dubos of a French Special Intelligence Unit, the B.C.R.A. Dubos was not his real name, since it was the one he had carried during the resistance, but I never knew him by any other. He looked exactly as did the famous actor Eric von Stroheim, portraying a Prussian officer on the screen. He had close-cropped gray hair, carried a riding crop, and almost always wore a monocle. He spoke perfect German, and had escaped five times from prisoner-of-war camps; three times in the First World War, and twice during this one. He was a direct man of very few illusions, and I did not feel my digestion would stand witnessing the questioning he invited me to attend. I told him so, which seemed slightly to offend him. "But my dear Ayer, we are not such barbarians as you imagine. I give you my word that we shall not lay a single finger, not even the little one on this filthy pig of an Alsatian."

He was literally true to his word. The door to the Colonel's office swung open and the prisoner walked rather arrogantly in, and behind him a guard. The Alsatian was tall, blond and muscular, dressed in the clothes of a farmer. Dubos at once ordered him to kneel on the thin brass edge of the fender before the fireplace, and to extend his arms rigidly to the side, "And do not let them sag, I warn you, not even by so much as one tiny millimeter." Colonel Dubos then placed his revolver on the desk before him, lit a cigarette and leaned back. "And now we wait and see," said the Colonel. "We will see how long this arrogance will last."

The prisoner was tough. The pain of the sharp metal biting into the tendons at his knees must have been excruciating, the ache to shoulder muscles nearly unbearable; still he held out for a remarkable length of time. Finally, one arm began to sag. Dubos quietly picked up his gun and sent a bullet crashing under the man's armpit. "Up, I said. Keep them up."

A little later, he repeated the performance. The Alsatian's thigh muscles were by now visibly trembling and he was twisting slowly in agony. His face was drained of color and covered with sweat drops. Dubos was on his fourth cigarette and second coffee when the man at last grunted, "I will talk. I will tell you who and where the others are."

Afterwards, the Colonel explained to me, "You see, my dear Ayer, you Americans are not realistic. You would have been polite. You might have taken days and this one pig might have cost the loss of thousands of your own men." I am not certain that the Colonel was entirely accurate, at least insofar as concerned the Third Army; not if one report I saw was typical. This was from a roadblock checkpoint, and Uncle George showed it to me with obvious delight. It read in toto, "One sentinel, reinforced, stopped seventeen Germans in United States uniforms. Fifteen were shot and two died suddenly."

To a trained counterintelligence officer, which Colonel Sheen most certainly was, the facts available pointed to one inevitable conclusion. They also fitted what has been a basic maxim of intelligence since the beginning of military time. This is: To estimate what the enemy hopes or intends to do next, look to see what he is making the maximum effort to find out. In other words, if the Germans were committing their best line-and-parachute-dropped agents all behind one area it was logical to conclude that this was where they intended next to strike.

Oscar Koch's credentials in the words of his chief were: "I ought to know what I'm doing. I have the best damned intelligence officer in any United States Command."

On November 23, the Koch periodic report G–2 of the Third Army had this to say:

The five re-formed Panzer divisions (1 SS, 2 SS, 9 SS, 12 SS, 130 Panzer) of 6 SS Army, though not as yet contacted on any Front, appear to have moved from their Westphalia concentration area. This powerful striking force, with an estimated 500 tanks, is still an untouched strategic reserve held for future employment. These five reconstituted Panzer divisions of 6 SS Panzer Army and the six re-formed Para divisions of 1 Para Army constituted a formidable strategic reserve for coordinated counteroffensive employment. Also, the constantly expanding crop of Volksgrenadier divisions in Germany gives the enemy another eight Infantry divisions capable of commitment in the West by December 1.

And on December 7 and 11 the following:

The most important factor regarding the enemy's reserves continues to be the large Panzer concentration west of the Rhine in the northern portion of 12th Army Group's zone of advance.

Over-all, the initiative still rests with the Allies. But the massive Armored force the enemy has built up in reserve gives him the definite capability of launching a spoiling offensive to disrupt Allied plans.

There is ample reason to believe that Dixon was equally good at his job. And all three agreed. In a meeting at SHAEF at which I was present Colonel Sheen presented their combined views, as I thought eloquently and well. An opposite British view, however, prevailed. It was expressed by the ranking officer present, Assistant Chief of Staff General Kenneth B. Strong of Supreme Headquarters A.E.F. His analysis was that the weakest link in the Allied chain was the French-held area near Colmar and that the American positions to the north were too strong for the Germans to dare to attack and, furthermore, that the Nazis did not have the logistical back-up to support a major drive toward Bastogne. Ergo, the attack, if any, would be to the south. Strong's view was reinforced by that of General Edwin L. Sibert, G–2 12th Army Group. This should have been viewed as a weak reed. I knew this General as a most pleasant person, but as an intelligence officer he was, perhaps, lacking in the necessary vision or imagination. Admittedly, as early as October 3, 1944, the weekly intelligence summary, 12th Army Group, had this to say "The most significant occurrence in enemy dispositions during the past period is the apparent withdrawal of the majority of the enemy's armored units for regrouping and re-forming in Germany, thus supplying him with a sizable mobile reserve." Later, however 12th Army group completely reversed its position, either to conform to the views of SHAEF or under influence of the masterfully written but tragically wrong "appreciations" of Montgomery's British 21 Army Group.

The prevailing estimate then ignored the fact that there were no real military objectives to the south. Whereas to the north, and not too far away, lay Liége, Antwerp and access to the sea. And it had ignored hard evidence. What, apparently, had been heeded was the voice of British 21 Army Group and Field Marshal Montgomery. His intelligence summary of December 12 read as follows:

It is now certain that attrition is steadily sapping the strength of German forces on the Western Front and the crust of defence is thinner, more brittle, and more vulnerable than it appears on our G–2 maps or to the troops in the line. Two outstanding facts support this unqualified statement:

The first is that there is ample evidence that the strength of the Infantry divisions that have been in the line on active sectors since the beginning of our offensive has been cut at least 50 per cent and several other divisions are known to have been virtually destroyed . . . The second fact is that while the enemy's minimum replacement need in the face of our offensive is 20 divisions a month, the estimated total available to him from all sources, for the foreseeable future, is 15 divisions a month.

These two basic facts — the deadly weakness of the individual Infantry Division in the line, plus the inevitability of the enemy falling still further in replacement arrears — make it certain that before long he will not only fail in his current attempt to withdraw and rest his tactical reserve, but he will be forced to commit at least part of his Panzer Army to the line.

Further to this, on the 15th of December Field Marshal Montgomery published not his G–2's but his own personal "appreciation." It contained the following categorical language: "The enemy is at present fighting a defensive campaign on all fronts; his situation is such that he cannot stage major offensive operations. Furthermore, at all costs he has to prevent the war from entering a mobile phase; he has not the transport or the petrol that would be necessary for mobile operations, nor could his tanks compete with ours in the mobile battle."

On the very next day the Germans without a doubt "committed" their armor to the line, ten full divisions of it, plus thirteen paratroop and infantry divisions. It was tactically brilliant, strategically an inevitable but calculated gamble to buy space and time. What is more, the offensive nearly succeeded in its primary aim; to drive through Liége to Antwerp and the sea, and it killed a mercilessly large number of our soldiers.

One thing is certain, for a while at least Von Rundstedt threw almost all Allied camps into a stage bordering on hysteria. This was true even in Paris where I was, observing Christmas Eve. Because I was out after curfew, wore no insignia of rank, had a GI haircut and spoke fluent French, which U.S. officers were not supposed to do, I was arrested as a German spy by some all too trigger-happy French MP's. I straightened the matter out in time and was able that night to do what I had all along intended to do.

Who was right before the battle and who wrong has long since ceased to matter except to family members of those who fell needlessly before Von Rundstedt's successfully vicious attacks during those deadly cold December days. What was done, and how, and by whom to remedy the situation will remain, however, a classic of military logistical and command history to rank with Hannibal's crossing of the Alps. It has all been written before, but the rough outline is worth noting again for the light which it throws on George S. Patton, Jr.

By the time Patton was summoned to confer with Eisenhower and Bradley, he and his staff particularly "Maude" Muller his G–4, had already spent forty-eight hours planning exactly what troops he would move how, where and when to come to the relief of Bastogne and beleaguered elements of the First Army. On the 19th of December, he informed his commander in chief that he could attack with three divisions quickly — by the 23rd. It was not believed that this was possible or that three divisions were enough. Patton was, however, sufficiently convincing and so confident that he carried the day.

Furthermore, he was better than his word. He attacked on the 22nd. Think what this meant. He had to move three armored divisions, plus supplies, plus supporting artillery, in a 90° movement, then a distance of 125 miles along ice-coated or mud-slick roads. Some idea of the magnitude of the operation may be gained from realizing that there were committed in this attack 88 battalions, or 1056 guns of 155-mm. size or bigger. That is a lot of artillery, and implies a huge tonnage of shells to move over one hundred miles. As a matter of fact: from December 18 to the 23rd 133,178 motor vehicles of varied types traversed a total of 1,654,000 miles; 32 truck companies moved 62,000 tons of supplies; and 19,928 miles of communications field wire were laid and maintained. Of course, the fact that he rescinded all blackout orders and forged northward with all vehicle headlights blazing was strictly unorthodox, but very swift. He again "had not taken counsel of his fears." This from Stonewall Jackson was one of his favorite and most often quoted phrases, this and the great Marshal Turenne's classic remark, "Did my knees know where I should this day take them, verily they would tremble."

In any event, after twenty days of fierce fighting the German withdrawal became a rout, and on January 16, the Third Army made contact with the First in the person of Patton's old love and as first formed, his personal creation, the Second

Armored Division, now commanded by Major General E. N. Harmon who had so brilliantly served with him in North African days.

It will be recalled that after the Third Army troops had been moved into position along the icy, snow-blocked routes, they were for a little while impotent because of almost zero visibility and consequent lack of aerial reconnaissance or air cover. It will also be remembered that George Patton directed that a prayer which he had ordered written and then, himself edited, be offered asking more clement weather for battle, and that certain religious purists criticized him for this act. No matter. It was quite consonant with this man's character, experience and beliefs to offer such a prayer to his god of battles. After serving him so long he could not now believe that his warrior's deity would let him down. And it is a fact of history, that the next day, the fogs and the clouds lifted, and aided by the bombs and firepower of General O. P. Weyland's planes, the Nazi attack was rolled back and the heroic defenders of Bastogne soon relieved. It could be said that there and then began the final dissolution of the armed defenses of Hitler's Third Reich.

Throughout the war Uncle George had high respect for and worked most closely with the Tactical Air Commands. This was particularly so on the continent and with General Weyland's XIXth Tactical Air Force. The two men worked as a closely coordinated and deadly team like the swordsman and archer of ancient battles. My friend, then an Air Force Major, Harold E. Watson, thus illustrated the point: "I was more or less in the technical intelligence business for XIXth TAC and we had taken over a Zeiss lens and camera factory near the German border. I wanted to keep it operating since we needed both reconnaissance cameras and the German know-how. A detachment from Third Army showed up one day, however, with orders to close the place down. I refused to comply and violence nearly resulted.

"Within a matter of hours I was summoned to the Patton presence and asked who in the god-damned hell I was, what in the same did I think I was doing and what was my excuse for existence.

"I explained as best I could, mentioning that I was with O. P. Weyland and had been flying over your uncle's head for quite a period of time. At this he interrupted, 'Oh, you're one of those fighting sons-of-bitches who flies when he can't see and massacred all those Nazi tanks. Well goddammit get out of here and go steal all the camera gear you need.'

"I didn't think it appropriate right then to tell him that I wasn't a combat pilot."

Possibly the most succinct evaluation of the role played at Bastogne by the Third Army's commander was made by Gerd von Rundstedt himself in an interview with Patrick Mitchell of the *Stars and Stripes*. It was simply, "Patton, he is your best." This can in a way be adequately footnoted by another authority whose opinions carried respect and who referred to "the extraordinary military efficiency of General Patton's Army." This was Sir Winston Churchill commenting on the Battle of the Bulge during a speech before the House of Commons on January 18, 1945.

Early in February after the Battle of the Bulge was over, and after Montgomery had publicly claimed to have won it, Third Army was still slogging forward toward the center of the Siegfried Line. The resistance was desperate and the progress deadly and slow. Furthermore the combined Chiefs of Staff had decided that General Eisenhower should make the next main effort in the north under Montgomery, using chiefly the U.S. Ninth Army to which several Third Army Divisions were to be transferred. When Patton learned of this he had several things to say of which two were quite typical. First, as recorded by then Colonel Robert S. Allen, seriously wounded and much decorated combat intelligence officer, he entertained his planning staff by mimicking a Field Marshal Montgomery briefing: "I shall withdraw and regroup, thereby deepening my zone of fire. I shall dispose several divisions on my flank and lie in wait for the Hun. Then, at the proper moment, I shall leap on him like a savage rabbit."

Second, in reporting the situation to his corps commanders, he concluded as follows:

"Eisenhower received this order at a recent meeting with General Marshall and certain other members of the Combined Chiefs of Staff in southern France (Marseilles). At this meeting, Eisenhower was told where the next major Allied offensive would be made, what it would be made with, and who would command it.

"Third Army will be required to transfer several divisions to Ninth Army. We will get the bad news later. Whatever it is, we will comply promptly and without argument. General Bradley is merely executing orders and can't help himself any more than we can. It is very obvious now who is running the war over here and how it is being run."

When a corps commander put in some caustic comment regarding Hq Ninth Army Patton shook his head.

"I know how you feel, and personally I agree with you. But whatever we may think of Ninth, we must never forget that it is an American Army. It is one of our Armies and it behooves us to do everything we can to help it."

George Murnane told me of a more pleasant aftermath to the Battle of the Bulge. "After the slapping incident 'Hap' Gay, who was at the time Chief of Staff to Patton, was also in the doghouse. The Supreme Command felt that somehow, in his position, he should have been able to prevent the incident. Accordingly, when the Third Army was formed, your uncle was told that he could not have Gay as Chief of Staff. General Hugh Gaffey was given that position and Gay kept on as Deputy Chief in name only. He really was, however, still in fact the Chief of Staff and it was he and Muller who directed the incredible work needed to plan and organize for the strike against Von Rundstedt in the north.

"After it was all over Eisenhower came to Patton's headquarters for dinner. We had hardly seated ourselves when I saw him look General Gay straight in the face and heard him say, 'Hap, I wouldn't be much of a man if I couldn't admit I was wrong. You did a magnificent job. I am recommending your promotion to Major General and giving you back your job as Chief of Staff.' "

Murnane added: "You know, in looking back, I have a hunch that Eisenhower and Patton really understood each other very well in spite of the fact that your uncle must have sometimes driven his boss almost crazy."

CHAPTER XV

"A damned fine war"

LESS than two months later I was still engaged — not in attempting to prove (for that a great many fine intelligence agents collectively had already done), but in trying to make higher authority believe what the Russians were in many areas planning for the postwar world. This was according to the instructions J. Edgar Hoover had given to me and to the F.B.I. agents under my orders in the European Theater. Since, however, intelligence personnel in Europe were officially forbidden to report, much less investigate, anything that our Red Allies were up to, our job was somewhat frustrating and ulcer-causing. It was, therefore, a gift from the gods to receive a classified message to me at SHAEF, which, in its entirety, read: GET OFF YOUR DEAD BUTT AND COME UP HERE. WE'RE ABOUT TO HAVE A DAMNED FINE WAR — of course it was signed "Patton." Unfortunately, he was not my commander, but also fortunately, I held a position in which I could write and sign my own orders. They took me, if not with the speed of sound, at least by the rapidity of jeep to Third Army Headquarters in Luxembourg. The next few days contained so many moments of importance that many of their details will never be forgotten.

In brief, what came next certainly was a fine war, if such a term can ever be properly applied to brutal battle. Patton had, at long last, acquired the supplies and support which, had he received them five months earlier, would, he felt certain, have taken him crashing across the German Rhine, straight to the heart of the Reich, straight into Berlin. But now he would have to fight for every yard of terrain; across flood-swollen rivers, through mud, and into the mouths of cement-protected camouflaged cannon — and against an enemy desperate in its as yet unacknowledged throes of death.

In the major operation which followed, George Patton proved his point, "The German hasn't the slightest idea what I'm going to do next. Therefore, when the time comes, I'm going to whip hell out of him." Not only did the Germans not know; at one point, they were very nearly one hundred per cent wrong in their estimate. So also, to a lesser extent, was Supreme Headquarters where, so Uncle George later told me, it had been strongly doubted that he could do what he planned with the forces available to him. Since, in the General's own opinion, the battle for Trier which followed was one of the main turning points of the war, I shall give here a condensed version of his own account of the action drawn jointly from what he told me personally, and from what he wrote for friends and family in *War As I Knew It*. It represents a most typical Patton reaction to a challenging set of strategic and tactical circumstances.

The city of Trier was the key point and major railhead of a heavily defended German triangle — and hence a very bothersome block in the path of our attack toward Coblenz and the Rhine. On the twenty-fifth of February, I had in for lunch, Generals Troy Middleton, Walton Walker and Hugh Gaffey. General Omar Bradley called and asked if he and General Terry Allen could come down also. I coached the three Commanders and General O. P. Weyland of our Air Forces, on persuading Bradley to let us continue the use of the 10th Armored Division for the purpose of taking Trier. I am sure that Bradley agreed with us, but felt he had to carry out orders. However, we persuaded him to let us continue the attack until dark on the 27th, provided General Eisenhower would let me call the 90th Division, which was not actually fighting for the purpose of abiding by the rule. Had we been refused permission to continue this attack, the whole history of the war might have been changed, because the capture of Trier was one of the turning points.

I again got Bradley's consent to attempt a breakthrough east of the Prum River, if and when an opportunity offered. Both Bradley and Allen were much pleased, I am sure, in fact Allen so stated, to be among a group of men who were eager to fight.

The above is from Patton's own written account. What he told me in person that he had asked for, and this is confirmed in General Harry Semmes' book, was permission to essay "an armored reconnaissance in force." There is no such term in the military lexicon, a fact of which Uncle George must then have been fully aware; and so was Omar Bradley. Obviously, both men must have been smiling at the time, since each, on this point, understood the other's problems very well.

Patton's account continues:

The sequence of events leading up to the capture of Trier is of interest because it violates the normal conception of how generals plan. The initial attack on the

Saar-Moselle triangle had been started by the XX Corps for the purpose of breaking in the 94th for battle. Then, on the nineteenth, Walker, who had a very good sense of timing, called to say that, with the assistance of an armored division, he thought he could clear out the triangle. As will be remembered, I borrowed the 10th Armored and things went moderately well, until we had forced the crossing at Saarburg. It then occurred to both Walker and me that we had never intended simply to take Saarburg, but had our eyes fixed on Trier, so we continued.

On the twenty-sixth, the XX Corps was not doing much, as it had been violently attacked east of the Saar and north of Zerf by the German 2nd Mountain Division, and at that time it looked as if we would have to turn east to remove that division. On the other hand, the XII Corps was doing very well with the 4th Armored which was units left at the Kyll River in the vicinity of Bitburg, while the 5th and 76th Divisions were approaching the Kyll. Knowing this, I conceived the idea of moving the 4th Armored south behind the 70th and the 5th Infantry Divisions and attacking Trier from the north. General Gaffey, temporarily in command of XII Corps, pointed out the difficulty from a logistical standpoint, of moving the 4th Armored, and suggested using the 76th Division, which was on the right, reinforced by the tank battalion of the 80th Division, which was resting.

The lesson to be gained from this is that successful generals make plans to fit circumstances, but do not try to create circumstances to fit plans.

There was more to it than this. In executing the move it

was necessary to pass part of one division through the supply
train of another. This was difficult, but it badly confused the
Germans to find a unit which their intelligence had told them
positively was on one flank suddenly appearing on the other.
Likewise, the enemy had estimated that the 10th Armored,
now halfway to Trier was to attack in a southeasterly direction to get behind the Siegfried Line, a logical and safer maneuver. In fact, this division struck to the north and thereby
compounded the existing Naxi confusion.

Patton continues:

> I called Bradley at dark (on the 27th), as I had
> promised, to tell him that I was not yet in Trier, but was
> within eight kilometers of it and asked if I could keep
> on. He told me to keep on until he was told by higher
> authority to stop me, and added that he would keep
> away from the telephone. [There follow details of the
> next day's operations which are largely technical.] On
> the first of March at 1415 Walker called up to say the
> 10th Armored Division was in Trier and had captured
> a bridge over the Moselle intact. The capture of this
> bridge was due to the heroism of Lieutenant Colonel
> J. J. Richardson, now deceased. He was riding in the
> leading vehicle of his battalion of armored infantry
> when he saw the wires leading to the demolition charges
> at the far end of the bridge. Jumping out of the vehicle,
> he raced across the bridge under heavy fire and cut the
> wires. The acid test of battle brings out the pure
> metal.

Uncle George told me, "You just can't tell until a man is
really under fire. You know that brave little son-of-a-bitch

was under reprimand and faced a possible court-martial for something that had nothing to do with combat."

I called Generals Smith [Bedell Smith, Eisenhower's deputy commander] and Bradley and told them Trier was ours. Both seemed very pleased.

Uncle George told me, "Bradley always thought I could do it, even if the rest of them didn't. Do you know what I did, when Trier fell? I picked up this phone right here on my desk, got Bradley on the wire and said, 'Brad, I just took Trier, what do you want me to do, give it back to the Germans?'"

I have asked General Bradley about this. He told me: "I cannot remember exactly what words he used, but it would have been perfectly typical of George to have said something just like that."

On my first evening of this visit, Uncle George was dicussing the earlier stages of this battle. He told me, among other things, "You know, Freddy, the psychology of the fighting man is a strange thing. Early, well before dawn, I watched men of an almost green division, soaking wet and cold, cross a swollen river in the face of steep hills packed deep with concrete gun emplacements, machine guns, mines and barbed wire. They crossed without hesitation and walked right through that concentration of fire. They never hesitated. Later in the day, I came across another oufit stalled along an open road. Do you know what was holding them up? A length of yellow string tied across their path between trees. No one dared touch it. I guess it's the unknown a man is scared to face."

One phenomenon Uncle George seemingly had never be·

fore been afraid to face was the varied behavior of women. He loved them and could be extremely gallant to them. But now in a combat theater, he would not have any female — whether eight years old or eighty — around his headquarters. He was convinced, and so told me, that those with whom he was unpopular at home had been trying and would continue to try in some way to destroy him. He felt that it was quite possible for someone to use a woman and a slanted press release to blacken his reputation. His conviction may have been based on fact. I simply do not know. Obviously, he was unpopular in certain quarters and did have a constant and often expressed feeling that someone or some group of persons was "out to get him."

I know, for instance, that he told me then, and later told his wife and children, that the beautiful Marlene Dietrich had warned him that his fears were well founded. I did not then press him for details and can add none today. I believe, however, that there exists sufficient evidence to show that a small handful of reporters did, in fact, try to make George Patton look either evil or stupid. Whether this was done on their own, or at the instigation of others, I still cannot say.

What seemed important to me at the time, however, was that Miss Dietrich, that most lovely lady, had been entertaining troops of the Third Army and was to dine that night in Luxembourg. She was no rear echelon entertainer and she did not perform, as did too many others, nearly naked, as a tantalizer to men who had available no women of their own. She wore olive drab slacks and the equivalent of an Eisenhower jacket and in them she went where the fighting men, and some of the fighting, actually were. In fact, that afternoon she had been performing in a large barn when an 88-

mm. shell ripped from side to side through the eaves. By one of the accidents of war, it failed to detonate. Her immediate reaction was to tell her audience that she intended to continue her performance; that is, if anyone present cared to stay. Needless to say, the house remained full.

George Patton considered Marlene Dietrich and Bob Hope to be the finest personages of the entertainment world, because they really thought first of the troops and not always of themselves. He would not, however, invite La Dietrich to dinner with him — not at least there, in the combat theater. I am still glad that he would not do so, since he assigned his aide, Colonel Charles Codman, and me to escort her to dinner with the Burgomeister of Luxembourg. She was not only beautiful, she was a lady; charming, well informed, kindly and considerate, a magnificent conversationalist, fluent in three languages. The house in which she was billeted was the same as mine, but mine was the better room, since it did not have a gaping shell hole in the ceiling. This was one time when I was more than delighted to exchange the better for the worse.

The early part of the next morning was devoted to detailed briefings by the various members of the staff. The conclusion was that the front was extremely fluid. This, the General interpreted correctly as "You mean, everything is as confused as hell and nobody is really sure where the Germans are. Well, I tell you what I'm going to do. I'm going to drive through Trier to see how things are, and then go find out exactly where this damn war is today."

This he did, in a command car, in the rear section of which was a swivel-mounted .50-caliber machine gun. General "Hap" Gay and I followed in another vehicle similarly equipped. General Gay had only one eye and was described to me by Patton as "one of the bravest men who ever lived." I think he had already proved this. He would do so again in this war and was later to become a great leader of troops in Korea.

On a rubble-blocked, still smoking street in Trier, we ran into General Walton Walker, Commander of XX Corps. He likewise said he was on his way to find out where the war was. Walker was another great officer, short, rugged and appropriately referred to as "the Bulldog." He was, after the war, to fly from Texas to Luxembourg at his own expense to be present at the burial of his beloved chief. The weather was so bad, however, that he was not able to land. All he could do was to fly above the dank overcast, the length of the long funeral cortege. Still later, he was to be commander of our forces in Korea during that "police action" and also to be killed in a tragically needless motor vehicle accident, exactly eight years to the day after George Patton's death.

Shortly after leaving Trier we found the war, or at least a most representative part of it. It was made rapidly clear why operational reports had been confused, since suddenly we found ourselves on a dirt road with mortar shells coming at us from both sides and falling uncomfortably close. This condition was the result of two German outfits firing blindly at each other. My reaction was to get out and crawl under the car, but this, among the company present, was clearly a reaction to be suppressed. Patton, having carefully studied the situation, slowly dismounted, strolled over to our vehicle to say: "Hap, in my considered judgment, the thing to do is get the hell out of here, drive home and have a drink."

On the way to this highly desirable goal, we came upon a

situation which more than justifiably triggered the Patton temper. A long column of weapons, vehicles and men clogged a main road to a depth of more than a mile, and this column was completely motionless, a perfect and defenseless target for German artillery should it be spotted by any of their reconnaissance aircraft. It was motionless because at the head was a motorized 155-mm. rifle jammed at a road turning beneath a concrete railway overpass. The officer in command was about halfway back along the column, from which point he had attempted to shepherd his charges. The colloquy between the two men was brief and very one-sided. "Colonel, you can blow up the goddam gun. You can blow up the goddam bridge, or you can blow out your goddam brains, and I don't care which."

A little further on Patton spotted, before any of us, a tall man in dusty civilian clothes walking by the side of the road. Within seconds, he shouted, "Stop the car and cover that man." The man was ordered over. Patton looked him up and down, then called him to attention in German. The man in automatic reflex snapped to a rigid stance. "You are an Army officer, are you not?" Patton snapped at him.

"Ja wohl, mein General."

Orders were given to have him taken to the nearest P.O.W. camp. I then asked, "How in hell could you know what he was at that distance and so quickly?"

"Goddammit, Freddy, if after all these years I can't recognize a soldier when I see one, I should turn in my uniform."

CHAPTER XVI

A general wants to weep

I THINK it useful here to describe Patton's expressed attitude toward the captured, as even this viewpoint would help
make him a target for criticism. He fully respected any and
all who had fought bravely and their best. I remember his
telling me of the capture of the citadel at St. Malo. One of
the most determined and heroic German defensive actions
in the early days on the continent was the resistance of the
garrison of this stronghold. There Colonel von Aulock and
not quite four hundred men held out for a very long time
against overwhelming odds and nerve-shattering point-blank
heavy-caliber artillery fire. When, finally, further resistance
became clearly futile, the defenders surrendered. Uncle
George described this: "The officers marched out with Von
Aulock at their head, in dress uniform, cleanly shaved and
proud as hell. They may have been short of water, but they
must have had plenty of brandy. General Macon's men on
our side had had a pretty rough time and were very tired.
I think the Krauts were damned happy, however, to give up.
But that Von Aulock, there was one soldierly son-of-a-bitch.
He and his men were not like another bunch, a complete

German division we surrounded. Their general sent over a message begging that I have my troops fire over a few phosphorous rifle grenades. Can you imagine why?"

I couldn't.

"Well, it was simple. He wanted to be able to report back to his Fuehrer that he was surrendering before hopeless odds, but only after being mercilessly incinerated by huge phospherous bombs dropped by our Air Forces."

After the war was over and various enemy military leaders such as Marshal Kesselring and Gerd von Rundstedt were interned in the vicinity of Bad Tolz, it was openly reported in the press that Patton wanted, or said he wanted, to invite them to dinner. He was quoted as wishing to sit down to discuss their battles, using salt cellars and spoons to illustrate the varying tactics. For this, he was severely criticized, a criticism he could never understand. He could not see why the practice of gallantry from the days of knighthood, or even that of air battles of World War I, could not be carried over to the present. In an instance such as this, I am not sure that I can either. After all, it was only a few years later that I stood, as part of a welcoming committee on the steps of the river entrance to the Pentagon to shake hands, after the man had been saluted by an honor guard, with a German air force general who had shot down forty-two Allied planes during World War II. Uncle George would have approved of this since he saw no reason why an honorable enemy could not, after defeat, become a friend.

Still, to Patton, there were others among the enemy who were not honored, but detested. He told me, for instance, of when his men had captured, hiding ignominiously in a wine cellar, the Gestapo general who had been in charge of the Province of Lorraine. "I called him a degenerate, murdering coward, then ordered: 'Throw the filthy bastard into the deepest, filthiest, dampest cell you can find.' "

In complete accuracy he was not, as Uncle George described him, a "Gestapo general" — but he was SS Brigade Fuehrer Anton Dunkern and as such a party member, rather than an officer of the German regular army, as well as military governor of the province. He was correctly reputed to have committed as well as condoned atrocities against the civilian population of the area.

Patton interrogated this man himself. Captain James B. Hallett, his chief of counterintelligence, described the scene to me.

Your uncle appeared dressed in heavy field boots and announced, "I always wear boots like these when I'm anywhere around you SS Nazi bastards. You will stand at attention when I speak to you and you will preface every answer to me with 'Sir.' "

Dunkern was fat, pasty-faced and had little pig eyes. Although of the SS, we found out later that he did not have the usual tatoo of his blood group under the left armpit; thus he was not of the Waffen-SS, who were combat troops, but merely a political officer. Somehow your uncle sensed this right away. He really tore into him and the dialogue as I remember it went almost exactly like this:

"I have captured a number of German generals," he began, "but you are the most sordid son-of-a-bitch of them all. You aren't a soldier at all. You're a goddamned party official. I ought to turn you over to the French."

Dunkern protested. "Under the Geneva Convention," he

whined, "that is not permitted. I am an American prisoner."

"How come you surrendered? Why didn't you die for the Fuehrer as you forced your troops to swear they would do?"

"I had no chance. The door suddenly opened and one of your men stuck his gun into my stomach."

"I'm surprised he was able to pull it out again," said Patton, eying Dunkern's sagging belly. "Our records show that you committed some very grave offenses in Lorraine."

"I did nothing I am ashamed of. I may have made some mistakes, but only those of human judgment."

"What do you mean, human judgment? Are you talking about Nazi judgment, or the judgment of decent people? What about the hostages you shot?"

"There were times," replied Dunkern, "when that was necessary for the protection of the Reich."

Your uncle's voice rose the way it always did when he was excited. "The war crimes commission will decide that" — then he turned on his heel and directed the guard "take the dirty bastard away and throw him in the deepest cell we have."

I think Dunkern was happy at that. He'd really expected to be taken out and shot.

An acquaintance of mine, Bernard Poore, then a combat intelligence officer, once told me of uncle George's reaction to the capture of another ranking German general, this time of the regular army.

I went into the "presence," feeling pretty damned proud of myself, saluted and identified myself.

"Well, Colonel, what the hell do you want?"

"I wish to report, General, sir, that we have captured General So-and-so and wish to know what we should now do with him." [Poore did not of course say General So-and-so. It is simply that I have completely forgotten the man's name.]

Well, Freddy, you know that high-pitched voice of his — it cuts right through you, and it cut through me.

"So what, Colonel, you know what you can do with him. You can shove him, that's what you can do."

I felt as important as a punctured balloon, and sort of mumbled, "Yes, sir," then turned to leave the room. I'd just about reached the door, when he spoke again — "Goddammit, Colonel, come back here. Sit down. Have a cigar and tell me all about how it happened."

Sometimes you'd want to kill the old man, but you'd have to end up loving him.

George Patton had read about a code of conduct as a little boy, studied under it and lived by it all the rest of his life. "The highest privilege of citizenship is to be able to bear arms for your country." He could not and would not condone atrocities, but he could not see that a German soldier had committed any crime for living by the same code as his own. He would not have understood some of the sentences meted out at Nuremberg to certain military leaders who, without committing atrocities, had simply carried out orders.

After we had "gotten the hell out of there and driven home," we had the drink, in fact, several of them, then dinner. This time, it was an excellent meal, in sharp contrast to those in Patton's mess at Nancy. George Murnane told me that Nancy was probably one of the poorest messes in the whole United States Army, because, "among my other duties, I was also mess officer." Not so at Luxembourg. All meals in the Third Army were by now good insofar as was possible, under some very varied circumstances. Patton never directly quoted Napoleon that "an Army marches on its stomach," but he did realize the tremendous effect on morale of good chow served hot. For example, even under the miserable sleet and snow-choked skies and in the face of vicious enemy action in the Bastogne area, on Christmas Day, 1944, every single soldier of the Third Army had a hot turkey dinner complete with the traditional trimmings. He demanded and often received effort beyond the possible to this effect: "There's too many so-called mess cooks who couldn't qualify as goddam manure mixers. They take the best food Uncle Sam can buy and bugger it all up."

The reason why such a thing did not happen here, and that the Third Army's food was well handled and prepared, was the quality of the man in charge. The chief mess officer was Major Edward P. Creed, another friend and neighbor, who was, as his father before him, and is himself today, the operator of the finest catering service on the North Shore. I have been curious as to how he ended up with Patton, and recently told him so. Here is what he had to say.

I enlisted in the Army immediately after Pearl Harbor and ended up as Chief of the Cooking School in the Quartermaster Corps. As you realize, I've known the Patton family practically all my life and handled both girls' weddings. In fact, during the war I used to get letters from your aunt, telling me how the General and the two sons-in-law were mak-

ing out. Your uncle tried to get me as early as before the
invasion of North Africa, and again before the Sicilian campaign. I am told he finally put the bee on General Sommer-
vell, who was running the Services of Supply. Anyway, I
joined him just before he went into Normandy.

For the first four months, I hardly saw him or his headquarters at all. He had very definite ideas about where the
most important work was to be done and ordered me to do it.
Naturally, if you know your uncle, this was in the evacuation
hospitals. Each division had one and the Army always had a
strength ranging between twelve and fifteen divisions. I was
in charge of running the preparation and serving of all meals
in all of them. Then one night, and I can't remember exactly
where I was except that it was a 150-mile jeep ride to Luxembourg, "Hap" Gay called up and told me to get myself and
baggage there, and right away, the old man wanted me, the
General's mess was in sad shape.

From then, I was in charge of that as well as the twenty-six
Third Army Headquarters' messes. I was with him all the
way through Germany and to Bad Tolz in Bavaria. When he
was relieved of his command of the Third, a fool move I'll
never understand, and transferred to the Fifteenth Army, I
was again in charge of all the hospital messes as well. Your
uncle asked me to stay on for another month, although I had
more than enough points to go home, so that I could help out
for General Truscott. Much more than that month went by
and still no orders to go home. And so one day I drove up to
Frankfurt where your uncle was, for the moment, acting
Theater Commander. He asked me, the way he would,
"God-dammit Creed, what are you doing here — I thought
I told you to go home?" I told him my orders hadn't come

through. He said: "You'll have them in just exactly one and a half minutes."

I asked him if there was anything I could do for him or send him from home. He told me, yes, he was much interested in a Catholic orphanage outside of Frankfurt — I can't remember the name of the place — and could I send over a bunch of hard candy for the children. Naturally, I did so, two hundred big bags of the stuff. By the time it got there, the General had had his terrible accident. Just the same, when Mrs. Patton got over there, the candy was delivered in his name to all the little German kids. She saw to it herself. That's the kind of people your aunt and uncle were.

Possibly in emphasizing other things, I have failed to make it clear that Uncle George was a deeply religious man. The Bible was his companion and the church his refuge. He did, however, hold some very firm ideas about the proper role of a chaplain. "There are too many of these weepers and wailers who can just barely stand up like men, and then prate about 'Those of ye who will this day die,' and so on, to some poor bastards who are already scared half to death as it is. What they need to be given is courage, and told that with God's protection and their own effort, they will live to sire litters of children — no, as a matter of fact, one litter apiece should be enough. It looks better."

He often took quick action in the matter of chaplains. Once when I had some work to do in General Everett Hughes' office at ComZone, his personal assistant, Mrs. Prismal, a schoolmistress-like but still sparkling Briton, handed me a document. "I think this will amuse you. The poor man brought it in his own shaking hand here today when he arrived for reassignment."

"This" was an extra copy of the orders of a major in the Corps of Chaplains. The sheet bore a very short notation. "This man can neither preach nor pray. We don't want him" — obviously, it was signed *Patton*. Since, as Rudyard Kipling would have said, "that is another story," I here refrain from comment on the educated British Intelligence Service practice of assigning female personal assistants to key American military leaders. After all, if you cannot trust your allies, whom can you trust? Nevertheless, it is comforting to know for certain what they really say behind your back.

After dinner, on the evening of the day near Trier, a movie was shown which drew some pungent comments about the taste of the Special Services. I cannot remember the title or even what it was about. No matter; the General ordered the projector shut off before the thing ended, and no one complained when, instead, a nightcap was poured for all. Afterward the Staff said goodnight and filed away toward bed. I started to follow them from the room, but made it only so far as halfway to the door. The Patton treble stopped me there.

"Just where the hell do you think you're going?"

"I'm going to bed, sir."

"And why?"

"Because I'm tired."

On this evening Uncle George did not himself seem tired or in the least discouraged. Now his eyes were brightly alert and his whole manner radiated vitality. Now he was back in battle and once more on his way to Berlin. Furthermore, he had defied Colonel Odom and was again smoking cigars. When he was not, even the faithful "Willy" guardedly kept his distance. Yes, Patton was in a good mood and quite his old self once more. I could tell this also by his voice when he then said to me, "The hell you're tired. You're too young to be tired, you're not going to bed. You're going up to my room, take a bottle of bourbon and a handful of cigars out of my footlocker. We're going to drink all the bourbon, and smoke the cigars, and we're going to have a talk. Then you can go to bed and that's an order."

"Yes, sir."

Under certain circumstances, as I have mentioned, it was quite impossible to call this man "Uncle George." This was clearly one of them. So, the order was obeyed.

The bourbon was gradually drained, the cigars were one by one reduced to ashes. The General talked and so at times did his nephew, but mostly only in answer to some very probing questions. Goodnights were exchanged in the vicinity of 3 A.M. I do not think it wise, therefore, here to record everything that was said.

Some things, some ideas, however, still indelibly remain in my mind and are, it seems to me, worth repeating; for instance: "Yes, I know, people ask why I swagger and swear, wear flashy uniforms and sometimes two pistols. Well, I'm not sure whether some of it isn't my own damned fault, but, however that may be, the press and others have built a picture of me. So now, no matter how tired, or discouraged, or even really ill I may be, if I don't live up to that picture my men are going to say, 'The old man's sick, the old son-of-a-bitch has had it.' Then their own confidence, their own morale, will take a big drop.

"I get criticized, every day, for taking needless risks by being too often right up in front. What good is a dead general?

they ask. I say, what damn good is a general who won't take the same risks as his troops? Maybe you don't know about Paddy Flint [Colonel Harry A. Flint, killed in Normandy]. He knew that nobody on earth has yet been able to push a piece of wet spaghetti from behind. Things were all confused and a tank outfit was bogged down, too scared to move through the hedgerows. Well, up sauntered Paddy carrying a swagger stick and asked, 'What's the matter with you bastards, need an infantry escort?' Then he marched out beyond them toward the Germans. Do you think they didn't follow? Do you think they didn't wipe up the Nazis? Of course, Paddy ended up getting killed, but for that outfit and the men who have heard about it, he isn't, by God, dead, he's immortal. Yes, a dead general can do some good."

When George Patton learned of the death of this friend on July 25 in Normandy he arranged for him to be buried in a coffin, a rare thing on a battlefield, and himself attended the burial service at Ste. Mère Eglise. He then had the dead soldier's personal effects sent to his widow via General Everett Hughes in England. To the last entry in Flint's diary he added a personal tribute to the man as a friend and a fighter. He wrote Mrs. Flint a long personal letter mentioning that he was sending photos of the church and the grave, but adding that he would do this later under separate cover because she might not want to look at them right away. After Patton's own death his former aide Charles Codman personally mailed to the widow the flag which had been draped over Paddy Flint's coffin, a thing Patton had intended to do in person when at last he returned home.

Here is a part of what Mrs. Flint wrote to the family concerning General Patton, after telling of the above examples of his kindness.

This is a very inadequate effort to express my regard for the friend that George Patton was. He was my friend and more especially the friend of my husband Paddy Flint. Probably only his family and those closest to him really know this great soldier. Loyalty to them and to his profession were his outstanding qualities and I am sure had he been faced with the necessity of a decision he would, without hesitation, have held his integrity as a soldier above all else. Few people, outside of his family, knew the gentleness, the true courtesy, the almost puritanical uprightness and devotion to his religious convictions that were the real George Patton. Many of his friends had evidence of these traits. Underneath the seemingly rough and tough exterior was the thoughtful, sympathetic, almost boyish man.

I have always had the conviction that the "Blood and Guts" manner, the tough talking, was really a sort of "Whistling in the Dark" which he had from the very first contrived to serve as a kind of apparatus to build himself into the person he wanted to be as a soldier; that he thought a soldier *had* to be strong, physically, mentally, morally (and he was all these); that he believed a soldier should be unmoved by fear, suffering, the sight of death, blood, any horrible or vile thing; *that he must endure.* This, it has always seemed to me, was the motivation back of all the rough, profane, and at times almost vulgar manner and speech.

I wish the people for whom he fought, deeming it an honor and a privilege to do so, could know what manner of man George Patton really was, that underneath the rough-spoken, cold-blooded exterior he was a gentle and kindly person who had to make himself tough to do the job he had. He wasn't born that way.

That evening in Luxembourg Uncle George had something to add about the Normandy terrain.

"You've heard and everybody at home has read about hedgerows, but they don't even know what they are. Let me tell you something about them. They're largely composed of an earth bank and grapevine stumps three hundred years old and a foot thick, with long tough roots. A tank can't go through them, but it can lumber over. The wily Kraut knows this and it doesn't take much of an anti-tank rifle to go up through the soft belly of a tank. It sort of takes the drive out of our tankers when they come up against this. Somehow, you're less brave when you keep feeling all the time that the first place you're going to get steel fragments is right up between your legs.

"I fixed this by having my armorer weld razor-sharp steel rails in a V out front of the tanks like a plow. Nobody else thought of this, but I did and it worked. Hell, it could cut through those hedgerows like a bullet through cheese. When poor Paddy was killed, I didn't have them yet and nobody dared move." (Actually, according to Patton's own account, written at the war's end, the 3rd Armored Division invented this "tank spade" in its rough form, and then it was later perfected by Colonel Thomas F. Nixon, Chief Ordnance Officer for the General throughout the war.)

Uncle George continued, "There isn't any defense that can't be overcome somehow or other. Every day something happens to remind me of it. Hell, even though armor-piercing shells just bounce off some of its steel-domed pillboxes, we still managed to get through the Siegfried Line. The whole Trier battle ought to give the pacifists something to think about. They ought to remember that Troy fell, and so did the walls of Rome. The Great Wall of China was a near perfect example of futility, just as has been every damned defensive fortress up to and including the Maginot Line, the German West Wall and now this one. A leadership that takes on a defense mentality is dooming its own people to extinction."

By this time, I had worked up the nerve to ask about something which had always bothered me. "Why do you do it, Uncle George? I just heard you admit that you swagger around and rant and swear and wave pistols, but the effect on morale doesn't sound like a good enough reason. Why do you get off such god-awful statements that get repeated and quoted in the press?"

Uncle George leaned forward, pointed his cigar at me. He was not smiling.

"Okay, Freddy, you asked, so I'll tell you. In any war, a commander, no matter what his rank, has to send to sure death, nearly every day, by his own orders, a certain number of men. Some are his personal friends. All are his personal responsibility, to them as his troops and to their families. Any man with a heart would, then, like to sit down and bawl like a baby, but he can't. So he sticks out his jaw, and swaggers and swears. I wish some of those pious sob sisters at home could understand something as basic as that." Then he did smile. "And as for the kind of remarks I make, why sometimes, I just, by God, get carried away by my own eloquence."

And, of course, we had talked of less elevating, but no less interesting subjects. He told me, "When we moved in here, I went looking for a proper building for our headquarters. I took a young major with me. His name doesn't matter any more, but I thought then he might make me a good junior aide. We were going through this old château which had been closed up for some time. Finally, we reached the master bedroom. It was quite a place, a huge mirror along one wall, a great big four-poster bed, and on the ceiling, above it, another full-length mirror. Well, you won't believe it, but the kid asked me, 'General, what in the world were those mirrors for?'

"Well, he never became one of my aides. Somebody that ignorant could never make it." Then, as not only an alliterative but also a philosophical afterthought, "You know, I've always believed, and never yet been proven wrong that a man who won't ———, won't fight."

It is worth noting in this context, that George Patton, later in Germany, believed in the nonfraternization policy only to a limited extent. He was quite open about this. "Anything my men have fought to capture, they are, by God, entitled to." This principle, coupled with a massive distribution of penicillin, had two salutary effects. The Third Army had in addition to the lowest casualty rates, the lowest incidence of V.D.; and its morale remained exceptionally high.

After another swallow from his glass, he went on with some pungent advice about the care and management of women, especially wives. In a gently expurgated and paraphrased version, it was this. "When you come home after a long period away, the usual thing is to hang around the house, and have the neighbors in and reply to a lot of their damned fool questions they really don't care to hear answered. Furthermore, any natural thing you do or feel like doing is going to get you a 'sh — be quiet, you're going to wake up the children,' or 'not now please, in a quarter of an hour, the Bullslingers are coming over here for tea.' No, the thing to do is load your wife into a car, drive to the nearest good hotel and stay there for two or three days. Don't even let her go outside. She'll tell you it's a hell of a poor idea, but it isn't. She won't admit it, but she'll be pleased. She'll know you give more than a damn for her and are still a man."

He then returned to a discussion of the future. What did I intend to do when the war was over? I told him in effect that I didn't think it was going to be over, not really, since there was still the menace of the Russians. At this, he leaned back and smiled. "By God, Freddy, you can pour us another drink. You've earned one and I need one, because maybe you've learned something by being over here after all."

Then he became more serious. "We've got a President who's a great politician and who pulled things together, when they had to be. But God damn it, the man has never read history. He doesn't understand the Russians and he never will. They're Mongols, and they're Slavs and a lot of them used to be ruled by Byzantium. From Genghis Khan to Stalin, they haven't changed. They never will and we, we'll never learn, not anyway until it's too damned late.

"There's another thing people in our government can't understand. They can't even understand the German. It is either that or they're too much influenced by the Jews who understandably want revenge. Look at this fool unconditional surrender announcement. If the Hun ever needed anything to put a burr under his saddle, that's it. He'll now fight like the devil because he'll be ordered to do so. They'll do that, the Germans — hold out when there isn't even the ghost of a chance. You remember my telling you years ago about the Kaiser's old veteran machine gunners? We had to kill all of them. Not one surrendered. And each one was in the best uniform he had in the trenches, was wearing all his medals, and had the photos of his family lined up on the concrete ledge in front of him. That's what will happen this time. It will take much longer, cost us more lives, and let the Russians take more territory. Sometimes, we're such God-damned fools, it makes me weep.

"Nevertheless, pretty soon now, the Germans will be finished, also the Japs, and you're going to have to make up your mind what you're going to be. All this talk about a Bavarian redoubt with half a dozen fresh Hun divisions ready to rise full armed, as did the men from sown dragon's teeth, out of underground barracks to save Hitler at the last, is so much hot air. There just aren't enough young male Germans unaccounted for and left alive to man more than one more division than those we already know exist. Some people can't even do simple arithmetic. Even if they can they'd rather take counsel of their fears. No, this will soon all be over, and you'll have to make up your mind what it is you want to do."

I told him what I then thought were my aims. These answers are, however, unimportant; first because this is George Patton's story, not mine; secondly, because I did not achieve those aims. What may, however, be important here, is to repeat again some of his comments, since they were to such an extent more than a partial index to the principles by which he conducted his own life. They included anew the reference to the ability to recognize fate. "You have to turn around and know who she is when she taps you on the shoulder, because she will. It happens to every man, but damned few times in his life. Then you must decide to follow where she points." It was then that he told me of what has been recounted earlier, how General Allenby had talked to him about the gold of luck and his awareness of destiny.

"You have to be single-minded, drive only for the one thing on which you have decided. Then you'll find that you'll make some people miserable, those you love and very often yourself. And, if it looks as if you might be getting there, all kinds of people, including some you thought were your loyal friends, will suddenly show up doing their hypocritical Goddamnedest to trip you, blacken you, and break your spirit. Politicians are the worst; they'll wear their country's flag in public, but they'll use it to wipe their behinds in the caucus room, if they think it will win them a vote. I know. I've lived a lot longer than you, and I've seen what I've seen. I wish I could get some of the bastards into the front lines here, it might be even better than making them read some history."

And then we talked of many other things, until at the last we came to that which was to him both the end and the beginning. "Now there's almost nothing to stop me. We have fresh divisions arriving. We've mastered the air. We have, after some tough lessons, the best weapons in the world. We can soon march into Berlin, Vienna, Prague and Belgrade, with people throwing flowers in our path. But from Washington or London or somewhere, they'll stop us. Otherwise, it might offend the damned Russians. Before that happens, I hope I get out of here to fight the Japs. If not, I'm going to resign and tell the people in my country what is the truth."

He ground out his last cigar, rose easily to his feet. "And now, by God, we can go to bed. See you at breakfast."

CHAPTER XVII

"I am across the Rhine"

★ ★ ★ ★

I MUST admit that having gone to bed with almost everything but my boots on, I awakened far, far too early for my condition. I was awakened, in fact, by noises from the next room. Walking over to investigate, I found Uncle George, stripped to a pair of shorts, doing vigorous calisthenics before a wide open window. This was on a bleak and snowy March morning after only three hours of sleep! I withdrew in silence to compromise with a shave and an ice-cold shower. I still felt far from the rosy glow of healthy youth. If the General felt otherwise he concealed it exceedingly well, managing heroically, if profanely, to face some fried eggs which were semi-liquid, far below the usual standard of his mess. He did not even disguise them with chili sauce.

This was March 7, the day that he was to review a green division just now being moved into the line a little north of Colmar. It was some distance away and the trip required, therefore, an early start. There was an icy drizzle, occasional sleet and much wind. The vehicle was, as usual, the open command car. The drive was altogether an unpleasant prospect, and it lived up to expectations.

Sergeant Mims, the General's regular driver, had committed what was known to Patton and the staffs as his "quarterly atrocity," so that he was for the moment in the guardhouse. Uncle George told me that, each time, this was a completely voluntary act on Mims' part. It prevented for a while his chances of promotion and thus he could remain a driver — and as a driver continue to pilot Patton. The Army assignment system is sometimes strange. A staff sergeant may not drive for an officer, but it was permissible for a general in the person of "Hap" Gay, who sometimes chose the role, to serve as rear gunner on his commander's jeep or command car.

In any event, the driver was one unfamiliar to Patton, who was dressed in only an Eisenhower jacket buttoned tightly down over a brown wool sweater. This was his only concession to the cold. After about half an hour, Uncle George noticed that the driver was turning a light shade of blue and that from time to time he shivered. Reaching forward, he tapped the man on the shoulder: "Corporal?"

"Yes, sir?"

"Are you cold?"

"Yes, sir."

"Do you have a warm sweater?"

"No, sir."

The General leaned back, unbuttoned his jacket, turned to me, "Help me out of this damned thing," after which he peeled the sweater over his head and handed it forward to the driver, "Well, Corporal, you have one now."

This was the kind of small action which was entirely typical of the Patton behavior. It may have been a bit dramatic, even deliberately so. It was nevertheless of a piece with his hospital visits, which he hated with a sick dislike, his appearances at the very front, and equally important, his trips to the dreary areas where mechanics struggled in knee-deep mud to repair or replace the tracks of his tanks. Even if only two men witnessed the event, as in the case of the sweater, somehow the news managed soon to spread the length and breadth of the Army. This is one reason why the General was loved by the enlisted men, although at times actively disliked by certain of his officers. He was completely intolerant of what he felt was inefficiency or stupidity on the part of any one of them, no matter how high in rank. Also, he drove his officers and expected them to drive as hard as he drove himself. Sometimes this was an almost unbearable pressure for even a much younger man, especially one who had not deliberately trained all his life for battle.

That forenoon, Patton stood in the open city square to deliver a speech for an entire division, one about to go for the first time into the line. Listening and watching, I was not overly warm, even in my field coat with liner. The General, however, stood bareheaded, dressed, it seemed to me, as he would have been indoors, and now without his sweater. His remarks bore certain overtones of a much earlier diatribe in England, but stressed a few points new to me. One of these comes easily to mind: "If any instructor back home told you to hit the dirt when enemy rifle or machine fire started, he was asking you to come over here and commit suicide. The German is no fool. He will shoot over your heads at a given spot, you'll dive to the ground, he's got his mortars zeroed in, and you'll end up so chewed apart, even the buzzards wouldn't touch you. The thing to do is to keep running forward and to keep firing. The Hun won't expect it, and he'll be more scared than you are. The way most new soldiers use their rifles, they are no more use than a pecker is to the Pope."

When I reminded him later at lunch that he had been "carried away by his own eloquence" again and of what he had said, he groaned, "Oh, my God, now I guess I'll have to write a letter of apology to the Vatican!"

His second talk was to the assembled Field Grade Officers of the division. It followed traditional Patton lines on tactics and also placed heavy stress on the responsibility of officers for the comfort and morale of the men under their command. He repeated something said many times before, but nonetheless important: "Sometimes getting hot food, or an extra pair of dry socks, up to every damned man in the lines, may be more important to victory that another ton of ammunition."

Toward the conclusion of his speech, I noticed that he was very intently studying one tall young officer. Suddenly, he pointed a finger at him. "You, Major. Yes, you're the man I'm talking to. Take off your helmet and step forward."

Obviously bewildered, the Major did as he was told.

Patton beamed. "By God, I was sure of it. You just about have to be a Merle-Smith. Am I right?"

"Yes, sir."

"Well, you're a beautiful young man. But I can tell you you're nowhere near as beautiful as your mother. I want to talk to you later."

Major Merle-Smith must have wished he could sink quickly into the ground. This being impossible, he merely flushed, and said, "Very well, sir," and backed away. This was Van Sanvoord Merle-Smith, Jr., an ex-schoolmate of mine at the Hill School in Pennsylvania, whom I had totally failed to recognize until he stood bareheaded before the General. Patton later appointed him a junior aide. Merle-Smith told me, "You know it was the damnedest thing when he talked to me next. He remembered every single thing Dad had done, what battles he had fought in and what decorations he had won, even the names of the other members of the family. The man had an incredible memory. Of course, he didn't ask for me as his aide until quite a long time later. I think it was about the middle of August. I had already accumulated more than enough points to go on home and be discharged. But there was no question what I would do when George Patton called me up and asked if I would stay on and serve with him. You just don't turn down a chance like that."

It required rare courage and endurance to be any form of aide to Patton. He had a quick and sometimes unreasonable temper, and its lightning was most likely to strike those who stood nearest him. Evidently "Pat" Merle-Smith did not lack in courage, since some years after the war he accepted, and held until recently, the position of Headmaster of the Foxcroft School for Girls in Virginia.

After lunch with the divisional staff, we drove back to Luxembourg where Patton climbed into a reconnaissance aircraft to study the approaches to the front, and also to try to locate some famous old castles which would appeal to his sense of history. When he took these excursions it worried his staff. The recon planes of those days operated at low altitude, and troops on both sides of the line were inclined not to trust anybody, since a recon plane often meant a spotter for an artillery barrage about to crash down. So all troops had itchy trigger fingers when they saw any such aircraft. This day, however, they did not, and Uncle George found himself a splendid castle on top of a rugged-sloped conical hill.

After returning to headquarters, he talked about it, observing that it almost certainly was Castle so-and-so of King Otto the something-or-other, and built about such and such a time. No one was prepared to argue with him, but at the news, Colonel Charles Codman left the room hurriedly. Later, in the evening, I asked him why.

"I know the old man when he goes historical. He's going to go out and visit that place just as sure as sure can be in the morning. It's bound to have been a German observation post and the bastards always leave a place like that booby-trapped. I had to give orders to have a team go out right away to delouse it. Sometimes keeping up with your uncle is enough to kill off two men half my age."

The late Charlie Codman was a true gentleman and a gallant officer, and for his pains had some unusual assignments. That night, for instance, he had to meet Generals "Tooey" Spatz, Hoyt Vandenberg and Jimmy Doolittle at Airfield "A," where their message had told him they could land. They set down, however, at Airfield "B" and arrived finally at headquarters, all eight or nine stars of them, seated in the rear of a truck. They were not annoyed, but Patton was, very. He made it quite clear to poor Codman that it didn't matter a good God damn whose fault it was, he should have covered both airfields, just in case. I knew how he felt. My father's mind has always worked the same way.

The Colonel was also chief wine steward for the Third Army mess, occasional historian, often the diplomat in residence, and sometimes courier. Later on, for instance in the very last days of the war, he was sent posthaste to Paris and the Bibliothèque Nationale to extract the accounts of Napoleon's Battle of Leipzig, a city which Patton hoped soon to invest. He had said, "The Germans are going to defend it the same way but I'm not going to attack the same way as Bonaparte." Uncle George never had his chance at Leipzig. The lines were ordered stabilized and the war came to its end.

No, Uncle George was never to take Leipzig or Prague or Berlin, but he did cross the Rhine. It gave him great pleasure especially in the light of the timing and attendant circumstances. It also greatly pleased General Bradley who likewise bore no love for Sir Bernard Law Montgomery. Early on the morning of March 23, Patton telephoned 12th Army Group to announce the news to Bradley who had just started on his first cup of coffee. According to Bradley's own account, Patton said, "Brad, don't tell anyone, but I'm across the Rhine. I sneaked a division over last night. But there are so few Krauts around they don't know it yet, so don't make any press announcements." Later in the morning, Patton's liaison officer with us came into the briefing room with a broad grin on his face and made this report: "Without benefit of aerial bombing, ground smoke, artillery preparation, and airborne assistance, the Third Army at 2200 hours, Thursday evening, March 22, crossed the Rhine River." This was a dig, of course, at Monty's huge and time-consuming preparations to the north. This recitation left out two things. One, Monty had also assembled an enormous fleet of landing craft of various types. Two, this was the time that George Patton did piss in the Rhine and have the photograph taken to prove it. Also, no more than twenty-four hours later, he changed his mind and asked General Bradley to make an announcement of the crossing. Uncle George wanted full credit when credit was due. And it certainly was to the credit of the 23rd Regiment that it made the initial crossing with a casualty list of eight dead and twenty wounded.

It was only a few days after the crossing of the Rhine that Patton's son-in-law, then Colonel John K. Waters, comes back into the story. He had, you will recall, been captured near Kasserine Pass in Tunisia. Then he had been moved from one P.O.W. camp to another, each time farther to the east, finally arriving at Lublin in eastern Poland. Then the tide of battle had turned west as the Russians crunched forward, and the group of prisoners were moved before them. Eventually, self-preservation became to the German guards more important than duty. They threw down their rifles and ran, leaving the prisoners to fend for themselves. According to what Johnny later told me in the hospital, his treatment and that of his fellow prisoners at the hands of the German civilian population was infinitely worse and more brutal than it had been in military custody. This may even be understandable since, toward the end of the war, the saturation bombing raids of ours and the Royal Air Force were taking a sickening toll of the noncombatants. I was told, for instance, when we entered Frankfurt, by an intelligent and seemingly unemotional French Displaced Person that at the end when one of our flyers parachuted into that area from a crippled plane, he was clubbed or stoned to death by old men, women and even children. Furthermore, she told me, "And I knew exactly how they felt."

In any event, most of Waters' group, of which he was the senior officer present, managed to escape German hands. Johnny did not. A fellow colonel became much too ill to move onward, therefore Waters stayed with him alone and both were recaptured and taken to a P.O.W. cage in Hammelberg, Germany.

On March 26, a task force of infantry and fourteen tanks headed out from the bridgehead across the river Saar and drove toward Hammelberg, where intelligence had reported there was a P.O.W. camp filled with Americans. The tank force was from the 4th Armored Division and commanded by Captain Abraham Baum. A Patton aide, Major Alexander C. Stiller, who had been one of his tank sergeants during World War I, accompanied the group. They ran into very heavy fire and lost more than half their personnel of 229 men before they managed to reach and break through the stockade. For a brief period they succeeded in taking the town and liberating the camp. Then a superior force, consisting of tanks and paratroopers, overwhelmed the Baum force and recaptured many of the prisoners. Waters, as senior U.S. officer among them, came forward with the white flag only to be shot through the lower abdomen at point-blank range by a fanatical young Nazi. He told me that had it not been for the later devoted care of a Serbian medic among the prisoners, working with virtually no supplies, he would certainly have died. This I can easily believe since when I saw him first at the base hospital after a stronger U.S. force had again taken Hammelberg, he weighed only about 95 pounds in contrast to his fighting weight of 175. Later, when Johnny was chief of our military mission in Yugoslavia, he managed to locate the man who had saved his life and again to thank him and bring gifts to his family. Waters is today a four-star general and as of this writing, head of the Continental Defense Command.

Because of the rashness of Patton's attempt, the tragically
heavy casualty list, but most of all because his son-in-law
had been one of the prisoners, the General was most severely
criticized.

I do not know whether Uncle George had known beforehand that John Waters was in the P.O.W. camp at Hammelberg. I do know that he told General Bradley that he was
not aware of Waters' presence until nine days later when
Hammelberg was recaptured by our forces. From experience
in intelligence work, I think he should be believed. In those
days, many tales of atrocities against U.S. prisoners were
common fare on the front. Most commanders' immediate
human, and humane reaction was to try to free the men as
rapidly as possible. Also, I cannot remember a single instance, during those days of movement and confusion, when
a command was aware of the identity of individual prisoners
in any individual P.O.W. stockade of whose existence they
had just learned. Be that as it may, I also remember what
Patton said in answer to criticism. He said it in open anger:
"God damn it, has anyone ever known me knowingly to send
a force insufficient in strength for its assigned task? Furthermore, no one who knows me would believe that I'd sacrifice
Stiller to save my own brother." He was, however, privately
much depressed by the whole business and so told General
Bradley. The latter, in telling of this event, said, "Your uncle
was very upset. I felt that he had made a mistake but did
not criticize or reprimand him. Failure itself was more than
enough punishment for George."

I think that Bradley's analysis was absolutely correct. Also,
his handling of this incident again helps to explain the basic
relationship between the two men. General Bradley, in

talking to me, put it this way: "You know, people who knew George well have told me they had heard him, at least in private, cursing out everybody from the President on down to some sloppy yard bird, but that he had never spoken that way about me." I can confirm the truth of this and can understand why.

Uncle George, however, never quite forgave himself for the Hammelberg disaster. As mentioned in his own account *War As I Knew It*, he wrote, "I can say this — that throughout the campaign in Europe, I know of no error that I made except that of failing to send a combat command to take Hammelberg."

In addition to the liberation of territories, Allies and his own troops, there was one act for freedom for which George Patton became famous in at least one enemy nation, Austria. Now the event has been retold on film for all the world to see, by Walt Disney, and its principal actors are horses — the beautiful white Lippizaner stallions of Vienna.

In early spring of 1945, Vienna came under heavy bombardment. Colonel Alois Podhasky, commander of what is called the "Spanish Riding School," managed somehow to wangle rail transportation and smuggle the horses from that city to the little mountain town of St. Martin's. Even there, there was danger to them, since fodder was desperately short and near-starving refugees looked on the sleek white horses as an obvious supply of meat.

When elements of the Third Army entered the town, an officer recognized the Colonel with his charges and at once sent word back to Patton's headquarters. Naturally, the General sent for the great riding master and arranged for him to put on a show of *haute ècole* for visiting Under Secretary of War Patterson, and for himself. At the conclusion of the performance Podhasky rode up to face Patton, who was standing at attention. His speech was possibly the briefest on record, simply, "We ask your protection."

The answer was almost as brief. "Magnificent. These horses will be wards of the United States Army until they can be returned to the new Austria."

But there were other Lippizaners. The mares and foals without which the breed would surely perish were still one-hundred miles distant in Czechoslovakia at a town named Hostoun, towards which the Russians were racing fast. These facts were flashed to Uncle George by Colonel Charles Reed, Commander, 2nd Cavalry Group, which was in the area. The orders he received were simple, "Get them."

Reed did so by sending a force across the Czech border and herding the white horses back into Austria. Naturally, the Russians complained most bitterly, which bothered Patton not at all. In fact, he announced to all who could hear, that the beautiful white horses were worth far more and were much nicer than Soviet generals.

Last year, when my daughter visited Vienna, she went of course to see the Lippizaners. She told me that someone had advised Colonel Podhasky that she was the grandniece of George Patton and that she was therefore treated as visiting royalty and told, but with more emotion and in more dramatic detail, the story outlined above.

There was, however, one area in which neither George Patton, nor anyone else in our armies could effect a rescue; and it was in an area where the resulting conditions often struck at the heart. My friend John H. Perry of Cincinnati, Ohio, and then a Captain of Artillery with the 26th Infantry,

told me of one sad transaction in which he had been involved.

We had, as you remember, been stopped near Linz, and
were on VE-Day in May 1945 headquartered near Hohen-
furth in Czechoslovakia. On either the 8th or the 9th it came
as my responsibility to accept the surrender of and be responsible for what was left of the Third Hungarian Army. That
is to say some 16,000 troops. This army was a very colorful
collection; they had retreated through Hungary before the
Russians and so managed to pick up some of their families on
the way. I remember thinking of it as sort of a comic opera
army with some of the most beautiful women and horses I
have ever seen.

There had, of course, been nothing comic about their experiences against the Russians in the Ukraine, and their
general, whose name I can no longer recall, was an outstanding character. He was a great and educated gentleman and
clearly a very brave man. Over the ten days or so that he
and his men were in my charge we became friends and had
a cocktail together nearly every evening. He had some fas-
cinating stories to tell.

Then came the sad news. As a matter of fact, for the
Hungarians it was tragic. I was ordered from higher echelon
to turn these poor people over to the Russians — obviously
somebody very high up's political decision.

My friend the general knew what it meant: "You know,
of course, that this signifies enslavement or death, or both,
for us."

I told him I was afraid he might be right. He then said
that he had two requests to make of me. The first one was

that I return their revolvers to him and his two deputy commanders. When I seemed to hesitate he said, "Oh, it's not
what you think. When we have to turn over our poor people
we must have our sidearms as emblems that we still command the authority. They are not to shoot ourselves with."

I was not sure that I believed him but did as he asked. Of
course, the Russians immediately took the revolvers away.

The general's second request was this: "I have struggled
against the Communists at home, and I have fought them as
best I could there and in the Ukraine. I know them well. I
have kept a diary of all this — in fact I have kept one all my
military life. I wish that you would take it and see to it that
it reaches your General Patton personally. He understands
the problem and he is the general I have studied the most
and whom I admire the most in the world."

I told him I would and was sad then to say goodbye. I
made the mistake of sending the general's diary back through
regular channels — so I wonder if it ever reached him, or
his family.

I told Perry at the time that I was willing to bet the papers
never reached their destination. Later I checked with the
surviving members of the Patton family. They had not seen
a trace of the diary; they had in fact never even heard of it.

The luster in Europe of the Patton name is not a surprising
thing, but it is something to think upon. I have often found
it true that on meeting many people on the Continent,
the General's memory is revered by allies and those whose
lands he freed. He is spoken of with admiration even by
former enemies whose troops he crushed. Sometimes it has
seemed that he was more appreciated abroad than in his

own country. All the way from Normandy and Coten-
tin peninsulas, southeast to Paris and on toward the west
bank of the Rhine, are concrete mileage markers carrying
the inscription "Route de la glorieuse 3m^e Armée Améri-
caine," and it is called "la route de la liberation" since that is
what it was. And on the Patton grave at Hamm, the Luxem-
bourgers, even in winter, still daily place fresh flowers.

CHAPTER XVIII

"I have spent my gold"

★ ★ ★ ★

AFTER spending far too few days on temporary duty with the Third Army, I was forced to return to more clandestine, if far less interesting, pursuits. It had been easy for me to see why Patton's enlisted men loved him, some of his officers occasionally hated him, and all were loyal. I came away as convinced as was the General, himself, that he could do what he had always sworn he would do — lead his mighty army triumphantly into Berlin. He felt there was nothing in the field which could possibly stop him. He was on his way to triumph for his country and for the things in which he believed.

It was not fate, but deliberate human intervention, that was to turn triumph into tragedy. It is difficult, even today, accurately to place the blame for this tragedy at any particular feet. It was the work of many minds, operating over a long period under heavy and diverse pressures and seemingly unable to adjust preconceived notions to fit altered circumstances. Some of these minds must have been stupid, others misled, and possibly a handful of ill intent toward the West. The chain of causation runs all the way from the Quebec

Conference, on through misjudgment of the Russians and miscalculation of their intents, and ends in the ultimate observance of a politico-military decision not to drive on to Berlin. No one, except the Soviets, today can doubt — certainly not the Satellites or the Germans themselves — that it was a tragedy.

It was also a tragedy for the West and for the Czech people that Patton, after crashing through the Palatinate and on to Pilsen, did not invest Prague. He knew even then, as his own writings attest, that the Russians would take over the country. No, whosoever the fault, it was not Patton's. He carried out the job assigned to him, and more beside, with drive and imagination. His lifelong training, and his training of the officers and men of the Third Army, proved their worth in these last weeks, for then and forever.

George Patton had moved his troops, material and supplies over tremendous distances often against a most determined, sometimes desperate opposition. He had taken calculated risks. He broke the tactical conventions of warfare and in so doing broke the enemy's back. He had, in fact, nearly always "known exactly what the Germans will do under a given set of circumstances" and the Germans did not know what he was going to do next. And he had indeed "whipped hell out of them." The total in enemy casualties was great and his own were remarkably small. The figures, taken from the official Third Army records, are shown at the top of the next page. These figures do not include the prisoners taken after the fighting stopped. Uncle George said that he did not think it was sporting to count them in the score.

Concerning the non-battle casualties, he remarked to me

	Third Army		Enemy
Killed	21,441		144,500
Wounded	99,224		386,200
Missing	16,200	P.O.W.'s	956,000
Total	136,865		1,486,700
Non-battle casualties	111,562		
	248,427		
Light tanks	308		1,529
Medium tanks	949		858
Guns	175		3,454

on two occasions, "The two most deadly weapons in the German arsenal are our own armored half-track and the Jeep; the half-track, because the boys riding one go all heroic, since they think they're in a tank; and the Jeep because we have so many god-awful drivers. Also, the Kraut has a filthy habit of stringing wires at windshield level between trees. He does it on roads he figures we may move troops on at night."

Having done the things he had done, Patton stood poised on an extended front stretching from Kassel in Northwest Germany to Pilsen in Czechoslovakia and Linz in Austria. He was in command of fifteen divisions, most of them battle-hardened and confident, a few fresh but eager to go. He was backed up by unchallenged might in bombers and tactical air command. He had it in his power to slash through anything before him like a cavalry saber through a pumpkin. That cavalry saber, honed to as fine an edge as any in history, was held by a muscular arm and poised to strike. But it never did. He did not take Prague and many other centers he felt were vital to United States interest. He did not take them because, as he told the press, "I was ordered not to." The surrender terms were agreed to, the papers signed. The war was over.

Some men felt at that time that the seeds of tragedy had been sown. To my knowledge only one military leader spoke out loudly to say it, not once, but many times. I want to tell of the first time. I think it still important that there exists even this short record of how it was.

The date was I am quite sure, the 11th of May, 1945, when the war in Europe was only three days ended. I had returned to Paris for a few days to confer with my deputy and some of my personnel in an attempt to reorganize our intelligence operation on a so-called peacetime basis. Five of us were in conference on the fifth floor of 15 Avenue Mozart, formerly the apartment of the Counselor to the Nazi Embassy until we had "liberated" it. We were interrupted by the stuttering ring of our only operational telephone. Don Daughters picked it up. Within ten seconds, his face had registered disbelief, amazement, and finally, near shock. In silence he passed me the hand set. I put it to my ear.

"This is your uncle, God damn it." There existed no doubt whatever, after these six and one half words, that it was. "I'm over at Everett Hughes' room and I want to buy you a drink. Now get the hell over here."

"Yes, sir. I will right away."

General Hughes' billet was in the Hotel Majestic on Avenue Kléber, perhaps four hundred yards from the Arc de Triomphe. In the living room of his suite were assembled eight or nine people, including four generals, two aides and some sort of Presidential Assistant, from the White House. His face and name, I am glad to say, have vanished from my memory. Everyone seemed in good spirits except Uncle George. This was perhaps because everyone but him was enjoying good whiskey. Patton, on the other hand, held a glass of milk and a soggy chicken sandwich, eying both with more than obvious distaste.

He turned to me. "Go make yourself a stiff one and don't stare at me. That God-damn Hughes won't let me have any bourbon. It's unchristian."

General Hughes grinned. "Of course I won't. George has brought back some recaptured French battle flags to return to Les Invalides. He has to make a speech and kiss Charles de Gaulle on both cheeks. I'm afraid of what he might say."

"Who, de Gaulle?"

"No. Your saintly uncle."

Patton, seated in the corner easy chair shoved the milk glass and sandwich aside, growled at them and lit a long cigar. He drew deeply on it, then took it from his mouth, leaned tensely forward, pointing the cigar like a weapon at his host.

"Well, by God, Everett, I'm going to say it now. It's all a God-damned shame. That's what it is."

Someone asked, "All what's a God-damned shame?" I had never seen Uncle George so deeply upset. He answered in that high, penetrating voice and that voice trembled, "I'll tell you. Day after day, some poor bloody Czech, or Austrian, or Hungarian, even German officers come into my headquarters. I almost have to keep them from going down on their knees to me. With tears in their eyes they say, 'In the name of God, General, come with your Army the rest of the way into our country. Give us a chance to set up our own governments. Give us this last chance to live before it's too late, before the Russians make us slaves forever.'

"That's what they tell me, and every damned one of them has offered to fight under my flag and bring their men with them. Hell, a German general offered his entire air force, the Third, to me to fight the Russians if necessary. Of course he had hardly any planes left, but he had pilots. By God, I would like to take them up on it. I'll feel like a traitor if I don't."

There was an uneasy stir in the room. Most of us sensed what was coming next. None of us quite dared to interrupt. Patton went on, "These people are right. They won't have a chance. We've signed away their lives. By God, we ought to tear up those damned fool agreements and march right through to the eastern borders . . ."

"Uncle George, for God's sake," I heard myself blurt, "you can't talk that way here."

He glared coldly at me. "Yes, I can. I'll talk any damned way I want. I know what we ought to do. We promised these people freedom. It would be worse than dishonorable not to see that they have it. This might mean war with the Russians, of course; but what of it? They have no air force any more, their gas and munition supplies are low. I've seen their miserable supply trains, mostly wagons drawn by beat-up old horses, or oxen. I'll tell you this," he again aimed the cigar at General Hughes, "the Third Army, alone, with very little other help and with damned few casualties, could lick what's left of the Russians in six weeks." He paused here for a few seconds. "You mark my words. Don't ever forget them. Some day we'll have to fight them, and it will take six years and cost us six million lives."

This, of course, was three months before the incineration of Hiroshima.

It was also a little more than four months before George Patton would be removed from the command of his own Third Army and placed in charge of an army of paper.

Some three weeks after the fateful meeting at the Hotel Majestic, George Patton went home to Massachusetts for a short leave, which was to be his last. He went to a triumphal welcome. And he went to say some of the things which he believed. All his actions during those brief days on his native soil were wholly typical. I was not there, but I know what happened.

There was a great crowd at the military airport at Bedford, Massachusetts on June 7 to greet Patton, a great crowd, and his wife, children and in-laws. The pictures show him surprisingly youthful, wearing his four stars, his ribbons splashed across the left breast of his tunic, and smiling an overpowering smile. The photo of him and Aunt Bea at the very first moment of reunion seems to me a classic. There can be no question in the mind of anyone who looks at it about how these two felt about each other.

There was no question either about how the people of Massachusetts felt toward the General. The motorcade to Boston was triumphant. So also was the one to the Hatch Memorial Shell on the Charles River Esplanade. To some in Washington he may have been a villain. To those who lined the roads to cheer him he was their own hero. I still have the front page of the Boston *Daily Record* for June 8. It carries

headlines two inches high which read: FRENZIED HUB HAILS
PATTON. This was no less than a true description of what
happened.

You can see him yourself if you try. Square-shouldered,
trim-waisted, proudly erect, his uniform immaculate and perfectly fitting, all brass and leather highly polished, the ribbons of his medals almost ablaze in color. You can see him
in the lead car, as I have seen him in other places, a knight
returned from the crusades, after the liberation of Acre, after
the slaying of the heathen, but still a knight who had as yet
no intention of laying down his armor. This is as he then saw
himself, even after the death, the horror and destruction of
two years and eight months of personally witnessed war.

You can also see him, if you try, as did Anne, my wife, as
she stood on a street corner on the route of parade through
Boston.

"I had left our apartment on Otis Place and just sort of
wandered down to the Charles Street corner where the caval-
cade would go by on its way to the Hatch Shell where Uncle
George was going to make a speech. When they finally came
in sight, there he sat in the lead car — looking like Alexander
the Great, Caesar and Napoleon all rolled into one, returning
from their wars. I was just standing there with a whole mob
of people. He turned and looked our way, then, it seemed,
straight at me. Suddenly he shot his right hand into the air
in a command to halt, and some junior officer came over to
me on the sidewalk. Meanwhile, of course, the entire parade
had come to a stop, and I wasn't a bit sure what was going
on, not until he had me seated in the second car with Aunt
Bea. I was embarrassed as the devil and it didn't help any
when he grinned that grin of his and said loudly enough for

everyone to hear 'God damn, I always did have a quick eye to recognize a pretty girl.' "

Uncle George certainly did have a remarkable memory for faces and the keen eyesight that gave him the capacity for quick recognition. It was demonstrated in this instance as in the case of "Pat" Merle-Smith. There is one more I would like to tell about because it suggests in addition another quality of the man.

Carl A. Russell of Beverly, Massachusetts, who is a taxicab driver, told me this story in April of last year. "When I was a kid I used to help on the milk wagon; that is, I got to deliver the bottles to the back stoop. One morning around 5:30 I'm delivering at the Patton place in Hamilton. The Colonel's in riding clothes about to get on a horse. I set the bottles down with quite a bang and he raises hell with me for making so much noise so early in the morning and stamps away leaving me a little shook up. About fifteen years later I'm manning an antiaircraft gun for the Seventh Army in Sicily when the General shows up in all his glory and comes right over to me, claps me on the shoulder and tells me that I'm doing a fine job. Then he takes a closer look and says, 'By God, I think I've seen you somewhere before.' I'm a little paralyzed and don't say anything. Then he says, 'Goddammit, now I know who you are. You're the little bastard that I chewed out for rattling those God-damned milk bottles.'

"And I saw him again later, right on the edge of Germany. I can't remember the name of the place but we were moving up forward, to a much too forward observation post; suddenly there comes Patton himself. This time he talks to one of the other men, he says, 'Son, I haven't had a damned thing to eat since breakfast, do you have any spare rations?' The man says, 'Sure, General,' and hands him a can. Patton starts to eat some of the goop, then his eyes fill with tears and he hands it back. He wipes at his eyes and says, 'I love every God-damned bone in your God-damned head.' What a character he was."

You can see and hear the man speak his heart, in his speech at Boston when he came home that day. But he said only part of what he burned to say. Twice at least some of that speech has been rerun on nationwide TV in a half-hour program purporting to tell the story of Patton and his Third Army. If you have seen that film you will probably remember the tall figure, the lined face, the earnest words, but above all, the strange mixture of soaring pride in the men he led, together with the unshed tears which stung his eyelids and burdened his voice and heart. He talked of the men in the Third Army, of the training they had undergone, the desperate nature of the enemy they had faced and the heroism with which most all of them had faced it. He said, speaking to parents and families of these men, "And no matter what you may have read, no matter what they tell you when at last all who survived have returned here, you who have stayed at home will never be able to understand how terrible some of it really was." He then went on to say that no matter how frightful war might have been it was something which could well come again and that we had best keep our ranks filled and our other defenses strong. This speech was short, shorter I believe than the speaker had intended — since, when he had said, "Let us not so much mourn the dead as thank our God that such men have lived," he sat down seemingly too emotionally shaken to say more.

That night and thereafter George Patton said, to the limit

General Noguès
and G. S. Patton, Jr.,
at Residency just after
French surrender.

An autograph, some-
where in Tunisia.

Landing in Sicily.

Across France to . . .

Belgium and
Prince Baudouin.

Luxembourg, March 1945.

"And that was for
the Rhine," March 23, 1945.

Bedford Airport, June 1945. *Below:* G. S. Patton, Jr.,
Frederick Ayer, Beatrice Ayer Patton.

June 1945
—Boston,
Massachusetts.

G. S. Patton, Jr., and Beatrice Ayer Patton,
July 1945. This was his last time aboard.

June 1945, back home at "Lake Vineyard" in California.

Beatrice Ayer Patton, Tufts College, Medford, Massachusetts. Universal Military Training Speech, 1952.

Hamm, Luxembourg. "Not by the last bullet."

of what was officially permitted him, what he had come to say.

I have kept the seating list of the great dinner in the Ball Room of the Copley Plaza Hotel — the seating list, that is, for about 220 of the more than 500 who attended. It still makes interesting reading. In addition to the obvious military representatives and members of the immediate family there were, for instance, present at the head tables: Mr. and Mrs. Charles Francis Adams, he a former secretary of the Navy with a name as old as Massachusetts and national history; Miss Mae Bartley, formerly a maid in my grandmother's house and then Superintendent of Nurses at the Beverly Hospital; Mr. and Mrs. George F. Booth, he the assistant superintendent of the farm at "Turner Hill"; Mrs. Donald Cassells, daughter of General Brewster, who had been a friend of Patton's father; Colonel and Mrs. Charles R. Codman, already mentioned; Miss Mary A. Crowley, nurse to Frederick Ayer in 1914-15, to Miss Annie Wilson later, and then for my youngest sister when she fell ill; Commissioner Lawrence Curtis of Boston; Miss Mary A. Curtis, then well over sixty and still riding to hounds; Major General and Mrs. Guy V. Henry of Virginia, he the next to last chief of mounted cavalry; Dr. and Mrs. Franc D. Ingraham, he the Chief Neurosurgeon in Boston Children's Hospital; Dr. and Mrs. Peer P. Johnson of Beverly; M/Sgt. William G. Meeks, Patton's colored orderly; Aunt Bea's sister and her husband, Commander and Mrs. Keith Merrill; Mr. and Mrs. Gordon C. Prince of the *Arcturus* voyage; Mr. and Mrs. Joseph Salerno of the Massachusetts Federation of Labor; Lieutenant Colonel N. W. Rice, my mother's brother; and Count Francesco Mario Guardabassi, husband to one of my father's nieces, who had been a portrait painter, a singer at La Scala, big game hunter, and soldier of fortune. There were fourteen generals and a scattering of governors, ex-governors, lieutenant governors and judges. But there were also nineteen sergeants and four privates first class. Of course the intermediate ranks were also well represented. The important point, however, was that only a very few of those seated were invited because protocol demanded it. They were there because George Patton wanted them to be, and for no other reason. He was that night to see all but six of these people for the last time.

George Patton believed that he had lived before, believed that he would again, knew that he had the gift of *déjà vu*, and enough instinct to recognize the fates. He felt that he was among the handful of men in the whole world who had these gifts. Now he was home after three years in the front ranks of battle, home safe, triumphant and still secure in his glory. And yet, what did he tell his cadet son George, now a lieutenant colonel with Silver Star, his daughters, Beatrice and Ruth Ellen? He told them, in effect, "I am soon going back to Germany, to the peaceful occupation, but I'm saying my final goodbye. Because I'll never see you again."

Here is how Ruth Ellen described it. "We were all in the living room of my house on Garfield Street in Washington, Bea and George and myself. Mother was upstairs packing his things. It was the night before Daddy was to go back to Germany. His exact words were, 'I am never going to see you again. I know this. I am going to be buried in foreign soil.' One of us said, 'Oh, Daddy, don't be silly. The war's all over now.' He said, 'Yes, I know. But my luck has all run out now. That gold Allenby used to talk about is gone. I've spent it all. I have not been a good enough man in my life to be killed by a bullet like General Bee at Manassas. I don't know how it is going to happen, but I'm going to die over there.' None of us said anything until he went on, 'Promise me one thing, let me be buried over there. In God's name don't bring my body home.' Of course we promised."

This last admonition to his children was nothing new. Uncle George had always left instructions that he should be buried in the country where he fell. "That's where any soldier would want to be; and it will remind people there forever of who it was fought to set them free." He was also fond of quoting Napoleon: "The boundaries of a nation's empire are marked by the graves of her soldiers." He often said, "Why goddammit, to bury a soldier anywhere else is simply to cater to a bunch of sniveling sob sisters retained by those carrion-eating ghouls, the coffin makers and undertakers."

Was this final scene with his family one of self-sympathy? Of self-dramatization? Maybe so. And maybe not. I have asked Ruth Ellen about it and she said this: "Sometimes Daddy talked just to hear himself, sometimes to shock people. But when he talked like that time he gave me the shivers. Sometimes he saw things other people couldn't see. I think that was one of those times."

So do I.

Ruth Ellen told me of another thing which happened during her father's brief visit home. "I had, as a volunteer, charge of one of the saddest wards in the Walter Reed Army Hospital. It was the one for multiple amputees. Still, I wanted Daddy to come see what I was doing and also to help cheer up some of those poor men. So he did. He came in like a one-man parade, although he plain hated hospitals.

Then he stood silent and looked around for a minute, and burst into tears. When he could speak, all he said was, 'By God, if I'd been a better general, most of you men wouldn't be here.' "

Certainly he was somewhat of a ham. He never denied this himself, not even in the early days when he practiced his "war face" in front of a mirror. Certainly he also enjoyed making startling statements, even outrageous ones, for their shock value. Nevertheless there were those things which he deeply believed, and in these beliefs he was constant.

Then in 1945, as he always had, he believed in universal military training. He believed it the simple duty of every man so to serve and so to train himself. He believed that the democracy, the shared burden, the strict discipline of two years of army life was a strengthener of personal and national character. He often said that any man reached his single best in battle, and he himself looked on war as a crusade. Now, however, was added a compelling historical reason for compulsory universal military service. He had told me of it while still in Germany. "You just wait and see. The lily-livered bastards in Washington will demobilize. They'll say they've made the world safe for democracy again. The Russians are not such damned fools. They'll rebuild; and with modern weapons. But if we have compulsory universal military service, if we vote for it first at the polls, or in Congress, then in years to come the rest of the world will know we mean what we say."

You will remember that at the time most church leaders were opposed to universal service, many felt it to be dangerously disruptive of home life and dangerous to the morals of the young. Nevertheless, those of them who had listened to and talked over the matter with Patton were afterwards somewhat shaken in their views. He was a most persuasive advocate.

In July of 1945, one of the men with whom he wished particularly to discuss the matter was Archbishop (now Cardinal) Richard J. Cushing of Boston, and an old acquaintance of Patton's own friend, Cardinal Spellman. Patton asked my father if he could arrange an appointment; and Father said he could. The General then informed the War Department of his intent, one certainly in the best interests of the Army itself. From Washington, however, he called Father on the phone. "Fred, if you've made that appointment with Cushing, cancel it. I've just been told to keep my mouth shut and that I'm a warmonger."

Uncle George was understandably angry and dismayed. He told my father at the time that this official muzzling had nearly caused him to resign from the Army so that he might go before the nation and speak his piece on the true nature of the Soviet menace, and the need for the continuance of full-scale national preparedness and alertness.

One of Uncle George's greatest problems certainly was an inability or unwillingness to restrain his public speech. He felt so strongly on various subjects that he was driven to speak out, even when his opinions ran directly in opposition to announced national policy. I talked at some length recently with General Omar Bradley on this subject. He said, "Yes, your uncle didn't care who was listening when he had something to get off his chest. I agreed with him most of the time, especially in his feelings about Montgomery's arrogance and too great caution. I agreed even more about the nature of the Russians and the dangerous decision not to drive on into Berlin, Prague and other capitals. But, even as a commanding general, he was under orders of the civilian administration and had no right publicly to disagree. I don't know how many times I told him, 'Dammit George, you're going to get yourself in a terrible doghouse if you don't keep your mouth shut.' Ike told him the same thing."

I then asked General Bradley what he thought would have happened had Uncle George lived, either to remain in the Army or as a civilian free to speak his mind. Would he, for instance, have behaved as had General Edwin Walker, who was officially punished for spreading the Birchite doctrine? The General answered, "He would never have behaved like Walker. He was far too intelligent and far too brilliant and thorough a historian. He read more history than any man I ever knew. I'm afraid, however, he would have gotten in trouble eventually. He would have liked some of the things that went on even less than I did and he would have spoken out, not within the chain of command, or in testimony to Congress where those things belong, but in public. As for being a civilian, I simply don't know. After he had spoken his piece, I can't imagine what he could have done with himself, a man driven by such tremendous energy."

Patton was always the geopolitician, the domestic politician almost never. It is questionable whether many people would have listened, even to a national military hero, and even if they had listened whether they would have believed, or taken action. People in those first days of peace did not want to hear any unpleasant truths. They wanted to be left alone quietly to reassemble their war-disrupted existences. They would not then have relished being shocked from their complacency. Later on it took the full power, glory and eloquence of Sir Winston Churchill at Fulton, Missouri, to begin that process.

Perhaps it was better for him that Uncle George died when he did, even if not by the last bullet of his last battle.

Patton was criticized, right in his own home town of Hamilton, Massachusetts, for what he said in July of 1945 to an audience of high school students. Standing before them, resplendent in all his medals, stars and sashes, he said, "You young men and young ladies may well be the soldiers and sailors, the airmen and nurses of this country's next war for survival. As such it befits you to keep your minds and bodies strong, to study the history of your country and of those who would destroy it. There are those who will not agree when I talk of the necessity of a strong citizen's army — that advocating it is an act of belligerence. Well, let me tell you this. I am sixty years old and never in all those sixty years have I known of a single fire that was prevented or put out by discharging the fire department."

It is hard today to conceive of a mentality which could take umbrage at such remarks, yet in 1945 it existed. Perhaps it still does.

Prior to the Hamilton speech Uncle George had made a very similar one in his other home town of San Marino, California, where he had gone to visit his sister Anita as well as other relatives and old friends. I have heard an eye-witness account from Mrs. George Kreissmiller, also of San Marino. "He received a hero's welcome and deserved it. He looked positively magnificent walking up there in full regalia and his flashing stars and medals. The speech he made was inspiring, but whoever was responsible for the welcoming arrangements did a most inappropriate thing. After the

General had been introduced and before he spoke, the representative of some Cub Scout group toddled up and presented him with a huge bouquet of flowers. He handled it like a ticking bomb, shifting it from side to side and from one hand to the other. Finally, he couldn't stand it any longer, and interrupted his remarks to put the thing down, then grin broadly and say, 'I know I've made a lot of widows during my life, but this is the first time I've had to stand around looking like a damned bride.' "

CHAPTER XIX

"Bloody but unbowed"

GEORGE PATTON returned to Germany in the middle of July to see, especially in Berlin, what others had seen and were to see from that time forward. In a letter home on July 21 he wrote, "We have destroyed what could have been a good race and we are about to replace them with the Mongolian savages and all Europe with Communism."

Pat Merle-Smith has told me of what took place during a second Berlin visit in the first week of September 1945. "The Russians were putting on a military review for all four occupying powers. Your uncle was seated next to Marshal Zhukov and I, naturally, was with the standees a few rows below. I heard quite clearly what was said when some huge Soviet tanks passed by. 'My dear General Patton, you see that tank, it carries a cannon which can throw a shell seven miles.' Patton answered, 'Indeed? Well, my dear Marshal Zhukov, let me tell you this, if any of my gunners started firing at your people before they had closed to less than seven hundred yards I'd have them court-martialed for cowardice.' It was the first time I saw a Russian commander stunned into silence."

On August 18, exactly twelve days after our first atomic bomb was dropped on Hiroshima, George Patton made an interesting analysis. On that date he wrote to his wife, "The use of the Atomic Bomb against Japan was most unfortunate because it now gives a lot of vocal but ill-informed people — mostly fascists, communists and S.O.B.'s assorted — an opportunity to state that the Army, Navy and Air Forces are no longer necessary, as this bomb will either prevent war or destroy the human race. Actually the bomb is no more revolutionary than the first throwing stick or javelin, or the first cannon, or the first submarine. It is simply, as I have often written, a new instrument added to the orchestration of death, which is war."

Also in August he wrote home on another key matter, a problem of which his handling was to help pave the way to his professional undoing. "To keep busy, fortunately I also have to occupy myself with the de-Nazification of Bavaria, and the recruiting of the industries of the German people so that they can be more self-supporting."

As mentioned, neither of these goals was exactly easy to achieve, especially since they were by their natures close to mutually exclusive. Also, the Morgenthau plan for the agrarianization of Germany had not quite been abandoned; but it was scarcely implemented in Germany, especially Bavaria, since there was a saving clause in the basic directive. It read, in effect, "The above is subject to the discretion of the Commander in the field." However, part of the spirit remained. It was a spirit which for a time caused sickening frustration to many Americans and British stationed in Germany. Anyone who had studied even basic economics could see what would be the inevitable result if Germany did not rapidly rebuild. The economic well-being of more than 50 percent of Europe depended on the viability of German industry. Without it hunger, unemployment, and empty warehouse shelves were bound to follow. And when this became true Communism could enter unhindered through the unlocked door.

In the light of his knowledge of history, his educated distrust of the Soviet, George Patton was fully aware of these things. It is certain that he did not react kindly to the situation. It is even more certain that he did not always act or speak with moderation and discretion. It was inevitable that he should finally make certain statements which would outwardly justify his professional execution. It had I believe for some time been decided that Patton must go. And on September 28, he went.

It is now reported, as it was said at the time, that George Patton's downfall came as a result of his remarks about de-Nazification. It will be remembered that all men with Nazi affiliations were ordered removed from all positions of authority, including the running of waterworks, power stations, medical laboratories, subway systems, even hospitals. Obviously doing this could result only in a paralyzed halt to what little organization for daily existence still remained in the bomb-shattered country. Patton said, according to some reports and as he later repeated to my father, these words: "It's just as if the Democrats in power at home threw out every Republican who held any kind of civic job or vice versa. Nothing would run."

It will be remembered also that what he was quoted as saying was "Nazis and anti-Nazis. Why it's only the ins and the outs, just like Republicans and Democrats at home." I was not present in Bavaria and cannot say. I have, however, discussed the matter with two men who were: the Honorable Carl McArdle of Washington, D.C., then of the *Philadelphia Bulletin* and later Assistant Secretary of State for Public Information, and Van S. Merle-Smith, Jr., aide to the General. Merle-Smith remembers the incident clearly. "That was at the end of a tough day, the 26th of September, when your uncle and I had just come back from visiting a Displaced Persons' Camp in which a hunger strike and rioting had been going on. The refugees had made such an incredible pigsty of the place that the General had to stop the car on the way home and vomit. Upon his return at the press conference someone asked him, 'General, do you know what is a Fragebogen?' [A questionnaire re party affiliations, prior employment, etc., a prerequisite to clearance for a job under the occupying powers]. Patton impatiently asked, 'Well, just what in hell *is* a Fragebogen?' Then there were some more leading questions and finally he made his unfortunate remarks — including, 'If there were an election I could be President of Bavaria.'

"As you know, I was with him almost constantly during those months from September until his death and I became convinced that there were certain correspondents who seemed bound and determined to distort what your uncle had to say, trap him into an unguarded statement, and somehow blacken him. If I were to guess, it was because he was so outspokenly against certain governmental policies. He trusted reporters too, you know, to keep his confidences; that is, protect him. It hurt him terribly when he felt they let him down."

McArdle told me this: "When I heard the report and saw the so-called transcript I, no more than any other reporter who knew the circumstances in Germany — or who knew

George Patton — paid the slightest attention. It wasn't even
a story worth filing. It was 'Pete' Daniell of the *New York
Times* who felt he had to blow it up into a story. It was a cruel
thing to do." Such was the temper of the times that obviously,
once the damage had been done, it was beyond repair. To his
credit, however, let it be recorded that one of the reporters
who had been present went later to the General's widow to
apologize. Aunt Bea told her family that the man, whose
name she no longer recalled, came to her to express his re-
grets for what had happened. According to Ruth Ellen, the
precise words were, "It is probably too late, but I want to tell
you, Mrs. Patton, how much I regret having had anything to
do with that fatal press conference. After I had spent more
time in your husband's presence and observed the problems
he faced and how he handled them, I came to admire him
greatly."

Aunt Bea's answer was typical and to the point. "It's still
too late."

I asked Raymond P. Daniell, now chief correspondent in
Canada for the *New York Times*, what were today his recollections of the matter. He wrote me a long letter largely con-
firming the story outlined above. I believe the last two para-
graphs should be recorded here.

> If it is indeed true, as you have suggested in your
> letter, that some correspondent called upon Mrs. Patton
> to express regret for what had happened, it was not I,
> nor do I know of anyone who did. That, of course, does
> not rule out the possibility nor indeed the probability
> that someone did. If there was, in fact, any movement in
> certain quarters to "get" General Patton, I certainly was
> not aware of it, although, as I have said earlier, there

was widespread talk, both among correspondents and officers, as well as among civilian representatives of various branches of the U.S. Government, of laxity in the enforcement of de-nazification throughout Bavaria. Whether the talk was set in motion originally by anyone with an ulterior purpose I have no possible way of telling. *In the light of present knowledge, I would not, however, rule out the possibility that such might have been the case originally,* although, by the time I decided to look into conditions in Bavaria, whatever pebble had been thrown in the pond, had created a ripple of very great dimensions. [Emphasis is the author's.]

You ask, if in the light of my own recollections and of history, there is any comment I would like to make. There is. While the story I wrote was fully justified, I would feel happier today about the whole incident if I had made a report to General Smith on my observations in Bavaria instead of writing the story for my newspaper. In justification, however, I would say that my mission there was to report the facts as I saw them and not to serve as an unofficial detective for General Eisenhower's Headquarters. My own opinion, for what it is worth, is that it was an unfair thing to take a great soldier and military leader as your uncle was, and assume that he would be as effective in the post to which he was assigned, after the military situation had become one purely of civilian administration. As a soldier who had served his country so valiantly and well in the field, he was, I think, impatient and out of sympathy with the rules laid down for political rather than military reasons. I may add that no field commander whom I met, during the campaign period and afterward, commanded greater loyalty from his staff.

Uncle George's own account of the event, written about three weeks afterward, is vivid and to the point. Whether right or wrong he did not budge from his convictions.

This conference cost me the command of the Third Army, or rather, of a group of soldiers, mostly recruits, who then rejoiced in that historic name; but I was intentionally direct, because I believed that it was the time for people to know what was going on. My language was not particularly polite, but I have yet to find where politic language produces successful government.

The one thing which I could not say then, and can not yet say, is that my chief interest in establishing order in Germany was to prevent Germany from going Communistic. I am afraid that our foolish and stupid policy in regard to Germany will certainly cause them to join the Russians and thereby insure a communistic state throughout Western Europe.

It is rather sad for me to think that my last opportunity for earning my pay has passed. At least, I have done my best as God gave me the chance.

Anyone who had listened to George Patton's often expressed feelings about the Nazis, or read of them, must have known that he hated them as "slimy scum," "filthy murderers," or for some reason as a favorite epithet of his, "those purple-pissing Nazis." The press, of course, understood this and should have realized that Patton's remark must have been somewhat distorted by being out of context. It was a meaningless verbal blunder, or even, under the circumstances involved, a reasonably true reflection of an actual and difficult situation. Once the infection of the report was planted and its poison spread, however, there was very little that Eisenhower or anyone else could do except relieve this man of his command. No one could leave unpunished a commander who was believed able airily to dismiss the ghastly crimes against humanity of the Hitler regime.

It is a sad fact that it is the nature of humans to listen to, believe, and repeat the bad, and to ignore the good. Hardly anyone seems to remember, although the event has at least twice been presented as excerpts from the documentary Army films on nationwide television, the fact that in March 1945 Patton had ordered the Mayor, City Council, and leading citizens of the city containing Ohrdruf to visit that dreadful concentration camp. There he literally forced them at gunpoint to witness at firsthand what horror they had permitted, even tolerated, by their smug assertions that they did not know what was going on. Patton did this almost at once after the camp's liberation, conducting the tour in person: to the gas ovens, past the hideous stinking cordwood stacks of corpses, past the few remaining skeletal, filthy, piteous walking dead. He did not let one of them turn his head away. He then set the dignitaries to digging graves until their hands bled. Later he reported, with a certain grim pleasure and evident sense of justice done, that the Mayor and his wife, upon returning home, had committed suicide.

It is perhaps too easy to forget the atmosphere of those days. It was during them that we signed the agreements at Yalta, recognized the Lublin Communist government of Poland, and chose to ignore the Soviet assassination of the country's freely chosen representatives. It was then that we decided to dismantle our armies in order to "bring the boys home," after inviting the Russians into the war with Japan which was already won, and then insisted on a coalition between Chiang Kai-shek and the Chinese Reds who were, after all, mere agrarian reformers.

Such events and the men who moved them nearly killed George Patton's spirit while he was still living and in health. His sword was taken away and he was given a pen which held no ink. He was given orders of silence, and these as a soldier he obeyed; almost, but not quite.

George Patton had a vision of a terrible future and tried to prevent it. In his own way he had worked to help achieve a West German reconstruction, without which there would exist a central European economic vacuum which would later call for billions of dollars in Foreign Aid. His letters showed his view. In one dated October 13, he wrote:

> As I stated before I cannot imagine a situation in which if the Devil and Mars had conspired together to produce a new war, they would have found a more happy set of circumstances. Poland is under Russian domination, so is Hungary, so will be Czechoslovakia and so is Yugoslavia, and we sit happily by and think everybody loves us. Already the atomic bomb has been countered and war will go on, and yet idiots have the temerity to criticize General George Marshall on the subject of war.

And again on October 19, 1945:

> I heard last night from a reliable source that when that eminent Tartar, Marshal Zhukov, arranged to fly to the United States, he refused to do so unless General Eisenhower or his son John accompanied him on the plane — by way, I suppose, of hostage. I think this is a very good sidelight on the mentality of the Russian

who, being totally dishonest himself, cannot believe that
anyone else is honest.

And on November 17:

It seems highly possible that the Russians have
spheres of influence in Korea, Manchuria and Mongolia.
Now, while in many of the states such as Czechoslovakia
and Austria, alleged democratic forms of government
exist, they are actually under the thumb of the Russians,
and it is quite certain that the Russians will not permit
any large-scale economic relations between the Bolshe-
vik-ruled countries and the rest of the world, because
if they did, too many foreigners would be able to look
behind the curtain and see what goes on in these Communist countries, because if the Communist people and
the rest of the world found out how Communism is run,
the leaders would either retreat or retire, *and retreat for
a Communist leader means death.*
One result of the Bolshevik conquest of half of Western Europe is that they have reduced the scale of living
in those countries to the Russian scale which is very low.

Patton is likewise reported by General Harry Semmes as
having also in October told his Chief of Staff, General Paul
Harkins, "I really believe that we are going to fight them, and
if this country doesn't do it now, it will be taking them on
years later when the Russians are ready for it and we will
have an awful time whipping them. We will need these Germans, and I don't think we ought to mistreat people whom
we need so badly."
The General said the same kind of thing to many, many
people during those months from May to October 1945. He

was completely consistent in the expression of his convictions. I have said before that he was not a diplomat. I think now I would like to change that statement to: He understood power diplomacy, but he was not a politician.

And yet, when relieved of his command, in a letter to Aunt Beatrice, he limited himself to this: "My head is bloody but unbowed. All that I regret is that I have again worried you. I have been helping Lucian [Truscott] to get the hang of the show and he feels rather depressed. I don't blame him.

"I was terribly hurt for a few days, but I am normal again."

Merle-Smith told me that he accompanied Uncle George to the meeting at which Eisenhower relieved him of his Third Army and Bavarian administrative command and was with him also on the drive back to headquarters after the painful scene had been concluded. He said, "On the way home your uncle was very calm and very humble. I am sure that he was very sad and felt that his lifelong career was over. We then had dinner together and during it he turned to me to say 'And now what is there left for me to do? I've obeyed orders and done my best; and now there's nothing left. I think that I'd like to resign from the Army so that I could go home and say what I have to say.' It was typical of your uncle at times to be so humble, to ask someone like me for his reaction. Mine was that to resign then would be an admission of error; the General agreed.

"Before he made his farewells to the Staff and turned over his command to General Truscott we were all expecting an explosion or at least rather spectacular dramatics. When the time came, however, he was very soft-spoken and carried the thing off with great dignity. He made about a two-minute speech which began, 'All good things must come to an end.

The best thing that has come to me thus far is the honor and privilege of having commanded the Third Army.' He then congratulated his men and staff, told us we would find in General Truscott every trait which could inspire loyalty and devotion. He concluded in this way. 'A man of General Truscott's achievements needs no introduction. His deeds speak for themselves. I know that you will not fail him. Goodbye and God Bless you.'

"The General did not weep, even when he handed over his Army's flag to General Truscott, or when all the troops sang 'Auld Lang Syne.' He was quite grim-faced when we left to board the train and obviously hurt. When we reached our compartment he took the seat by the window and sat smiling and saluting to the crowd on the platform. Finally he turned to me and said, 'Pat, I hope to God this train starts pretty soon, but until it does I'm going to sit smiling out this window even if it kills me.'"

Despite his outward demeanor George Patton must have been seething inwardly. His war was over. Japan had also surrendered. There was too little to do and too much time to think. Uncle George had all along recognized the nature and aims of the Russians but was forced to sit idly by while his government made what to him were dreadful mistakes in making concessions to the Soviets. It is quite easy to see why he traveled as much as he did during this period to call upon old friends and why he was so restless. It is harder to understand how he managed to keep his mouth shut even as much as he did.

I was at this time ordered from Berlin to Washington in order to see what we could salvage of F.B.I. plans for intelligence coverage of postwar Europe. I could not, therefore, remain aware of much of what Uncle George did, or really said. I will, therefore, not even try to guess and will content myself with telling the very little more which I know.

During the period from the middle of October until his death Uncle George did mainly the traditional things. He inspected divisions and their headquarters. He visited old friends like General Houdemon, hero aviator with a wooden leg, the last French pilot to be shot down by the Boche in World War I and among the last to have this happen in World War II. Writing later, Houdemon had this to say: "We saw each other one more time at my home a month before his death. Then America lost her greatest general, the greatest guarantee of her future security. France lost her best American friend, Pont-à Mousson her liberator and savior, and I my best friend of good and bad days."

Patton went also to triumphal receptions in Rennes, Avranches, Chartres and other cities liberated by his army and was made an honorary citizen of each, not to mention dozens of the smaller outlying towns. He thus collected almost literally sufficient certificates of honorary citizenship to paper the walls of a room. He took lunch with General de Gaulle, an event which Pat Merle-Smith described as austere, morose and worried. The dinner on the same day with his old friend General Alphonse Juin, who had fought the dreadful campaign in Italy was neither morose nor austere, but Juin was deeply worried. He feared the communization of Europe and even the possibility of direct Soviet military action.

There were other events which were not traditional at least in their details. One, I think, is outstanding. On a day in November for instance, Patton visited, as was his habit, one of the Enlisted Men's Clubs, this time in Mannheim. Merle-Smith (by now a Lieutenant Colonel) was with him. Among the soldiers present was a sloppily uniformed youth seated, a beer can in his hand, feet propped up on another chair. At the General's entrance, which was never a surreptitious business, he did not stir.

Patton whirled on him. "Goddammit soldier, don't you know enough to stand up when your commanding officer comes into the room?"

The youngster remained seated. "The joke's on you, General, I'm not a soldier any more. My discharge papers came through today."

"Then, by God, there's no excuse for you at all, since at least you might show your respect for my gray hairs."

The ex-soldier of six hours left very quietly.

As already recounted, Uncle George had gone to Berlin and later to Stockholm.

Pat Merle-Smith told me about the Swedish trip and of their visit to the King at his country place where he received them with all the informality of an ordinary suburban householder in shirtsleeves anxious to show off his rose bushes. He told also of Uncle George's reunion with the Swedish 1912 Olympic team against whom he had competed so well thirty-three years before. "I was not included in the festive party but I know that it was held at some 400-year-old inn on the edge of the city. It lasted very late and your uncle said he never had a better time in his life. Sometime during the festivities, fairly early I should imagine, they got out pistols and had a target shoot. The General shot a better score than he had posted for record during the games and brought it back to show around just as delighted with himself as a small boy with a silver cup won for bow-and-arrow shooting, at a summer camp. Things like that pleased him a lot, especially under the circumstances that the Swedes at the party had solemnly declared him their blood brother."

I know also that he did many other things to pass the time and suspect that he was eating his heart out. Although he had talked to Merle-Smith and to his family about resigning from the Army he had, apparently, late in the fall, shelved this idea, at least for the time being. I believe this to be true since early in December he was notified that he would be returned to the United States again to take command of his Third Army. It seems doubtful, however, that he would long have retained that command. What seemed to him our national blindness to Russian intentions, plus rapid and thoughtless demobilization, would soon have forced him to violent public speech.

He had obeyed orders in July in not speaking his thoughts to Catholic leaders. But then he had been exposed to the steel curb bit and the muzzle for only a few days. Constant restraint before the daily spectacle of what he considered irremediable wrong would have driven him nearly out of his mind.

CHAPTER XX

Not "by the last bullet"

I REMEMBER that December 9, 1945, was, in Massachusetts at least, a cold, gray day and that there was a light cover of snow upon the ground. My mother and father, my family and I were, however, warm inside a sturdy fieldstone camp house two miles from nowhere and grilling meat over a fine wood fire. All wars were over. Christmas was coming soon, and three generations of Ayers were happy. We were, that is, until Herbert Machon, my father's chauffeur, electrician, plumber, philosopher and friend, stepped in out of the cold. He had walked all the way to the camp on snowshoes. I could tell from his expression that he brought bad news.

"Mr. Ayer, the War Department has just called your house to say that General Patton has been badly hurt in an automobile accident and that he may not live."

My immediate reaction, other than grief, was to blurt out, "Accident, hell. It was murder. Those Communist sons of bitches killed him."

I know there were many others who felt that Patton had been murdered. There are some who still do. From all I have since learned I am convinced that they are wrong. There was, however, in the timing, if that be a proper word, a cruel irony. The date of the accident was December 9, 1945. All arrangements had already been made for the General to leave for England and thence for the United States for a Christmas leave with his family. The date scheduled for his departure from Germany was the next day, December 10.

Here, according to all firsthand accounts is what happened. Uncle George and General Gay were riding in the back seat of a staff sedan on the Frankfurt-Mannheim autobahn on their way to go pheasant hunting. An army truck coming from the opposite direction swung to its left to go into a side road. Both drivers swerved so that the collision was not head-on, but the cars did hit in a glancing impact. The staff car was somewhat damaged but was still drivable. Patton was thrown forward and hit his upper forehead either against the back of the front seat, or the crossbeam of the car's roof. The impact crushed vertebrae in his upper spine, resulting in almost immediate and nearly total paralysis from the neck down.

Logic as well as investigative findings dictate that this must have been an accident. One does not hit a car carrying the intended victim of assassination with a truck at low speed and from an angle. Nor does one normally choose a second vehicle as a murder weapon. It is uncertain, and it may be the murderer who is killed, not his target. Also, I was told that the driver of the truck in question felt such deep remorse that he later attempted to commit suicide. No, however tragic, it was not murder; it was fate, one of the fates in which George Patton had always believed had touched him with her bony hand. This time it was the last and lethal sister of whom he had spoken to his children on his last visit home in the month of July. The gold of his luck was run out. He had indeed spent it all.

Immediately upon news of the accident my father phoned Dr. Franc Ingraham, chief neurosurgeon of the Boston Children's Medical Center, who advised getting hold of Dr. Geoffrey Spurling whom he considered the best man for the case. Somehow or other, between them, Father and Dr. Ingraham managed to have a New Haven train stopped between stations and virtually kidnaped the surgeon to dispatch him to Patton's bedside. The next day Aunt Bea flew to London, en route to Germany, with instruction to take Dr. Hugh Cairns, top British neurosurgeon, with her. So rapidly had the War Department swung into action, however, that she discovered on arrival that Cairns had already left by army plane. On the next day, as already related, I saw my father off while he suffered a 104° fever from his mass of simultaneous inoculations. He went on the overnight Boston–New York train, a ghastly enough method of travel under normal circumstances, since it is known to the regular customers as the "rock crusher." Father told me that the crowning blow came the next morning at the Harvard Club where he stopped to freshen up and eat a breakfast. "I felt like the wrath of God and looked forward to at least a nice hot bath. I undressed, turned on the tub, and by God there wasn't any hot water." Nevertheless, he caught his plane and reached the hospital in Heidelberg on the next day.

Uncle George now called on all his great strength, and for the last time. Even with most of his lung capacity paralyzed, he fought back at death for twelve full days. Both surgeons told my father and Franc Ingraham has told me that in the light of the nature of his injuries any man with a less furious will to live would probably have died within the first two or three days. As a matter of fact, it was believed after ten or eleven days that he might live. He seemed to be getting stronger. My father and Merle-Smith have both told me this and that at times the patient seemed quite cheerful. I doubt that he could have realized that even were he to live it would be at best as a half-paralyzed man in a wheelchair. I hope he did not. At the end pneumonia put an unbearable load on Uncle George's heart and he died on December 21, 1945. His very last words were to his wife, "It's too dark, I mean too late."

Earlier he had talked at length with my father of things which I think it best to leave private between them. He did, however, turn to him, almost at the very end to say, "This is a hell of a way for a soldier to die." Perhaps so; perhaps also George Patton's god of battles had on that day shown mercy on this his constant servant.

What more is there to tell? You know now of the funeral train so often stopped in the journey in the cold dead of a December night, saluted at a score of places by flower-bearing French honor guards and also honored by the bareheaded silence of defeated Germans. You know how the bereaved widow spoke graciously in reply to those tributes at each point of halt. You know of the plane carrying Walton Walker droning unseen and unseeing above the winter clouds as that general did all he could to say farewell to his departed Chief. You know that this chief was buried as he wished in our own Military Cemetery and that even today his grave is never without fresh-cut flowers. Perhaps you do not know that at least once Winston Churchill laid a wreath against George Patton's plain white cross, a thing an American President is yet to do.

You cannot possibly know of what I heard on the day of his

death and, for the moment, thought was a most fitting epitaph.

On December 21, 1945, I was in Boston in the company of two Marine Corps officers. When the news was brought to us there was a moment of dreadful silence. I saw tears in the eyes of one very tough man. Then he shook his head, lifted his glass, "There died the best god-damned Marine the Army ever bred."

I have thought about this many times in the years which have passed and know that that brief statement told only part of the story and I have here tried to tell a little of the rest. Someday some military historian will write the fully documented biography of the General. By that time people named may have all been dead for many years, places mentioned of no importance any more, and events all but forgotten, and George Smith Patton, Jr., some faded photographs and one thousand pages of printed words. And so I would like you with me to take one last look at him.

Perhaps you see him differently, but here is how George Patton still appears to me. He was a man who trained and disciplined his mind and body nearly every day of his life for the role he had always known he was to play; a man who believed in the aristocracy of achievement and in the sanctity of his country's cause. He was conceited, sometimes ruthless, often inconsiderate and outwardly very, very tough. He was often too much the impetuous showman and yet a deep and careful thinker. But he was also magnificently well read, deeply religious, softhearted, emotional and easily moved to tears. He suffered a torment caused by the constant conflict between the educated, sensitive and romantic aspects of his nature, and his own image of what he was destined to be and toward which, perforce, he drove himself. He was most ma-ture in professional learning and experience; and yet in certain ways he never quite grew up. He was nearly always certain that he would succeed but often feared that he would not gain proper recognition. In most things he was both a pragmatist and a mystic. He was both self-sacrificing and self-indulgent. He made his own rules of war and by them he crushed the enemy, just as he had always known he would.

He came close to being a worshipper of his ancestors and believed that they were always with him. He felt inescapably the dictates of aristocratic and honorable traditions. He cared very little for public opinion and he spoke his convictions aloud. He was in this a rhetorician rather than a dialectician and so drove directly to those conclusions which historical knowledge, experience, upbringing and instinct told him were correct.

The late Professor Richard M. Weaver of Chicago University, in writing recently of John Randolph of Roanoke, might, I feel, have been describing George Patton when he said:

> He was a follower neither of men's opinions nor their fortunes, and he did not feel that a bold utterance needed apology. He was the kind of person who feels that he must be right since he knows that he is a great man. There is potential danger in this but also power. In some men this feeling is productive of blindness and conceit, but in others it is the very substance of proof without which the forms of logic are but dry perfections.

It was no dry perfection of logic but an inner certainty which assured George Patton that he had once worn the crested helmet of Greece before Troy and then had been the leader of a Legion; that he was the mounted knight in armor, and the kilted highland warrior. A sure knowledge of what was past armed him with a keen instinct for what was still to come. It was, I believe, for all these reasons that he became the most terrible striking sword of that which is no longer modern war. He was enfant terrible to some, and hero to others.

I opt for hero, since he lived life to the hilt in his belief that no matter what, "la noblesse oblige"; he lived his every year to the very end according to his own creed, "A citizen's proudest privilege is to bear arms under his country's flag." He believed throughout his life that he would be reborn to lead again in battle. Whether he will or not cannot be known. But one thing is sure. It would be a terrible thing for the country he served so well if George Patton were to prove to have been the last of his kind: the last leader who never took counsel of his fears.

Thus, here at the end, I take leave of Uncle George with his most favorite quotation of them all. It is from *Pilgrim's Progress* and was used by Beatrice Patton as the dedication to her husband's account of his final war. It seems to me even more appropriate at the end than it was at the beginning.

My sword I give to him that will succeed me in my pilgrimage, and my courage and skill to him that can get it. My works and scars I carry with me to be a witness for me that I have fought his battles who now will be my rewarder.

So he passed over and all the trumpets sounded for him on the other side.

Printed in the United States
89624LV00004B/76-99/A